MANAGEMENT OF HUMAN RESOURCES

MANAGEMENT OF HUMAN RESOURCES
A Systems Approach
To Personnel Management

William P. Anthony

Associate Professor and Chairman
Management, College of Business
Florida State University

Edward A. Nicholson

Associate Dean
College of Business Administration
Wright State University

Grid Inc., Columbus, Ohio

I.S.B.N. 0-88244-113-2
Library of Congress Catalog Card Number 76-8107

1   2   3   4   5   6   ⊠   2   1   0   9   8   7

MANAGEMENT OF HUMAN RESOURCES *was edited by Jane C.*
Foss; stylized by Elaine Clatterbuck, production manager. Cover design
was by Marcie Clark. The text was set in 10/11 Times Roman by Capital
Composition, Westerville, Ohio.

To Our Children
Cathie, Sarah,
Tonya, Allen, Daren

CONTENTS

Preface

PREFACE

People have always been a key resource for organizations. However, it has been only during the last few decades that academicians and practicing managers have begun comprehensively researching, writing, and learning about people and their organizational relationships from a management standpoint. From the somewhat naive approach of the human relations concept, we have moved to the "human resources" concept. We have begun looking at the total human resource situation in organizations, using the systems approach. We have begun identifying managerial strategies and processes that not only maximize organizational productivity but also human satisfaction.

The type of knowledge and skills required of managers in organizations have changed extensively over time. In the early stages of the industrial revolution, it was the entrepreneur, the innovator, who rose to the top of the corporation. He had the skill, knowledge, and strength of character to put a corporation together and make it grow. Soon after, the production manager specialist became more important. The corporation was formed, and people with technical skill and knowledge were needed to ensure that the organization ran efficiently. The next set of skills needed by organizations were financial and accounting skills. Those managers with knowledge of financial markets and accounting information were highly prized because they could help obtain the capital so the corporation could grow even more. Then came the marketeers. Corporations needed new markets and new products. The marketing concept received prominence and people with marketing skills soon found themselves at the head of major corporations.

Today is the era of the human resource manager. Managers who have the skills of effectively organizing, planning, controlling, and motivating the organization's human resources are greatly prized. Schools and colleges of business proliferate with courses in organizational behavior. Executive and management development courses cover such subjects as organizational development, organizational renewal, leadership, communication, motivation, and interaction management. Managers commonly identify various "people" problems as their most important problems requiring a solution.

Much of the initial study of people at work was done by psychologists and social-psychologists which evolved into the human relations school as interpreted by business professors and practitioners. The manager's role under this school mistakenly became one of "keeping people happy." Managers thought that if they could keep their people happy, their human resource management problem would be solved. We know today, of course, that job satisfaction is but one of a myriad of complex human resource management issues. The interpretation of the human relations school by most managers also erred in another way; most of the responsibility for human resource management was placed primarily with company personnel departments, and the focus of their efforts was directed toward operative and not managerial or professional employees. The practicing manager often thought that his duty in human relations was to keep his people happy and to be sure he got along well with his subordinates and that they got along well among themselves. Manpower planning, job structuring, reward systems, performance appraisal, and other personnel issues were all viewed as functions of the personnel department and of only tangential interest to the manager on the firing line concerned with getting out production or sales.

Personnel management books of this period tended to reinforce these perceptions on the part of practicing managers. The books took a strictly functional view of personnel management and explained ways of setting up and administering recruiting, hiring, manpower planning, health and benefit, wage and salary, and industrial relations functions in the company. These were usually viewed as the province of the personnel department, and its authority was limited primarily to developing and administering these functions for operative, not managerial, employees in the organization.

This perception is changing, and our book addresses this change. No longer is personnel resource management the sole function of the personnel department. No longer are personnel management issues just a discussion of a rather narrowly defined list of personnel functions. No longer are these issues applicable to operative workers only. To reflect these changes, the term "human resource management" has come into more prominent use. It is this term that we have chosen for the title of our book to reflect the approach we take.

Today's managers in every department and at every level of the organization are human resource managers. They share this responsibility with, and receive staff advice from, personnel departments. They are concerned with traditional personnel issues as they've been traditionally applied. But today's managers also are beginning to realize more clearly that human relations for the first line supervisor is not enough and that personnel management is not solely relegated to the personnel department.

We hope this book reflects this change in concept. We have addressed some traditional personnel activities such as recruitment and selection, job design and evaluation, and training and development, but by taking a systems approach and by treating the functions from a different perspective, we hope that we have conveyed the concept that every manager is a human resource manager.

Many people have assisted us in preparing this book, and any listing of people is bound to omit someone. However, we wish to thank Professors Steve Kerr of The Ohio State University and Terry Mendenhall, Kansas State College, for their thoughtful comments and criticisms of the manuscript. We also wish to thank Diane Boutwell and Beverly Pitts for their assistance in typing and editing the manuscript. Nils Anderson of Grid, Inc., has been considerate and encouraged our efforts throughout the preparation of the manuscript, and we appreciate his assistance. Philip Anthony of Owens-Illinois, Inc., provided much of the inspiration and basic philosophy through his example and discussions with one of the authors in particular.

Even though we have benefited greatly from this advice and assistance, any errors in the book are solely our responsibility.

THE SYSTEMS CONCEPT

In our approach to the study of human resources, we are taking a systems view because it facilitates the structuring of an overall framework that integrates the various facets involved in the management of human resources. That is, it allows us to consider the major forces both in the external environment and within the organization that affect the management of human resources. It allows us to establish an integrating framework to identify these forces, determine where and how they impact on human resources, and to determine the effect of these forces on the changing utilization of human resources in the organization.

This chapter presents an introduction to the systems concept. Concepts are defined, and their applications are made to organizations as systems. Chapter 2 applies these concepts to the human resource system of an organization.

DEFINITION AND EVOLUTION OF THE SYSTEMS APPROACH

Over the past three decades, many scientists in all fields have adopted the systems approach to the study of a particular discipline. We see the application of the systems approach in psychology, sociology, anthropology, physics, biology, chemistry, and in the business fields of marketing, finance, accounting, economics, and management. In the field of management, the systems approach developed first in the areas of operations analysis and computer sciences. More recently, it has been applied to the general study of management, information management, and to the management of human resources.

Since the application of the systems approach to management first evolved from the operations analysis and computer areas of management, many students believe that the systems approach means using mathematical equations, sophisticated quantitative methods, and computer technology. While the systems approach can be, and often is, expressed using mathematical notation, it need not be expressed in these terms. In this book we use some terminology from computer sciences, and we will make extensive use of diagrams and flow charts. However, we will not use the notation of the mathematician. While the quantification and expression of relationships in the field of human resources is a worthwhile pursuit, this application of the systems approach is better left to advanced courses in human resources management.

SYSTEMS DEFINED

Most individuals are familiar with the word *system* and use it in everyday language. We often speak of communication systems, economic systems, transportation systems, heating and cooling systems, electrical systems, and ecological systems. We even talk of cultural and social systems. The word system is used because it expresses the idea that each of these things is made up of parts and that these parts somehow interact with each other for some purpose. To express this intent in usage, we can *define a system as an organized or complex whole: an assemblage or combination of things as parts forming a complex or unitary whole.*[1]

This definition implies several ideas. First is the concept of *interdependency*. The parts that make up a system are interdependent with one another. If a change occurs in one part or set of parts, it affects all other parts in the system. For example, in a railway transportation system, the quality of the tracks will affect the efficiency of the engine and thus the overall performance of the system. Some parts of a system are more directly affected by a change in a given part or set of parts. The nature of the effect varies from a direct effect to an indirect effect depending upon the function of a particular part within a system.

A second implication of the definition of a system is the concept of *wholism*. This means that the system should be considered as a functioning whole. Changes in parts of the system and the functioning of elements of the system should be considered from the standpoint of the overall system's performance. In the railway transportation example, any changes in the quality of the track not only affects the performance of the engine but also has a rather direct affect on the total performance of the system. This concept of wholism also requires one to consider the performance of all aspects of the system when introducing change into one component. For example, we would not wish to design an engine capable of pulling a train at 120 mph unless the track were capable of handling speeds this high. Nor would we create track to handle speeds this high unless engines could pull trains at this speed. Finally, we would not even be interested in achieving these high speeds unless passengers, an integral part of this system, desired to travel this fast. All parts of the system must be considered.

SUB-SYSTEMS

Closely related to this concept of wholism is the analysis of sub-systems within a system. Sub-systems are a group of functioning elements within a larger system. It is a system within a larger system. In the railway example, the reservation and ticketing system is a sub-system of the railway transportation system. A given railway organization, such as the Chesapeake and Ohio Railway, is also a sub-system of the railway system.

The accounting system of the Chesapeake and Ohio is a sub-system of the railway system. In fact, the railway transportation system is a sub-system of the nationwide transportation system.

Therefore, the determination of sub-systems depends upon the level of abstraction desired at a given point in time for a desired type of analysis. If we are concerned with the overall functioning of our transportation system in the United States, we would be concerned with not only the functioning of the railway system, but also the system as it relates to the functioning of our airlines, truck, shipping, pipeline, and highway systems.

On the other hand, if we are attempting to improve the accounting system of the Chesapeake and Ohio Railway, we would be concerned with the information flows, financial statements, and use of an electronic data system within the accounting system. The accounting system would be the system and the other facets would constitute sub-systems. The determining factor as to what are considered systems and what are considered sub-systems depends upon the purposes and what we hope to accomplish through our analysis—or in other words, the analytical level of our analysis.

These relationships can be summarized for our railway example as shown in Figure 1-1. Of course this diagram could be carried to the extreme in either direction. It could be extended upwards to the business system, economic system, cultural system, and, after several more levels of abstraction, to the universe. It could also be extended downward to points of further specificity until we get to atoms and their parts. Consequently, in a technical sense, all systems are sub-systems of the universe, and all systems can be carried to the level of specificity of the atom. While these levels of abstraction and specificity are certainly necessary for some scientists (e.g. physicists, chemists), we in management are normally not interested in either of these two extremes of any system.

OPEN-CLOSED SYSTEMS

The concept of sub-system analysis leads us to a consideration of *open* and *closed* systems. An open system interacts with its environment, usually a larger system. A closed system does not interact with its environment. Most biological and social systems are open. The environment not only affects but is affected by the system. However, at any point in time, at a given level of analysis, a system may be considered closed, even though it does, over time, interact with its environment. This may happen, for example, when a system attempts to temporarily isolate or insulate itself from its environment.

Railway passenger service in the late 1960s had approached a closed system. It was difficult for potential passengers to make reservations; there was no advertising by railroads for passenger service; passenger trains were eliminated from runs; new cars were not ordered and old ones were not remodeled; and passenger train stations were closed. Railroads believed people would rather drive, fly, or ride the bus, and they also believed that by concentrating on freight service they could maximize their profit.

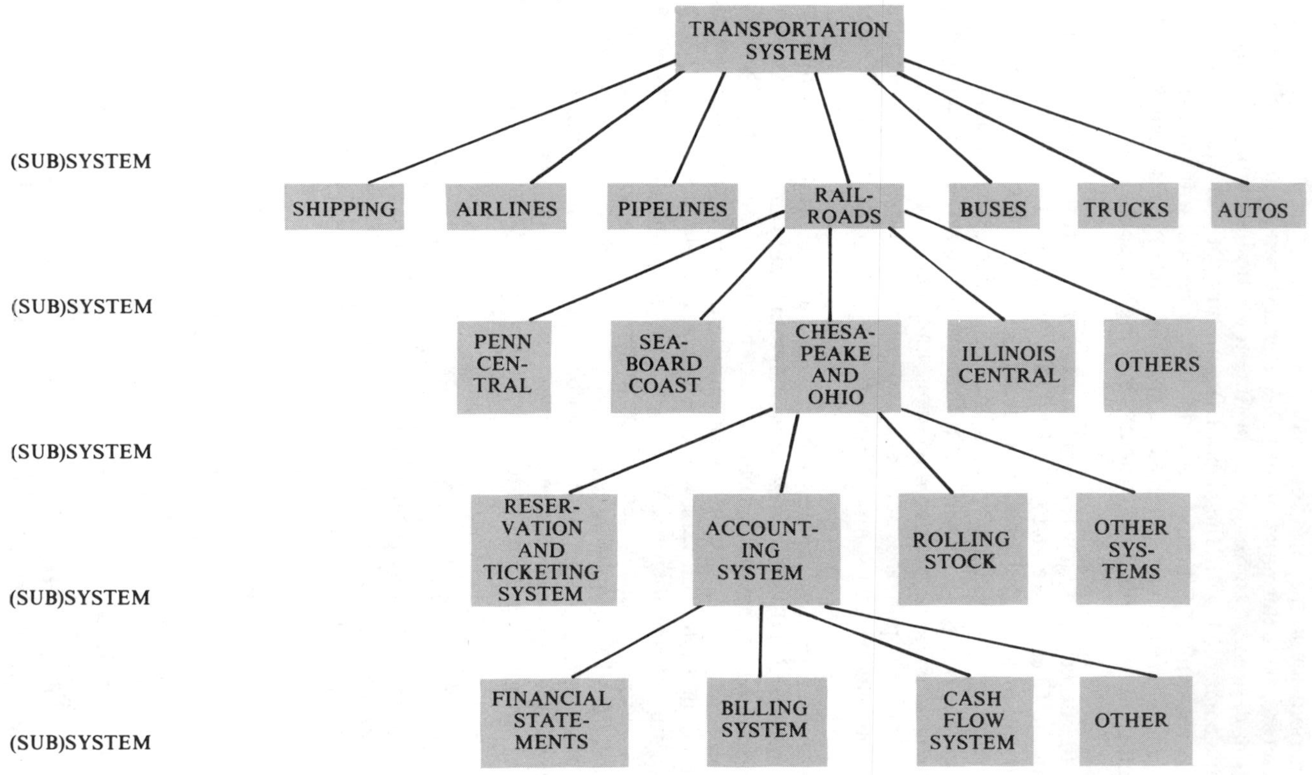

4

FIGURE 1-1 SYSTEM AND SUBSYSTEM INTERFACE

(SUB)SYSTEM

(SUB)SYSTEM

(SUB)SYSTEM

(SUB)SYSTEM

(SUB)SYSTEM

However, this changed when Congress passed a bill creating Amtrak and when the fuel shortage became critical. Now railroads have a toll free number for passenger reservations; they are advertising; new trains and runs have been added; new cars have been purchased and old ones remodeled; and train stations have been remodeled and new ones built. The system is now interacting more with its environment. Thus, for analytical purposes, it is appropriate to view the open-closed systems concept as a continuum rather than a dichotomy.

FUNCTIONALISM

Functionalism attempts to look at social systems in terms of structures, processes, and functions to understand the relationship between these components. It focuses on the question: How does the system work or function? It differs from a pure systems approach in that it attempts to *explain* rather than simply *describe* the operation of a system. It is part of a modern systems philosophy in management, however, in that we not only want to describe the operation of a system but also analyze it and explain why it works as it does and what can be done to change its operation.

A very useful concept of functionalism is the *functional-dysfunctional* continuum. When a part or sub-system of the system efficiently aids the system in its overall operation, it is termed *functional*. On the other hand, when a part or sub-system of a system hinders the overall operation of the system, it is termed *dysfunctional*. This concept is useful because it enables judgments to be made about the efficiency and effectiveness of sub-systems. It enables us to relate a given change in a part of the system to the overall operation of the system.

For example, salesmen in a business organization wish to increase the number of products sold. To do this, they may secure a higher level of orders than may be produced in a given time period with the firm's physical and human resources. They may also extend credit very liberally, thus increasing the possibility of poor credit risks. Thus, the salesmen's desire to maximize sales may be actually *dysfunctional* to the organization's goal of maximizing profit. To meet the higher orders of salesmen, marginal obsolete equipment may need to be put back into use; the work-force may need to work overtime; and product quality may suffer. A very liberal credit policy may significantly increase the bad debt loss experienced by the firm. Thus, these increasing costs may be significantly greater than the extra revenue generated by the higher sales. Profit would actually be less at the higher level of sales than at the previous level.

DYNAMIC AND STATIC SYSTEMS

Systems can be either dynamic or static. A *static* system is one in which no changes take place, while a *dynamic* system is one whose state changes over time.[2] A table is an example of a static system since it consists of four legs, top, glue, screws, etc. and changes very little over time. Most social and biological systems are dynamic with changes occurring over time.

Again, as with other systems concepts, this should not be viewed as a dichotomy but rather as a continuum. For a given time interval at a given level of analysis, a system may be considered rather static. However, over a longer time period at another level of analysis, it may be dynamic. In the table analysis, over a short time period (e.g. less than one year) the table is fairly static. However, over a longer time period (e.g. ten years), it is dynamic in that the varnish wears and cracks, the glue becomes loose and the legs wobble, and the color may change as it is exposed to the elements.

ABSTRACT AND CONCRETE SYSTEMS

An *abstract* system is a system composed of ideas or concepts. A *concrete* system is a system composed of physical characteristics. A mathematical formula is an abstract system. A particular manufacturing plant with its production process is a concrete system. Most social and biological systems are composed of both concrete and abstract elements. For example, a business organization is composed of physical and material resources as well as a philosophy, ideas, objectives, and operational policies.

BEHAVIORAL CLASSIFICATION OF SYSTEMS

Systems can be classified into one of four behavioral categories depending upon how they function:[3]

1. State-maintaining
2. Goal-seeking
3. Multi-goal-seeking and purposive
4. Purposeful

A *state-maintaining* system is a system that reacts in *a specific way* to a given internal or external event to produce the *same* external or internal state (outcome). It reacts only to changes. A home heating unit with a thermostat is a state-maintaining system. A humidistat is another example. The key element is that it reacts to change to provide a previously determined out-come or steady-state.

A *goal-seeking* system is one that can react differently to a given internal or external event to produce a different external or internal state (outcome). Such a system has a choice of behavior as opposed to the state-maintaining system. It seeks a goal or given end state. Systems with automatic "pilots" are goal-seeking.

Multi-goal seeking and purposive systems are ones that seek different goals in at least two different external or internal states. However, these different goals have a common property. Production of that common property is the system's purpose. Even though the goal is determined by the initiating event, the system chooses the means by which to pursue its goals. Many computer programs are multi-goal seeking and purposive. For example, a computer programmed to bill customers and pay bills of suppliers is multi-goal seeking in that it does what it does because of an instruction from an external source. It is purposive because the billing process (the acquisition or disbursement of funds) is a common property of the different goals which it seeks.

A *purposeful* system is one which can produce the same outcome in different ways and can produce different outcomes in the same way. It can change its goals under constant conditions, and it selects goals as well as means to achieve goals. A human being is a purposeful system, as is a family, fraternity, and most other social groups. Purposeful systems display a *will* and can make complex decisions.

INPUT-OUTPUT SYSTEM

Most biological and social systems are open systems as we have indicated previously. Since an open system interacts with its environment, it is often useful to visualize this sytem as being affected by (taking or receiving from) and affecting (contributing or giving to) its environment or other systems and sub-systems. Input-output analysis allows us to attempt to explain a system's relationship with its environment, as well as examine the internal operation of a system.

Input-output analysis involves the examination of a flow of materials, ideas, concepts, money, people, etc. from beginning to end through a system. It has six facets:

1. Determination of inputs
2. Determination of sources of inputs
3. Determination of the transformation process
4. Determination of outputs
5. Determination of users of outputs
6. Determination of the feedback process

A commonly used input-output diagram appears in Figure 1-2.

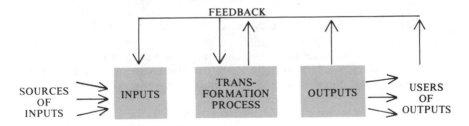

FIGURE 1-2 AN OPEN SYSTEM INPUT-OUTPUT DIAGRAM

Reading this diagram from left to right, we can begin with *sources* of inputs. These sources exist in the environment. They may be outputs of other systems or outputs of a sub-system of the same system. The several arrows indicate that the sources for inputs are often multiple and varied.

The *inputs* are the major and minor resources coming into the system. They are the essential building blocks of the system. They are what the system needs to operate. The *transformation* process of a system is the process that works on the inputs. It changes the inputs, hopefully by adding value to them. It does this to produce *outputs* or the end results of the system. These outputs are then used by the environment or by other systems or sub-systems.

The operation of the transformation process, as well as its results (outputs), are fed back into the system so that changes may be made in inputs and/or the transformation process in order to change outputs. *Feedback* can be generated from the users of the outputs (such as customers) and other external sources, or it can be generated by an internal source within the system. An example of an internal source for feedback is a quality control operation that inspects finished goods before they are shipped to customers. Feedback is provided to the system that may change the inputs and/or transformation process of the system.

THE ORGANIZATION AS A SYSTEM

An *organization* is an open, dynamic, multi-goal seeking, purposeful system that has elements of concreteness and abstraction. It consists of resources which are transformed into outputs for users. All organizations fit this description whether they be public or private, profit or nonprofit, business or government, socialistic or capitalistic, small or large, efficient or inefficient, or weak or powerful. They transform inputs into outputs for users.

Organizations make this transformation within a given environment. They not only are affected by this environment but also affect it. They receive their inputs from this environment, and their outputs are used by people or other systems in the environment. They are also constrained by factors in this environment. There may be constraints which come from sources of inputs as well as constraints that may exist in the social, legal, and political arenas of the environment. The economic system of the environment also provides many constraints, as does time and the state of technology.

The elements of an input-output analysis for an organization are found in Figure 1-3.

An organization's inputs consist of four essential resources: human, physical, financial, and information. Within each category of resources are found several types. For example, human resources include people with varying interests, abilities, skills, aspiration levels, and physical characteristics (e.g. sex, build, strength, color of hair, etc.). Physical resources include an organization's plant, office buildings, land, equipment, tools, raw materials, semi-finished goods, finished goods, and energy sources. Financial resources include cash, accounts, credits, a budget allocation, etc. that an organization uses in the purchase and utilization of resources. Information consists of data, ideas, reports, etc. which are generated internally or externally and inform the organization as to its inputs, transformation process, and outputs. It is a key resource in that its quality will greatly affect the utilization of other resources.

Perhaps the most important resource an organization has is its people or human resources. This is so because it is through working with people that all other resources are generated and utilized. Physical resources are obtained through dealing and bargaining with people. People generate data and analyze it to provide information. Human resources would

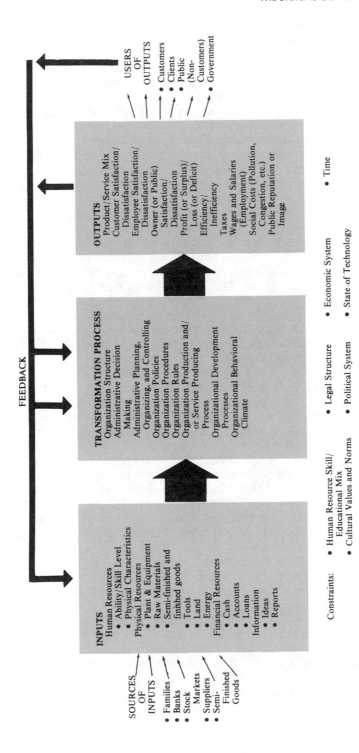

FIGURE 1-3 THE ORGANIZATION AS AN OPEN SYSTEM

probably be the most difficult resource to replace should an organization lose all its resources.

These resources come from many sources. Families produce children who are educated in schools and join the labor market. People immigrate from other countries. Individuals move from one geographic area of the country to another, from one industry to another, and from one skill or occupation to another. Banks, bond markets, and buyers of stock provide financial resources for the organization as do customer sales. Suppliers provide raw materials, equipment, semi-finished and finished goods as well as fuel or energy to operate the transformation process.

The transformation process is one whereby the organization adds value to the inputs. It involves the manufacturing or service-producing process of the organization. It also includes the way the organization structures itself; the policy, procedures, and rules it develops to run its day-to-day operations; the method and quality of its decision making process in allocating and utilizing resources; and the overall planning, organizing, and controlling skills of its managers. It includes the behavioral climate of the organization. The behavioral climate is the atmosphere of the organization as it affects motivation, commitment, morale, and productivity. Organizational development programs and processes, in another part of the transformation process, are the organization's training and education efforts for its personnel, which are directed toward improving overall system performance.

The end result of the transformation process is the organization's outputs. Most of us think of a product or service as the only organizational output. But a given organization produces much more than this. Wages and salaries are produced for employees. Profit or a loss is produced for owners (if a business). Employee, customer, and public (noncustomer) satisfaction or dissatisfaction is produced. Taxes are produced for governmental units (federal, state, and local). Social costs in the form of pollution, congestion, racial and sexual discrimination also are often outputs of organizations. Hopefully, another output will be efficiency and productivity.

These outputs are used by customers, in the case of business organizations, and by clients in the case of governmental and other public organizations. An organization's nonbuying public is also a user of some of an organization's output. For example, one may not own an automobile but he still may breathe the polluted air which an automobile produces. Government not only buys organization products and services, but it also receives tax payments generated by the organization's operations. Organizations often buy the output of other organizations.

Thus, we see that organizations actively interact with their environment in a dynamic manner. They obtain resources (inputs) from the environment, add value to these resources (transformation) to produce products and services (outputs) which are used by people in the environment. The next section discusses this process for a given organization, the state university.

THE STATE UNIVERSITY: AN EXAMPLE
OF AN ORGANIZATION AS A SYSTEM

Administrative analysis of state universities has heightened in recent years as a result of student disruptions in the 1968-71 period and the desire of legislatures for university accountability. As a result of this analysis, the image of a university is changing from that of an institution of ivory tower intellectual elitism dominated by pure scientists in the arts and sciences to a community-oriented, service-producing organization working through professional schools of business, education, medicine, law, engineering, social welfare, and public administration.

The university is also being increasingly viewed as an organization to be managed just as other organizations are managed. Recognition is being made that the managerial processes are universal regardless of the organization to which they are applied and the contexts in which they are applied.

Therefore, the systems approach to management can be applied to a university as can other management concepts. In this section, we analyze a state university from a systems perspective to indicate systems application to other than business organizations.

In many states, a state university may be considered a sub-system of the state university system which may consist of several other state universities as well as junior and community colleges. However, this does not affect our analysis, since the university in a state university system simply interacts with a slightly different environment than one not in the system. It faces different constraints, but within those constraints its operations are essentially the same as other universities.

Figure 1-4 indicates a systems view of a state university. The university uses the same four classes of inputs as does any organization—human, financial, physical, and information resources. However, the specific types of resources are different from other organizations. Human resources consist of a faculty, students, and a supporting or administrative staff. Physical resources include land, football stadiums, classrooms, computers, desks, chairs, audio-visual equipment, chalkboards, books, supplies. Financial resources include funds from state legislatures, private donors, corporations, foundations, student tuition, and federal grants. Finally, universities obtain and use information regarding the acquisition and utilization of these resources.

The primary transformation process of a state university is the generation (research) and dissemination (teaching, publishing) of knowledge. Since most state universities have graduate programs, they must be concerned with the generation of knowledge. Since they have students and a public to serve, they must also be concerned with disseminating this knowledge.

This generation–dissemination of knowledge is the transformation process of a university. It *occurs* within an organizational structure which facilitates the process. Policies, procedures, and rules exist to give meaning to the structure in facilitating knowledge generation and dissemination. Decisions are made to allocate resources on the basis of knowledge generation and dissemination. University administrators plan, organize, and

12

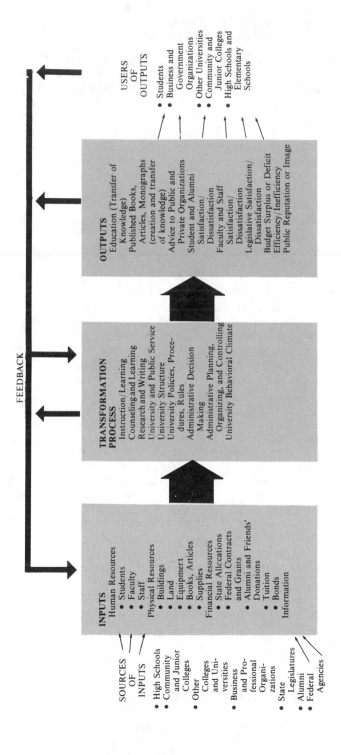

FIGURE 1-4 A SYSTEMS VIEW OF A STATE UNIVERSITY

control with a given structure to generate and disseminate knowledge. A behavioral climate is developed which provides adequate incentives as well as a reward and penalty system to encourage people to effectively generate and disseminate knowledge.

Thus, the key to the transformation process is the generation and dissemination of knowledge. Structure, policies, rules, procedures, structure, decision making, planning, organizing, controling, and a behavioral climate are a part of this process in that these factors facilitate the generation and dissemination of knowledge. Administrators exist to facilitate faculty and student activity; faculty and students do not exist to facilitate administrative activity.

The primary output of the process is education. Education manifests itself through various media. Students learn in classrooms and laboratories. Books and articles are published which students, managers, and the general public read. Public and private organizations receive advice from university personnel. Through this educational process, students and alumni are either satisfied or dissatisfied. Faculty and staff, as well as legislators and boards of regents, are also satisfied or dissatisfied. A university generates an image or reputation with the public which is another output of the process. Budget deficits or surpluses may be generated. The process may be done efficiently or inefficiently.

All of these are outputs of a university and need to be considered. Simply to view the output of a university as the generation of so many credit hours of instruction or the graduation of X number of students in certain programs at various degree levels is a much too narrow focus. While the number of students taught per quarter and graduated per year is an output, what is really being produced is education, not bodies. Student credit hours and number of graduates may be used as measures of educational output, but are not, in and of themselves, education.

The users of university output are many. Students use the knowledge generated and disseminated. Employers (government and business) hire graduated students and also buy university consulting services. Educational institutions such as other universities, community and junior colleges, high schools and elementary schools, use graduated students and the books, articles, and monographs produced. Other employers also use university-generated published materials.

Throughout the entire process, information is fed back into the system. Students, faculty, staff, business employers, state government agencies, alumni, foundations, and federal government agencies all provide information on the quality and quantity of outputs and on the effectiveness of the transformation process. This information is used to adjust university inputs and to change the transformation process.

One recent example of such a feedback process involves the twelve-hour teaching law that has been instituted in several states. This law states that professors must spend twelve actual hours per week in the classroom teaching courses. As such, it is a rule or regulation in the transformation process. It was passed because of the opinions of legislators that professors were doing "too much consulting and research and not enough teaching" and needed to be put back in the classroom.

The concern for this consulting/teaching balance heightened in the late sixties and early seventies when campus disruptions occurred. Many legislators believed that campus disruptions were at least partly caused by the fact that faculty members were "never around" to control the students. Another reason for this rule was the shortage of money experienced by many states to fund higher education. To make funds go farther, it was believed that "teaching productivity" should be increased. Consequently, as a result of the feedback, legislators took action to change a rule in the transformation process.

This rule change may have other effects in the system. The output mix may be changed. For example, there is less likely to be as much production of knowledge through research. The dissemination of knowledge through books and articles may also decrease. Advice to business and governmental organizations may be far less than previously. The purpose of the change was to increase the dissemination of knowledge to students through formal classroom instruction. The effort is to maximize this output at the expense of other outputs.

Of course such a rule change may be dysfunctional to the total operation of a state university. Good faculty members skilled in research, publication, and consulting may leave the university. Business and government organizations may be dissatisfied because they cannot obtain the quality and quantity of advice desired from universities. Students may be dissatisfied with instructional performance since course content becomes stale and out of date without research. Doctoral students may believe the quality of the doctorate program has deteriorated without a research base. University funds from federal agencies and foundations may fall off because no one is writing grant proposals for funded research. Research equipment, such as computers, and buildings may sit idle for lack of use. Basic research generated in the physical and social sciences, medicine, and engineering may not be performed and the state of knowledge of our society in these areas may not keep pace with our national needs and priorities.

The result of the twelve-hour teaching law is undetermined at this time. Yet this serves as an example of what may happen when change is made in an input or in a part of the transformation process based on feedback when all factors in the system are not adequately considered. One advantage of a systems philosophy is that its wholistic characteristic allows one to analyze the effects of change on total system performance and output generation and to analyze sub-system behavior as it interfaces with the broader system. The systems philosophy helps in determining functional and dysfunctional characteristics of the system and to predict these characteristics for a proposed change.

CONCLUSION

As seen in the university example, the systems approach has advantages as an analytical tool. However, it also has disadvantages. This chapter concludes by discussing the advantages and disadvantages of a systems approach to the study of organizations and points out some pitfalls which one needs to be cautioned against in using this approach.

ADVANTAGES OF A SYSTEMS PHILOSOPHY

As we have indicated, a systems approach enables one to consider an organization as a whole. The elements of the organization are clearly specified. Sub-system interface is explicitly considered, as is organizational interface with its environment. The flow of energy and resources through the input, transformation, output process is clearly depicted. The sources of inputs and the users of outputs are specified. The role of feedback in the system is given the importance it deserves. Thus, predicted consequences of changes made to an input or the transformation process can be more clearly stated in terms of how these consequences affect other inputs, other parts of the transformation process, outputs, users of outputs, and the quality and type of feedback.

The systems philosophy also allows for the integration of what may initially seem to be diverse concepts, ideas, or elements. Concepts or elements are synthesized into a system. A framework is provided in which there is a place for every aspect of an organization. The pieces of the puzzle are put together by using a systems philosophy.

The systems approach also allows for model building and easier graphic presentation of ideas. By focusing on flows and interrelationships of elements, we can develop models that better express the operation of an organization. These models may be expressed as a flow diagram or as a set of equations. Variables are specified, and the relationships of each variable to one another are made explicit. Since model building is the first step to empirical research, hypotheses generation and testing is facilitated.

The approach also allows for quantification of relationships between elements. The advantage of quantification is the preciseness offered in stating relationships. No longer do we rely on words, which have many meanings, to express relationships. Mathematical formulae reduce the semantic barrier in explaining relationships among organizational elements.

DISADVANTAGES OF A SYSTEMS PHILOSOPHY

Most of the disadvantages to adopting a systems framework as an analytical tool need not exist. However, they often do exist because of misunderstanding or misapplication of the approach. Therefore, users of this approach need to know what pitfalls exist in its application and how these might be avoided.

There is a tendency for some students and practitioners who apply the systems approach to advocate a more centralized administrative structure in organizations. This tendency towards centralization probably results from the wholistic aspect of the systems approach. Viewing the organization as a whole may tempt some individuals to concentrate decision-making power at the top of the organization with little delegation taking place. Because of the possible adverse behavioral consequences of centralization (which are more fully discussed in subsequent chapters), this temptation should be resisted.

The systems approach can also over-simplify organizational relationships. Both intra-organizational relationships (relationships among elements within an organization) and inter-organizational relationships (relationships between the organization and its environment) may be over-simplified. This probably results from the fact that the human mind may not be able to adequately express all relationships among elements through modeling. Most models of organizations that are developed, therefore, tend to be over-simplifications of reality. Exclusive reliance on these models at the expense of managerial judgment, experience, and other information can, therefore, have dysfunctional consequences. Models developed from a systems philosophy should be considered as tools for understanding a complex reality rather than completely representing the whole reality.

For many individuals, the systems approach may be too abstract and difficult to apply. This dilemma often results from the manner in which the systems approach is studied and applied. As we indicated previously, some people believe the systems approach is the same as the management science or computer science approach. This is not the case. Yet, when a systems approach is presented, it may be "heavily modeled," quantified, and abstract. This presentation is difficult to follow for readers not skilled in the use of mathematical notation. The key to overcoming this disadvantage is not to rely excessively on model building and quantification in studying and applying the systems approach.

Finally, the use of quantitative methods with a systems approach can present the illusion of finiteness. Very few relationships in the social sciences, including the study of organizations, can be stated with precision. Human beings and social interrelationships are so complex that we often do not specify all relevant variables and determine their cause and effect relationships, let alone determine the magnitude of those relationships. Therefore, one must be cautioned against relying on quantitative tools in applying the systems approach at the exclusion of basic description.

Given these pitfalls, however, the systems approach is a valuable analytical guide to the study of organizations. In the next chapter, we apply the systems approach to the study of a major sub-system of an organization—its human resource system. The concepts which we have developed in this chapter are applied to the acquisition, allocation, and utilization of human resources in organizations. The remaining chapters in the book focus on each element in the human resource system.

CASE 1
JUST THE FACTS

Any approach to making a decision should try to identify all relevant variables in the situation. A manager's first job is to get the facts. The problem is that no manager ever has perfectly complete information. Therefore, we all make decisions on the basis of incomplete information. The only hope a manager has is that he hasn't omitted an important fact in his decision process. But, in reality, a managerial decision is only an educated guess. Therein lies the disadvantage to the systems approach. This approach implies wholism, input-output analysis, and cause and effect. But it will never work because managers never have "whole" or complete information.

Questions

1. Does this statement reflect an understanding of the systems approach?

2. Do you agree with this statement? Why or why not?

3. To what extent does the systems approach improve organizational decision making? To what extent might it actually hinder efficient and effective decision making?

4. What are the alternatives to the systems approach in analyzing organizations and in organizational decision making?

CASE 2
THE "TECHNICAL" CHANGE

Captain Smith, the OIC of the voice communication (VOCOM) maintenance shop of the 47th Communications Group, noticed a marked decrease in the quality and efficiency of work being done in shop. Morale among the shift workers was low and getting worse. More complaints about the job, the shop, and other people were being filed. The physical appearance of most of the workers was in violation of the grooming standards set forth in Air Force Manual 35-10, and several men had recently been reprimanded. Much of the preventive maintenance work which had previously been done without question was now being "pencil-whipped" instead of actually being accomplished. Job turnover, both voluntary and involuntary, was rising rapidly, throwing the shop into a severe manpower squeeze. There was a great deal of conflict between the three shifts and the "permanent days" shift (former shift workers who were, for no given reason, placed on permanent day shift work and not subject at all to rotating shift work). However, despite the inter-shift conflicts present, intra-shift cohesiveness was very good, and absenteeism, which by all of the other given symptoms should have been very high, was virtually nonexistent for each shift. The only consistent "absenteeism" occurred on the "permanent days" shift, as they each took days off from time to time for various (not always good) reasons.

The VOCOM shop is responsible for performing routine, emergency, and preventive maintenance on secure (encoded) voice equipment for much of the North American Air Defense (NORAD) command headquarters. This involves the use of many telephone-type instruments which link the headquarters with their vital posts throughout the world.

About a year prior to the time the problem situation arose, the shop had changed over from a difficult, inefficient manual switchboard setup to a completely automatic switching unit. This switchover was well planned and well coordinated with all the shiftworkers. The new unit was far superior to the old manual unit which required an operator to connect all calls coming through. The automatic configuration freed workers from their operator-tasks to perform their required maintenance work, was completely compatible with the voice-encrypting equipment, was much less prone to failure, had a complete back-up capability in case of circuit failure, and provided the "conference call" capability not available on manual models.

Since fewer men were required under the new automatic configuration, action was taken to reduce the shop's manpower through the transfer of excess operators. Work under the new system went well.

Less than ten months later, with almost no warning, the shift workers were informed that the shop was returning to a new manually operated, switchboard system. It was installed and operating within a month and the still-superior automatic switch was dismantled and removed. The administrative NCOs on "permanent days" did not think about rescinding the manpower reduction request until after several transfer orders came down to the shop. When it was drawn up, it was delayed when it somehow got "lost" in papers stacked on SMSgt Jones' (the shop NCOIC) desk. The shop was severely undermanned, and several more critical personnel had transfer orders by the time the request was rescinded. This system also requred the presence of two "R" cleared personnel on duty each shift. Requests for clearances of this type for the remainder of the shop personnel were again delayed on SMSgt Jones' desk. Each of the three shifts had only two "R" cleared people, some of whom had transfer orders. The "permanent days" shift was completely "R" cleared, but none of them was put on shift work to help out the shifts. Thus, the two "R" cleared people on each shift were forced to work twenty straight shifts without a day off until some "R" cleared people were augmented to the unit for relief. There were a maximum of only five people on each shift, and since the two "R" people had to stay in the shop, the shifts had to rotate two to three people to cover work required outside the local maintenance area.

SMSgt Adams was the second highest NCO in the office, and he was concerned about the obvious work-accomplishment problems since the shop had been severely written up on the last IG inspection in several maintenance performance areas. He was, however, impeded by SMSgt Jones' position and tendency to delay making changes since he was to retire in about a year and didn't want to "make waves."

SMSgt Jones told the shift workers at a shop meeting that he knew they were "goofing off," trying to see what they could get away with. He promised swift, strict disciplinary action if they didn't "straighten up and fly right" until he retired and got away from the place. In the last IG inspection when asked for an explanation of the shop's writeups, Jones stepped aside and let the blame for the discrepancies fall squarely on the shift workers, saying the workers were uncooperative and refused to follow established shop practices and Air Force regulations.

Questions
1. Using the systems approach, what seems to be the major input (causal) and output (resultant) variables in this case?

2. Explain the inter-relationships between the making of a technical change in this situation and the changing human behavior.

3. To what extent are Jones and Adams each responsible for what occurred in the case? Why do you think Jones seems to "lose" papers on his desk? What should each of them do now?

4. What is Smith's responsibility in the case and what should he do now?

STUDY AND DISCUSSION QUESTIONS

1. What is the systems concept? How did it evolve?

2. Is a family a system? Why or why not?

3. Are human resources the most important resource for an organization? Is it also true that "through financial resources all other resources are acquired" and, therefore, are just as important as human resources?

4. Why might the systems concept be mis-applied by practicing managers?

5. Can you think of any other possibly dysfunctional policy changes besides the twelve-hour teaching law at your college or university?

6. From a systems perspective, what is the mission or purpose of a college or university?

7. Explain the reason why the systems concept was first applied in the computer and production areas of management.

8. Comment on this quote made by a manager in a management development program.
    This systems stuff is nothing but mumbo-jumbo. All a manager needs to do is treat people fairly and they'll be productive. There's no need to consider inputs, outputs, through-puts and all that crap.

9. From a systems perspective, could you actually diagram the sources, inputs, transformation, outputs, users, and feedback mechanisms of an organization with which you are familiar? Could you make such a diagram for a college class?

10. Is the systems approach as valid for studying a small organization, such as a local gas station, as for studying a large corporation, such as General Motors?

ENDNOTES

1. Fremont E. Kast and James E. Rosenzweig, *Organization and Management: A Systems Approach* (New York: McGraw-Hill Book Company, Inc., 1970), p. 110.
2. Russell Ackoff, "Toward A System of Systems Concept," *Management Science,* July 1971, p. 665.
3. Most of the material in this section has been developed from Ackoff, Ibid., pp. 665-67.

ADDITIONAL READING

Baker, Frank. *Organizational Systems: General Systems Approaches to Complex Organizations.* Homewood, Illinois: Richard D. Irwin, 1973.

Cleland, David I. and William R. King. *Management: A Systems Approach.* New York: McGraw-Hill Book Co., 1972.

Cleland, David I. and William R. King. *Systems Analysis and Project Management.* New York: McGraw-Hill Book Co., 1975.

Johnson, Richard A., Fremont Kast and James E. Rosenzweig. *The Theory and Management of Systems.* New York: McGraw-Hill Book Co., 1973.

Kast, Fremont E. and James E. Rosenzweig. *Organization and Management: A Systems Approach,* 2nd ed., New York: McGraw-Hill Book Co., 1974.

Sayles, Leonard R. and Margaret K. Chandler. *Managing Large Systems: Organizations for the Future.* New York: Harper and Row Publishers, 1971.

Shrode, William A. and Dan Voich. *Organization and Management: Basic Systems Concepts.* Homewood, Ill.: Richard D. Irwin, Inc., 1974.

THE HUMAN RESOURCE SYSTEM

The basic framework for the remainder of the book is presented in this chapter. Basic systems concepts developed in Chapter 1 are applied to the human resource system of the organization. The use of this approach allows the integration of both macro and micro concepts concerning human resources which have developed in the literature.

The focus is on the organization, which is viewed as dynamically interacting with its environment in the acquisition and utilization of its human resources. Particular emphasis is placed on the organization's processes of adaption to changes which occur in the macro environment.

THE HUMAN RESOURCE

As indicated in Chapter 1, the human resources of an organization can be considered the most significant input an organization utilizes. It is through human resources that all other resources are acquired and used. Decisions about human resources tend to directly affect the quality and use of all other resources.

Human resources differ in another significant manner from other resources. They have intrinsic value. As such, they are treated differently. Four basic assumptions regarding human beings are generally held in our culture:

1. *Individual differences*—While people have much in common, each person is unique in physical appearance, experiences, personality, aspiration level, attitudes, etc. Consequently, it's somewhat difficult to lump people together and generalize accurately about their behavior.
2. *A whole person*—A person is a system. He has ideas, a body, feelings, past experiences, and attitudes which mutually interact. When a person is employed in an organization all of his characteristics are brought into the organization, not just his hands or brain.
3. *Caused behavior*—All human behavior is caused. People do things for reasons, and there may be many reasons for a given act. The

reasons may not be recognized by the person nor may they be readily apparent to a researcher, yet they are there. To observe and explain human behavior is important.

4. *Human dignity*—People are of a higher order than other factors of production and need to be treated with respect and dignity. The foundation for this moral philosophy lies in the Judeo-Christian ethic of western culture. Human life, happiness, and the integrity of the individual are key values generally adhered to in our society.

In view of these assumptions regarding human beings, people are not "used" as are other resources in an organization. When we use the term "manage" or "utilize" human resources, we do not mean that they are used as are machines, buildings, tools, cash, or materials. Human beings have a will, free choice, and intrinsic value; machines, tools, and buildings do not.

The goal of the human resource management system is to create organizations that are both effective and efficient. Roethlisberger and Dickson, over thirty years ago, stated that:

> ... management has two major functions: (1) the function of securing the common economic purpose of the total enterprise, and (2) the function of maintaining the equilibrium of the social organization so that individuals through contributing their service to this common purpose obtain personal satisfactions...[2]

Therefore, the emphasis of human resource management must necessarily be on establishing systems that accomplish organizational goals (effectiveness) with efficient use of resources. In the past, organizations took this to mean production at the least possible economic cost. Consequently, efforts to increase efficiency often were directed toward reducing per unit labor costs. The adverse personal consequences of such action were ignored unless they resulted in some financial cost to the firm. Today, we realize that this approach ignores some very real and important personal as well as social costs that may be associated with personnel practices in organizations. This book addresses the efficiency of human resource management practices from the point of view of both economic and noneconomic costs and benefits which accrue to those in the larger system: the individuals, the organizations, and society as it pursues its goals.

SIMPLIFIED HUMAN RESOURCE SYSTEM OF AN ORGANIZATION

Human resources flow through an organization as do other resources. In Figure 1-3 we depicted an organization as a flow of resources through the input-transformation-output process. This section will focus specifically on the human resource flow through the organization.

A simplified diagram of the human resource flow is presented in Figure 2-1. This diagram simplifies the flow of human resources for

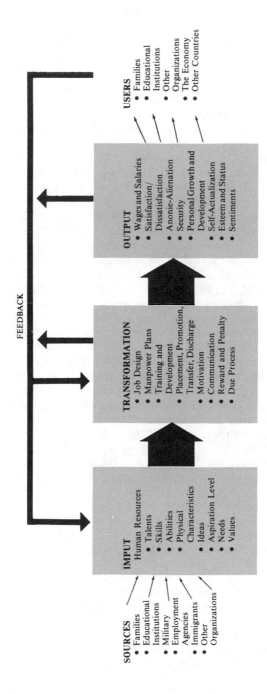

SOURCES
- Families
- Educational Institutions
- Military
- Employment Agencies
- Immigrants
- Other Organizations

IMPUT
Human Resources
- Talents
- Skills
- Abilities
- Physical Characteristics
- Ideas
- Aspiration Level
- Needs
- Values

TRANSFORMATION
- Job Design
- Manpower Plans
- Training and Development
- Placement, Promotion, Transfer, Discharge
- Motivation
- Communication
- Reward and Penalty
- Due Process

OUTPUT
- Wages and Salaries
- Satisfaction/Dissatisfaction
- Anomie-Alienation
- Security
- Personal Growth and Development
- Self-Actualization
- Esteem and Status
- Sentiments

USERS
- Families
- Educational Institutions
- Other Organizations
- The Economy
- Other Countries

FEEDBACK

FIGURE 2-1 SIMPLIFIED HUMAN RESOURCE SYSTEM IN AN ORGANIZATION

introductory analysis. Later in this chapter, a more complicated diagram is presented which develops Figure 2-1 more fully. The more sophisticated diagram serves as the outline for the book.

However, at this point, let us focus on Figure 2-1. As seen in this diagram, the human resources of the organization provide the skills, abilities, talents, ideas, and aspiration levels an organization needs to get its work done. These human resources come from the environment. Some of the sources in this environment include families, educational institutions, and other organizations.

The transformation process in using human resources involves several phases. First, the work of the organization is determined as it relates to the product or service to be produced. This work is the total productive effort of the organization needed to bring about a desired good or service. Then, jobs are designed based on this work analysis. Next, manpower plans are formulated for acquiring human resources to fill these jobs. People are trained and developed to better perform their jobs. They are also placed, promoted, transferred, and discharged as job requirements change. The organization develops a behavioral climate to bring out the highest levels of motivation in its human resources. A communication process is established to facilitate the coordination of human and other resources. Finally, a reward and penalty system is established to encourage good performance and discourage poor performance. Due process is applied throughout to attempt to insure the rights of the people employed.

While the primary output of any organization is the production of a product and/or service, we are interested in focusing on the outputs that relate directly to the human resources of the organization. These outputs mainly include wages, salaries, satisfaction, dissatisfaction, alienation, anomie, security, personal growth, and esteem and status.

Note that all these outputs are generated in an organization. Some of the outputs should not be generated but, never-the-less, often occur. For example, everyone is paid a wage or salary as a result of their productive effort. However, not everyone is satisfied in their employment relationships. For some, the dissatisfaction received from the job is so extreme that they are in a state of *anomie,* a state of normlessness. They feel there is no meaning to their life. Some are alienated. They rebel against the organization and perhaps society as a whole.

Most people receive security in their employment relationships. Often they also receive status and esteem through their jobs. If they can experience personal growth and development in their jobs, they may also achieve self-actualization. They become all that they can become and reach their full potential. Not many individuals fully achieve this through their jobs. Sentiments are developed among people working in the organization. Sentiments are feelings of liking or disliking among people in the organization.

The users of these outputs are the families of the people employed, educational institutions and other organizations, the economy, and other countries which receive the output produced. Wages and salaries buy goods and services from other organizations, which provide a level of security for the employee's family. Educational services are purchased from educational institutions. For multinational organizations, wages and salaries, security, and so on, are provided for people in other countries.

The attitudes of the users of output, as well as the output itself, are evaluated by the organization in its acquisition and use of its human resources. Organizations should continually monitor wage and salary structures to be sure they are competitive. This will help the organization determine if it is attracting quality human resource inputs. Levels of satisfaction, anomie, and need achievement of human resources should be measured frequently to determine if jobs should be redesigned or if changes should be made in reward and penalty systems, due process, communication, motivation training and development, placement, promotion, transfer, or discharge policies and procedures.

Note in this human resource system a dynamic interaction with the environment is occurring. Human resources are obtained from supply sources in the environment, and the outputs of the system are used by people and institutions in the environment. This aspect of the system is developed more fully in the next section.

THE HUMAN RESOURCE MODEL

The relationships presented in Figure 2-1 are developed in more detail in Figure 2-2. This model of the human resource system depicts the relationship the organization has with its environment and the internal processes of the organization involved in its acquisition and utilization of human resources. Emphasis is placed on the interaction of the organization with its environment and the organization's changing use of its human resources over time, as it attempts to institutionalize environmental demands made on it.

In discussing the organization's interaction with its environment, we will use the *macro-intermediate-micro environment* continuum.[3] The *macro environment* is "the broad system in which all the organizations of a given culture exist."[4] The *intermediate environment* is the environment that links a given organization with its macro environment. Some authors also refer to this as a "boundary spanning" environment in that the boundaries between an organization and its environment are "spanned" or "crossed" through the intermediate environment.[5]

The *micro environment* is the organization itself. This environment consists of the structure and internal processes and procedures of a given organization. In our analysis, we will especially focus on the decision-making process in organizations as they use human resources through time.

Since Figure 2-2 serves as the basic outline for the remainder of the book, it is important that the student have a clear understanding of this model at this time. Therefore, the rest of this chapter explains the relationships which exist in this model.

THE ORGANIZATION'S
MACRO ENVIRONMENT

The organization's macro environment is the source for the organization's human resource inputs and also receives the outputs generated by the organization. The macro environment influences organizational

26

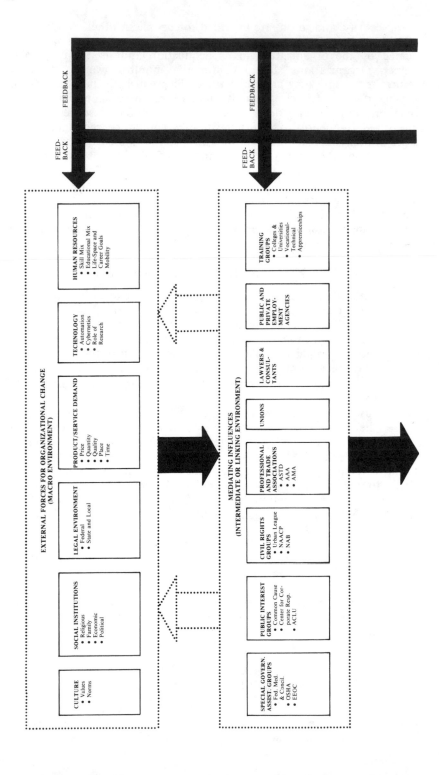

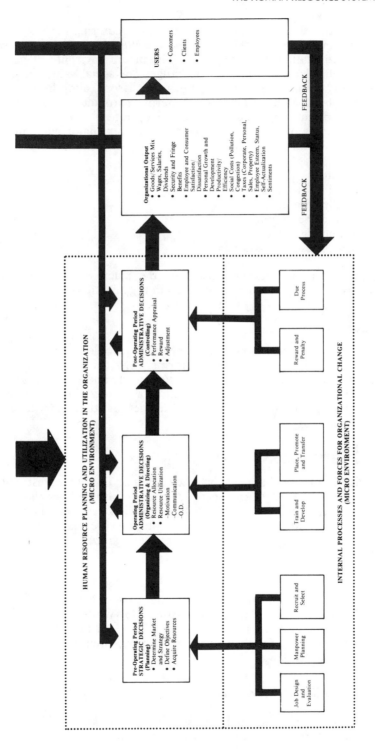

FIGURE 2-2 THE HUMAN RESOURCE SYSTEM

change. It may exert forces on the organization requiring the organization to change. An example of this would be the 1964 Civil Rights Act which forbids discrimination in employment. The macro environment may also prevent or hold back organizational change. The social values of honesty and integrity usually prevent organizations from adopting programs which may be unethical. Thus, the macro environment sets the broad parameters within which the organization operates.

For purposes of our analysis, we focus on six major components of the macro environment:

1. Culture
2. Social institutions
3. Legal environment
4. Product/Service demand
5. Technology
6. Human resource skill mix

These are the most relevant aspects of the macro environment which directly affect human resource utilization in organizations.

CULTURE

Culture is the underlying glue which holds people together and gives them their identity. It is the values, norms, roles, history, tradition, art, and language of a people. It tends to change slowly and provides a sustaining *raison d'etre* for what the people do in a society. In our model, we focus primarily on Western cultural changes as they impact on the organization.

SOCIAL INSTITUTIONS

Social institutions arise from the culture. They manifest cultural values and norms. While sociologists differ as to a list of basic institutions, they can be classified into four major categories: religious, family, economic, and political. We focus on how institutions are changing as culture changes and how changing institutions affect organizations.

LEGAL ENVIRONMENT

The legal environment consists of the laws of a society, including federal, state, and local laws and statutes. In Western culture it also consists of common law, or court-made law based on precedent. The legal environment also includes the values we hold regarding fair and impartial treatment under the law.

PRODUCT/SERVICE DEMAND

Customer/client needs and wants as they are manifested in demands for goods and services are the reasons why organizations exist. This includes governmental organizations as well as business organizations. These needs and wants direct organizational activity. They determine the product/service mix and the human resource mix needed to produce this product/service mix.

TECHNOLOGY

Technology is the state of the art employed in producing and delivering goods and services. It includes the level of sophistication of equipment and machinery and its use in the production of goods and services. It also includes the level of scientific advancement in a society that leads to the development of new equipment and processes through research and development. Technology has a significant impact in determining the human resource skill mix and its utilization in an organization.

HUMAN RESOURCES

People in an organization come from the macro environment. They have varying skills and aspiration levels. They have varying educational levels. They vary in the level of their career goals as well as the importance they place on these goals compared to other goals in their life. They also vary in their mobility, both geographical and occupational.

THE INTERMEDIATE ENVIRONMENT

The macro environment interacts with a given organization through an intermediate environment. This environment is a linking environment which spans the boundary between an organization and its macro environment. The intermediate environment manifests the macro environment to a given organization. Thus, it filters, blocks, as well as amplifies, aspects in the macro environment.

We will consider eight major groups in the intermediate environment:

1. Special governmental groups
2. Public interest groups
3. Civil rights groups
4. Professional and trade associations
5. Consultants
6. Employment agencies
7. Training organizations
8. Unions

These are groups with which an organization deals in its acquisition and use of human resources. These groups manifest the macro environment to an organization.

SPECIAL GOVERNMENT GROUPS

Governmental agencies enforce and interpret the law to an organization. These agencies include federal regulatory commissions such as the

Federal Trade Commission, Equal Employment Opportunity Commission, or Securities and Exchange Commission; federal assistance organizations such as the Federal Mediation and Conciliation Service; state regulatory commissions, such as the Environmental Control Board or the Public Utilities Commission; and city and county regulatory bodies, such as a zoning board, or planning department.

Organizations, be they private or governmental, increasingly interact with governmental bodies. The legal environment changes rapidly and organizations must continually monitor and, to some extent, influence new legislation which affects them. They must also understand and use the court system as needed to obtain important dispute settlements regarding legal interpretations.

PUBLIC INTERESTS GROUPS

During the past fifteen years, there has been a tremendous increase in the operations and political power of public interest groups. The better known groups which have exerted their influence include John Gardner's Common Cause, Ralph Nader's Center for Corporate Responsibility, and the well-known American Civil Liberties Union. These groups attempt to influence the legal environment and also to directly affect the policies of organizations. For example, in the early 70s at General Motors' annual stockholder meetings, Nader's Center for Corporate Responsibility raised issues dealing with the operations of General Motors in South Africa and the absence of minorities on the GM Board of Directors. Even though they technically lost the stockholder votes at these meetings, much publicity was generated, which resulted in GM adding a Black (Rev. Leon Sullivan) to the board of directors and in GM changing some policies in their South African operations.

The strength of these public interest groups are a new force with which organizations must deal. The ease with which these groups can focus public scrutiny on a given organization by effectively using television and press coverage for dramatic effect suggests that organizations must continually monitor, understand, and deal with these groups in the future.

PROFESSIONAL AND TRADE ASSOCIATIONS

Professional and trade organizations bring the organization into contact with organizations of similar industrial and occupational interests. These groups interpret industrial, trade, and professional developments to the organization. At the same time, an organization influences the activities of professional and trade associations through its membership. New developments in training and use of human resources often emerge through these organizations.

UNIONS

Unions have a significant impact on organizational use of human resources. Not only is the management of blue-collar operative (non-management) employees influenced by unions, but so is the utilization of professional, technical, and other white-collar occupational groups. The growth of unions in white-collar occupations and in governmental employment has been phenomenal during the past decade.

Unions provide both constraints and opportunities to management. They provide stability to many employee-employer operations and often serve to minimize and control conflict. Craft unions, through the hiring hall, often perform several personnel functions, such as recruiting and hiring, which would normally have to be performed by the employer. On the other hand, unions, especially those in strong bargaining positions, can gain significant concessions from an organization at the expense of organizational productivity or profitability. Management must maximize and capitalize on the opportunities presented by unions and must minimize the adverse consequences that might arise in the union/management relationship.

OUTSIDE CONSULTANTS

These individuals are used by organizations in dealing with the legal environment and for specialized study and advice on organizational markets, human resource use, and internal operational procedures. They provide skills to the organization on a temporary basis when needed to solve specific organizational problems. Thus, they bring much knowledge of the macro environment to the organization.

CIVIL RIGHTS GROUPS

Civil rights groups have had a significant impact on organizational human resource utilization of minority groups and women. These groups have not only directly influenced federal and state equal employment opportunity legislation, but have also taken action directly against specific organizations to bring about an end to discrimination in employment.

PUBLIC AND PRIVATE EMPLOYMENT AGENCIES

Employment agencies often represent the labor market for new employees to an organization. Human resources are filtered through and then directed to particular organizations by these agencies. They often close the gap between the job seeker and the vacant job.

TRAINING ORGANIZATIONS

High schools, vocational-technical schools, junior and community colleges, universities and professional schools, and apprenticeship programs provide the organization with its skilled manpower. The essential, basic training which organizations require of its human resources are not furnished by the employing organization but by these intermediate groups. In view of changing technology with its demand for changing and higher occupational skill levels, training and educational institutions will have an even more important role to play.

HUMAN RESOURCE PLANNING AND UTILIZATION IN THE ORGANIZATION

Organizations make decisions regarding the acquisition and utilization of human resources. The decisions are very directly influenced by the organization's macro environment as it is manifested to the organization through the eight major groups in the intermediate environment. The decisions are also influenced by the mission and objectives of the organization.

We can view the types of decisions made by organizations as being either *strategic* or *administrative*. Strategic decisions are those made to acquire and deploy an organization's resources to achieve objectives in the future.[6] These are crucial decisions because they tend to direct the overall effort of an organization. Most of these tend to be planning decisions and are generally made in a preoperating period. They usually deal with such areas as determining market strategy, developing operational definitions of organizational objectives, and resource acquisition. These decisions also tend to be *preventive* in nature in that they tend to anticipate and minimize the severity of problems before they happen.

The second type of decisions made by organizations are *administrative decisions*. These decisions are the routine, day-to-day decisions that are made in using an organization's assets.[7] Often these decisions are *curative* in nature. That is, they tend to be concerned with solving specific problems after they arise. These are the "fire-fighting" decisions so many managers complain about. These decisions tend to be organizing, directing, and controlling decisions.

In studying Figure 2-2, we see that organizations make these decisions through time.[8] Strategic decisions are made in the preoperating period for a given organizational program. During the operating period, administrative decisions predominate. Postoperating decisions are also administrative decisions and tend to emphasize the controlling function. Feedback from these decisions influence other decisions to be made in the preoperating and operating periods.

HUMAN RESOURCE UTILIZATION AND DECISION MAKING

With regard to the organization's human resource decisions, strategic decisions in the preoperating period tend to be job design and evaluation decisions, manpower planning decisions, and recruiting and selection decisions. Once decisions are made as to market strategy and organizational objectives, resource acquisition decisions are made. Jobs are designed to fulfill organizational objectives. Immediate and long term manpower needs are determined, including the skill/educational/ability mix needed. The recruiting and selection process begins.

During the operating period, administrative decisions are made to allocate and utilize resources. Human resources are trained and developed for specific job requirements. People are placed, promoted, and transferred in the organization as needed. Motivation, communication, and organizational development programs are designed and implemented.

During the post-operating period, decisions are made which evaluate the use of human resources. It is at this stage that individual performance appraisal is conducted. This performance appraisal process is usually tied to some reward and penalty system which includes salary adjustments, discipline procedures, and promotion and transfer decisions. In addition, decisions regarding training needs are developed to improve an individual's performance. Throughout these processes, due process to protect the rights of an individual applies.

The separation of organizational decisions regarding human resources into the three operating periods is somewhat artificial. Rarely can a given decision on human resource utilization be classified solely into one of these three categories. For example, decisions on placing, promoting, and transferring individuals are both operating decisions and post-operating decisions.

Yet, from an analytical view, it is useful to classify human resource decisions into one of these three categories to better understand the key decisions made with regard to these resources over time. It also helps to determine whether a given human resource decision is essentially a strategic or an administrative decision. Both types of decisions are important of course, but strategic decisions tend to influence the quality of administrative decisions.

For example, decisions regarding the design of jobs in the organization will have a major influence on decisions made to motivate employees. It is extremely difficult to motivate employees who have been placed in highly repetitive, rationalized, dead-end assembly line jobs. In fact, the whole thrust of job enrichment as a motivational tool requires the redesign of jobs to make them more challenging and hence more "motivating." Likewise, if poor recruiting and selection decisions are made which result in the acquisition of a poorly trained workforce that lacks needed skills, any training and development program the organization adopts will need to be quite comprehensive, time consuming, and expensive to provide the remedial training plus additional training needed.

Thus, it's important to focus on the key human resource decisions, which are often strategic decisions, and improve these first before attempts are made to deal with administrative decisions. Too often managers spend their time making day-to-day administrative decisions—"putting out fires"—at the expense of making strategic, preventative decisions which would have kept those fires from starting in the first place.

ORGANIZATIONAL OUTPUT

As the result of the decisions made in the human resource planning and utilization process in the organization, outputs are produced. These outputs include goods and services, wages, salaries and dividends, security and fringe benefits, employee and consumer satisfaction/dissatisfaction, personal growth and development, productivity and efficiency/inefficiency, social costs (e.g. pollution and congestion), taxes (corporate, personal, sales, property), employee status, esteem and self-actualization, and employee sentiments.

Some of these outputs are used by customers and clients in the macro and intermediate environments of the organization. They are also evaluated by these customers or clients, and the results of this evaluation process are fed into the major components of the macro environment, components of the intermediate environment, and into the organization itself. Feedback is also provided directly to the organization from the clients and customers of the organization. This feedback directly affects strategic and operating decisions that organizations make in acquiring and utilizing its human resources.

Some of these outputs are used directly by employees and their families. They are weighed and considered by these people and resultant evaluations are fed back into the organization's operating processes. Much of the feedback from employees is received indirectly by the organization. For example, dissatisfied employees may reduce productivity, increase waste, have more absences and tardiness, file more grievances, or even engage in sabotage. This is their way of manifesting their dissatisfaction to the organization without verbally communicating it directly to managers.

Thus, it is crucial for both public and private organizations to monitor and evaluate information it receives both directly and indirectly from its clients, customers, employees, and intermediate environment. Not only must this information be monitored and evaluated, but it must become a major input to future decisions. A comprehensive study showing poor employee attitudes and low morale is of little benefit if the results of the study do not somehow affect managerial human resource decisions. Labor market research studies showing noncompetitive wages for employees in the organization are worthless unless decisions are made to change the wage and salary structure to attract and hold competent employees.

It is essential for governmental and other public organizations to realize the importance of this feedback. Users of governmental services are rightfully called clients. This includes users of social welfare programs as well as students in state universities, high school and elementary students in public school systems, prisoners in rehabilitation facilities, and farmers who use the agricultural extension service. The attitudes and evaluations of these groups, as well as the attitudes and opinions of employees, need to be better monitored, evaluated, and the resultant information inputed to the decision process. This feedback evaluation is especially important for governmental groups since they often exist as monopolies and are not under the constraints of competition which private organizations usually face.

CONCLUSION

The organization exists to satisfy customer or client needs. It makes decisions regarding its human resources in producing goods and services to satisfy these needs. These decisions are influenced by the organization's intermediate environment which links the organization to its macro environment. These decisions are also influenced by the client, customer, and employee evaluation of the output produced.

The organization exists in dynamic interaction with its environment.

It obtains inputs from sources in this environment (through the intermediate environment) and it produces outputs which are used by people in this environment. As the organization dynamically interacts with its environment, it moves through time. It is as if "[the organization] throws its hook into the future . . . anchoring it in some intended destination toward which it pulls itself, purposively, modifying its activity and organization to achieve this end."[9] All the while it is pulling itself into the future, it makes strategic and operating human resource decisions.

Chapter 3 of the book looks at the organization's macro environment in more detail. The changing nature of the demands made by the components of this environment are analyzed as they affect human resource decisions. Special emphasis is placed on the interaction of the macro environment with the organization's intermediate environment.

CASE 1
ACCUREX CORPORATION

The Accurex Corporation was known throughout the metal working industry as a manufacturer of the highest quality precision measuring equipment. During and after the Second World War, Accurex invented and commercialized a line of gages which were widely accepted by industry. The gages were covered by strong patents and there was little competition. Each required some small design changes and Accurex design and manufacture were truly excellent. Over a period of years, as the product line matured and patents expired, competition became stronger, and profitability and market share began to erode. Top management decided after several fruitless attempts at improvement to make a change in supervision.

Mr. Dick Street, a young graduate engineer with two years' supervisory experience in another engineering department of Accurex, was assigned to correct the situation. Both the marketing group, who quoted the jobs, and the design group were made up of long service employees who had helped to build the product line through the early years. They had no formal engineering training, but were dedicated to producing a quality product.

Several of the designers told Mr. Street that they knew they sometimes took too long to design a gage, but the Accurex reputation was built on quality and that could never be compromised. Mr. Street was able to review the design of gages built by competition and talk with several key customers. He concluded that both Accurex and competitive gages performed a perfectly satisfactory job. But Accurex gages had more fancy features, features which did not contribute to the efficiency or accuracy of the gage. After careful thought he was sure this was the basic cost problem that must be addressed.

Mr. Street decided to call his entire group together and explain the changes he now felt were necessary. He indicated:

> I'm sure you all know that profits are becoming smaller, and we must make some changes to survive in today's business environment. We are designing frills and gingerbread into our gages, which cost

additional design and manufacturing time. It will be necessary for all of you to change your design techniques, eliminate unnecessary features and thereby reduce product cost. I'm sure I can count on each of you to do your part.

Three months passed, sufficient time for meaningful results, and Mr. Street was forced to confirm his earlier suspicions. In the three month period the situation had not improved at all. He had failed to effect any change in the way his group was designing gages.

Questions

1. What evidence exists that indicates that Street did not look at other important variables in the human resource system which were in operation here? Which variables did he overlook?

2. What factors in the macro environment had a significant influence on the issues raised here?

3. If you were Street what would you have done differently? What should he do now?

4. What relationship do decisions affecting the technical aspects of production in this situation have with the human resource system?

CASE 2
JOHNSON RUBBER PRODUCTS COMPANY

Johnson Rubber Products Company had decided to close its Akron, Ohio plant and built a new plant in Jonesborrow, Alabama. Union wage rates and an obsolete plant had driven the production costs sky-high, and the top management of Johnson believed their products could be produced cheaper in a new plant under nonunion conditions.

After several months of investigation, the company decided upon Jonesborrow as the site for the new plant. Jonesborrow was becoming an industrialized city and eleven other companies had located plants there over the last fifteen years. Not one of them was unionized.

A new plant would be constructed and some of the newer machines from the older plant would be moved down to Jonesborrow. However, the management estimated that about 60 percent of the machinery needed for the plant would have to be brand new and specially constructed. Herein lies the dilemma. The most efficient machinery would require very little skill to operate. While the company could thus capitalize on the low skill levels of the industrial workforce available by using these new machines, they were concerned about the problems that would likely crop up later. There were few jobs in the plant that would be highly skilled. The company estimates that only 10 percent of the jobs would require high skills if they went with the most efficient machines. Thus, their concern was with the opportunities for growth on the jobs they would be offering to the Jonesborrow community. The management of Johnson had heard and read about job enrichment and the problems caused by frustrated, bored workers in mundane, routine, unskilled jobs. They wanted to avoid these problems in their new plant. Yet they also wanted to use the most productive machinery.

Questions

1. How does an organization assess the human resources available to it from its macro environment?

2. To what extent do you think the Johnson Company based its decision to move to Jonesborrow because the skill level of the available workforce was low?

3. Is the basic dilemma in this case between maximizing production or maximizing worker satisfaction as the case suggests? Why or why not?

4. What factors should the company consider in reaching a decision on the new equipment? What are the most important factors?

STUDY AND DISCUSSION QUESTIONS

1. Is all human behavior caused? Can you think of any human activity or behavior which is not caused?

2. What do we mean when we say that "human resources are managed?"

3. Explain the macro-intermediate-micro environmental concept.

4. What are the major components of the macro, intermediate, and micro environments?

5. Distinguish between strategic and administrative decisions.

6. What are the components of the human resource system?

7. What are some outputs of a major corporation?

8. Are there any components of an organization's macro environment which can be managed?

9. What role do the groups in the intermediate environment play?

10. Do you feel that most managers treat their subordinates as if they have "intrinsic value?" Explain.

ENDNOTES

1. Keith Davis, *Human Behavior at Work,* 4th ed. (New York: McGraw-Hill Book Company, Inc., 1972), pp. 15-17.
2. F. J. Roethlisberger and W. J. Dickson, *Management and the Worker* (Cambridge, Mass.: Harvard University, 1939, paperback edition), p. 569.
3. See B. J. Hodge and H. J. Johnson, *Management and Organizational Behavior* (New York: John Wiley and Sons, Inc., 1970), pp. 3-13 for a more detailed discussion of this concept.
4. Ibid., p. 8.
5. See, for example, James D. Thompson, *Organizations in Action* (New York: McGraw-Hill Book Company, Inc., 1967), pp. 70-79.
6. Neil W. Chamberlain, *Enterprise and Environment: The Firm in Time and Place* (New York: McGraw-Hill Book Company, Inc., 1968), pp. 30-43.
7. Ibid., pp. 17-25.
8. Dan Voich and William Shrode, *Organization and Management: Basic Systems Concepts* (Homewood, Ill.: Richard D. Irwin, 1974) pp. 155-156.
9. Chamberlain, op. cit., p. 9.

ADDITIONAL READING

Beach, Dale S. *Personnel: The Management of People at Work,* 3rd ed., New York: Houghton Mifflin Company, 1970.

Dunn, J. D. and Elvis C. Stephens. *Management of Personnel: Manpower, Management and Organizational Behavior.* New York: McGraw-Hill Book Co., 1972.

Hicks, Herbert G. *The Management of Organizations: A Systems and Human Resource Approach,* 2nd ed. New York: McGraw-Hill Book Co., 1970.

Hodge, B. J. and Herbert Johnson. *Management and Organizational Behavior.* New York: John Wiley and Sons, Inc., 1970.

Megginson, Leon. *Personnel: A Behavioral Approach to Administration.* Homewood, Ill.: Richard D. Irwin, 1972.

Miles, Raymond E. *Theories of Management: Implications for Organizational Behavior and Development.* New York: McGraw-Hill Book Co., 1975.

Miner, John B. and Mary Geen Miner. *Personnel and Industrial Relations: A Managerial Approach,* 2nd ed., New York: Macmillan Co., 1973.

Seiler, John A. *Systems Analysis in Organizational Behavior.* Homewood, Ill.: Richard D. Irwin and the Dorsey Press, 1967.

Wasmuth, W. J., Rollin H. Simonds, Raymond L. Hilgert and H. C. Lee, *Human Resources Administration: Problems of Growth and Change.* New York: Houghton Mifflin Company, 1970.

Yaney, Joseph P. *Personnel Management: Reaching Organizational and Human Goals.* Columbus: Charles E. Merrill Publishing Co., 1975.

THE STRUCTURE OF JOBS AND THE LABOR FORCE IN AN INDUSTRIAL ECONOMY

In this chapter, we focus on the macro environment for organizations. This is the top part of Figure 2-2, reproduced here as Figure 3-1. We need to first understand an organization's overall environment, particularly the jobs, human resources and technology found in that environment before we can discuss the internal operations on organization.

To a great extent, organizations view the labor market as a pool of skills and abilities in the macro environment that will be tapped as the

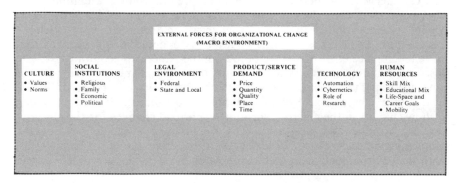

FIGURE 3-1   THE MACRO ENVIRONMENT

need arises. For most job requirements, employees with appropriate skills and abilities are readily available. From time to time, organizations will experience shortages of certain skills or find that the wage level is so high that they cannot "afford" to hire the type of people that are needed to fill the available jobs. The relationship between the organization's job requirements and the available pool of skills and abilities is typically viewed by managers as a sequential process whereby the organization first establishes the best job structure in terms of job content and task assignments, determines each job's worth in the production process, and then proceeds to hire and/or develop human resources that match these requirements. This is an entirely too static view of a dynamic, interactive process.

A much more realistic and comprehensive view of this exchange between the micro and macro environments affecting the employment of human resources needs to be considered. Economists typically point up four main determinants of labor supply: the size, age, sex, and educational composition of the population; the demand for goods and services in the economy; the nature of production technology; and the labor force participation rates of major sub-groups in the population. The employing organization views its role as that of offering wage and benefit levels that will affect the labor force participation rates of appropriate sub-groups. The population is considered as given; the demand for goods and services determines the level of employment in the organization; and the production technology determines job content and task structure. This conceptualization of the process requires that human resources conform (or be motivated to conform) to established jobs. Within the past decade, job design studies have emerged from many organizations that suggest we consider none of these factors invariant in the employment process. Rather, organizations should consider manipulating ". . . the configuration of technology as interpreted in task designs and assignments making up jobs, and to determine what variations are possible and what the effects of these are on personal, social, and organizational variables."[1]

In other words, the systems view of the employment process requires that we focus on the interactive relationship that exists between the pool of human resources potentially available for the labor force and the human resource decisions made by employers. The relationship is a complex one that requires careful attention to historical relationships and changes in values, science and technology, the legal environment, and society's institutions. The purpose of this chapter is to describe the changes that have taken place in the structure of jobs in the American economy over the last two-hundred years, why these changes took place, the role of employers in these changes, and what changes are likely to occur in the near future. The objective of this chapter is to promote an understanding of how changes in the macro-environment portend changes for the employing organization and vice-versa. The intent is to evoke a view of the employment manager's role in society as a proactive one in his relationship with the environment—not, as has too often been the case, a reactive one.

LABOR RESOURCES IN THE ECONOMY

From the vantage point of the typical organization, the population base is the starting point for manpower planning. The employment manager tends to view the population in some geographical area as a vast pool of talents, skills, knowledge, and potential abilities that must be attracted, selected, trained, developed, and placed to serve the requirements of the organization. This certainly is not an invalid view of his world, but it may be too simplistic a view. For to perceive a labor market as only another resource pool to be exploited efficiently fails to account for the important interaction that occurs between changes in the macro system and changes in employing organizations. The two systems interact in subtle ways and effect changes in an endless action-reaction chain. To understand some of the more important relationships, we move back in time to the mid-eighteen hundreds.

In 1850 the United States was in the throes of an industrial revolution. It was being transformed from an agricultural and trading nation into a great manufacturing nation. For example, in 1869 twenty percent of the national product was the result of agricultural production, nearly 16 percent was contributed by trade, and 14 percent by manufacturing. By the 1920s the manufacturing sector was contributing over 22 percent, agriculture had fallen to 12 percent and trade continued to provide about 14 percent of the national product.[2] What accounted for this change? Certainly changes in production technology, (e.g., the mechanization of production, the harnessing of steam power, the genius of assembly-line technology) paved the way for the United States to become a manufacturing nation. But, no less important was the fact that domestic markets for manufactured goods had grown as the population increased from 23 million people in 1850 to about 116 million in 1925.

Throughout the colonial period, there was a shortage of skilled craftsmen, especially on the Eastern seaboard. But beginning in the 1800s a rapid growth in immigration occured. Dulles points out that:

> In the first half century of our national history, approximately one million immigrants entered the country, but in the single decade from 1846 to 1855, the total was almost three million. Famine in Ireland and suppression of the revolutionary uprising on the continent accounted for a swelling stream of workers crossing the Atlantic, and there was an increasing proportion of mechanics and laborers, as contrasted with farmers, among these newcomers. They tended to settle in the east, drawn to the rapidly growing cities and manufacturing centers, and were available for all kinds of work, more often unskilled than skilled, at wages greatly reduced from anything which native artisans and mechanics considered essential for decent living conditions. Immigration, that is, was perhaps for the first time providing a labor surplus which counteracted the effect of cheap land and the frontier in drawing workers off from the eastern states. A pattern that was to become even clearer in the 1880s and 1890s, when the trend of immigration showed still greater gains and a further shift toward the ignorant, unskilled and poverty-stricken peasants of south-eastern Europe, was already outlined in the 1850s.[3]

This immigration added to an expanding domestic population and fed not only the demand for manufactured goods in the U.S., but made practicable the expansion of manufacturing using the newly invented production processes. Throughout our early history, the manufacturing sector of the economy was growing, but at a relatively slow rate compared to the 1800s. One of the important limiting factors was the availability of skilled labor to staff the handicraft industries. It is tempting to conclude that had the new production processes been "available" during the 1700s manufacturing would have grown rapidly during that period as it did in England. However, without a plentiful supply of cheap, unskilled labor the "technology" of mass production made little sense.

The Industrial Revolution brought about a situation where machines increasingly performed the skilled tasks of production with consistent and acceptable quality, thereby reducing the demand for the artisan and craftsman. The rationale of dividing complicated tasks into simple components and hiring unskilled labor to perform only these simple tasks elegantly suited the growing labor force of unskilled, technologically unsophisticated, uneducated immigrants from foreign lands and from domestic farms. Note that manufacturing grew not only because of scientific and engineering changes in the processes of production but because of the coming together of the forces of developing mass markets, both foreign and domestic, immigration, and the suitability of new management "technology" (division of labor and assembly line techniques) to conditions in both factor and product markets.

CHANGING OCCUPATIONAL STRUCTURE IN THE LABOR FORCE

Statistical data from the early industrial period is of questionable quality; however, Table 3-1 provides a reasonably accurate picture of the labor force in 1900. The U. S. economy was still dominated by agriculture, and nearly forty percent of the economically active were employed on the farm. The family farm was the major form of organization in this sector, and although farms were growing in size and output during the 1800s,

TABLE 3-1

OCCUPATIONS OF THE ECONOMICALLY ACTIVE POPULATION
1900-1950

	1900		1950	
Occupation	Thousand	Percent	Thousand	Percent
Professional, Technical, & Kindred Workers	1,234	4	5,081	9
Managers, Officials, and Proprietors, Exc. Farm	1,697	6	5,155	9
Farmers and Farm Mgrs.	5,763	20	4,375	7
Clerical and Kindred Workers	877	3	7,232	12
Sales Workers	1,307	5	4,133	7
Craftsmen, Foremen, and Kindred Workers	3,062	10	8,350	14
Operatives and Kindred Workers	3,720	13	12,030	20
Private Household Workers	1,579	5	1,539	3
Service Workers	1,047	4	4,641	8
Farm Laborers and Foremen	5,125	18	2,578	4
Laborers, Exc. Farm and Mine Workers	3,620	12	3,885	7
TOTAL	29,030	100	58,999	100

Source: U. S. Bureau of the Census, *Historical Statistics of the United States: Colonial Times to 1957* (Washington, D. C.: Superintendant of Documents, 1960), p. 74.

employment was declining as a result of the adoption of mechanized farming methods.

By 1950 agricultural output had increased greatly and was feeding a population that had doubled to over 150 million in fifty years and, at the same time was producing a growing surplus of food commodities. This growth in output was accomplished using fewer and fewer workers, and by 1950, only about eleven percent of the labor force was employed on the farm. During this half-century, the manufacturing, transportation, and service sector of the economy grew most rapidly, and unskilled and semi-skilled operatives, clerical positions, craftsmen, and foremen jobs skilled jobs and in professional and technical positions in the labor force, the dominate changes were in the growth of jobs that required moderate skill levels, some formal training, or education.

Table 3-2 projects these occupational changes through 1985. Note that the largest increases will occur in the professional and technical, clerical, and other service worker categories. Farm workers, private household workers, nonfarm laborers, and operatives will decline as a percentage of the labor force. The percent of the labor force classified as managers and administrators, while initially declining will remain stable from 1972-1985.

TABLE 3-2

**EMPLOYMENT BY MAJOR OCCUPATIONAL GROUP, 1960, 1972,
AND PROJECTED 1980 AND 1985**
(in thousands and percentages)

Occupational Group	1960	%	1972	%	1980	%	1985	%
Professional and Technical Workers	7,236	11.0	11,459	14.0	15,000	15.7	17,000	16.8
Managers and Administrators	7,367	11.2	8,032	9.8	10,100	10.5	10,500	10.3
Sales Workers	4,210	6.4	5,354	6.6	6,300	6.6	6,500	6.4
Clerical Workers	9,538	14.5	14,247	17.4	17,900	18.7	19,700	19.4
Craftsmen & Kindred	8,748	13.3	10,810	13.2	12,200	12.8	13,000	12.8
Operatives	11,380	17.3	13,549	16.6	15,000	15.6	15,300	15.1
Nonfarm Laborers	3,749	5.7	4,217	5.2	4,500	4.7	4,500	4.4
Private Household Workers	1,965	3.0	1,437	1.8	1,300	1.3	1,100	1.1
Other Service Workers	6,387	9.7	9,529	11.6	11,400	12.0	12,300	12.1
Farm Workers	5,196	7.9	3,069	3.8	2,000	2.1	1,600	1.6
TOTAL	65,778	100.0	81,703	100.0	95,800	100.0	101,500	100.0

Source: Neal H. Rosenthal, "The United States Economy in 1985: Projected Changes in Occupations," *Monthly Labor Review,* December 1973, pp. 18-26.

Even though percentages of certain occupational groups may remain stable, there will be an increase in demand as measured by total numbers for several groups. For example, 7,367,000 people were classified as managers in 1960 and made up 11.2 percent of the labor force. By 1985, over 10,500,000 people will be managers even though their percentage in the total labor force will drop to 10.3 percent.

These figures reflect a continuation of earlier trends. The greatest labor force growth will occur primarily in white collar occupations requiring some type of technical skill. Decreases will occur primarily in unskilled and semi-skilled blue collar occupations.

CHANGES IN FORMAL
EDUCATIONAL ACHIEVEMENT

These occupational changes have led to changes in levels of educational achievement of individuals in society. It is not clear whether the changing nature of occupations causes increased educational levels or whether changes in educational achievement cause changes in occupational structure. The way in which employers organize their resources in large part determines the occupational characteristics of the labor force. In the aggregate, the jobs that employers wish to fill now and in the future constitute the demand for labor. The skills, experience, and educational requirements of these jobs directly affect the supply characteristics of labor. Our educational system, job counseling, employment agencies, and employee training and development programs are oriented toward creating human resources that "fit" the jobs. On the other hand, many individual employers engage in manpower planning and design jobs around a supply of labor they assume is influenced more by personal values, social forces, political ideals, and changing economic conditions. While the view of the individual employer is not necessarily wrong, it fails to see the interdependencies between the way in which employers organize the factors of production and the influence this has on the supply of human resources.

To illustrate the point, since 1900 the tremendous increase in white-collar jobs that require post-secondary schooling has promoted the growth of higher education. As the supply of job seekers with more education increases, there is a tendency to increase the educational requirements of jobs because of concern for hiring the "best" people. On the other side, job seekers extend their schooling, in an effort to improve their marketability, which raises the average level of education of the labor force, which again feeds into employers who continue the cycle. This has produced many problems for employers and employees alike. Some employers have difficulty filling low-level jobs while at the same time some job seekers can not find employment because they are "over-qualified", or "over-educated."

These kinds of problems point up the need for manpower planners to consider the design of jobs and the use and development of production technology, not only from the narrow perspective of short-run efficiency in their organizations, but also from the view of the long-run needs of employees and society.

Therefore, changes in educational requirements of the job are both a result of and a cause for changes in levels of educational achievement. It is an interactive process, but more attention needs to be directed to the fact that educational requirements specified for an occupation are often a result of higher levels of educational achievement in the labor force. (This interactive process has resulted in higher levels of educational achievement among people in the labor force.) These changes are summarized in Table 3-3. This table indicates projected changes in levels of educational attainment for persons 25 years old and older in the civilian labor force to 1990. Note that the percentage of those with four years of college will increase from 7.4 to 12.7 percent. Those with five or more years will increase by even a greater percentage, 5.1 to 11.1 percent. Those with only eight years of elementary school will continue to decline from 16.8 to 3.6 percent. The portion with high school degrees will increase by about one-third from 27.8 to 41.2 percent.

Chart 3-1 shows the projected dramatic increase in the percentage of those with four or more years of college and the corresponding reduction of those with eight years of schooling or less. Note also the increase of

CHART 3-1

EDUCATIONAL ATTAINMENT OF THE CIVILIAN LABOR FORCE 25 YEARS OLD AND OVER, 1957-59 AVERAGE, 1970-72 AVERAGE, AND PROJECTED 1980 AND 1990

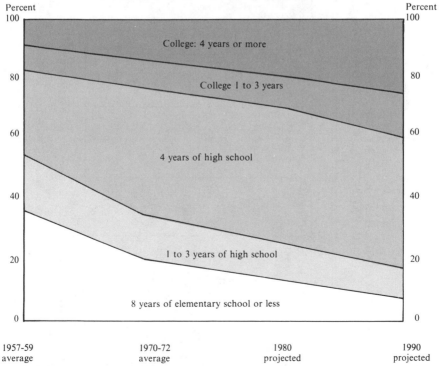

Source: Denis F. Johnston, "Education of Workers: Projections to 1990," *Monthly Labor Review,* November, 1973, p. 24.

TABLE 3-3

YEARS OF SCHOOL COMPLETED BY PERSONS 25 YEARS OLD AND OVER IN THE CIVILIAN LABOR FORCE, ACTUAL 1957-72, PROJECTED TO 1980, 1985, AND 1990 (percent distribution)

Year	Total		Elementary school			High school		College			
	Number in Thousands	Percent	Less than 5 years[1]	5 to 7 years	8 years	1 to 3 years	4 years	1 to 3 years	4 years or more	4 years	5 years or more
1957-59 average[2]	55,909	100.0	6.3	11.4	16.8	19.2	27.8	8.4	10.2	(³)	(³)
1964-65-66 average	60,067	100.0	4.1	8.7	13.4	18.9	32.8	9.6	12.5	7.4	5.1
1967-68-69 average	63,618	100.0	3.1	7.2	11.0	17.6	36.4	11.0	13.7	8.1	5.6
1970-71-72 average	65,655	100.0	2.6	6.4	10.0	16.9	37.5	12.0	14.6	8.3	6.3
Projected:											
1980	77,227	100.0	1.5	3.9	6.4	15.1	40.7	14.0	18.5	10.4	8.1
1985	84,731	100.0	1.0	2.7	4.8	13.8	41.3	15.2	21.2	11.6	9.6
1990	91,456	100.0	.6	1.9	3.6	12.5	41.2	16.4	23.8	12.7	11.1

[1]Includes those reporting no formal education.
[2]Total excludes persons whose educational attainment was not reported.
[3]Data not available.
Source: Denis F. Johnston, "Education of Workers: Projections to 1990," *Monthly Labor Review*, November 1973, p. 23.

those with one to three years of college. This can be partially explained by the great increase of persons who receive two years of post-high school education in community and junior colleges and in two-year post-secondary technical schools.

EDUCATION AND OCCUPATION

In general, rising levels of educational attainment have been associated with all occupational levels. Not only are there more people with four years or more of college in the professional and technical occupational categories, but the sales, laborers, farm managers, and farm laborers categories have also seen an increase in the percentage with four years or more of college education. However, the percentage with a college education in the farm laborer category is still insignificant at 1.8 percent.

Table 3-4 presents the percentage of people with high school and college educations for each occupational group. The greatest increases have occurred in the professional, managerial, and sales categories. Managers and proprietors in particular have increased by about 8 percent, the greatest increase in college education for any group. Increases in the percentages of workers with only a high school education were especially pronounced in blue-collar, service, and farms occupations.

TABLE 3-4

PERCENT OF WORKERS 25 AND OLDER WITH 12 YEARS OF EDUCATION OR MORE, BY OCCUPATION, 1960 AND 1970

Occupation	Percent with 4 years of high school		Percent with 1 to 3 years of college		Percent with 4 years of college or more	
	1960	1970	1960	1970	1960	1970
Professional and technical	16.0	17.5	19.7	17.8	55.4	58.4
Managers and proprietors	30.4	33.8	17.2	19.2	15.7	23.8
Sales	33.3	39.4	15.2	17.9	9.9	13.5
Clerical	47.6	54.6	15.9	16.9	5.7	5.9
Craftsmen	27.2	38.0	6.2	8.0	2.1	2.2
Operatives	20.3	30.4	3.2	4.1	0.6	0.8
Service	20.2	30.5	4.6	6.4	1.2	1.7
Laborers, except farm and mine	13.2	23.7	2.4	4.0	0.6	1.2
Farmers and farm managers	20.1	31.4	5.0	6.9	2.2	3.9
Farm laborers and foremen	10.3	18.6	2.3	3.4	0.8	1.8

Source: William V. Deutermann, "Educational Attainment of Workers, March, 1973," *Monthly Labor Review*, January 1974, p. 60.

EMPLOYMENT BY SECTOR

Thus far we have examined the occupational and educational relationships and projections for the labor force. Another important factor in the labor market which influences the structure of employment is the shift in the particular sectors which produce employment. In general, over the years, employment as a percentage of the total labor force has been declining in goods-producing industries (e.g., mining, construction, manufacturing) and increasing in service-producing industries (e.g., transportation, communication, wholesale and retail trade, finance, insurance, and real estate) and in government (state, federal, local). This trend is predicted to continue through 1985, although not at as pronounced a rate. Chart 3-2 indicates that government employment at all levels will continue to expand in terms of percentage of the labor force but at a decreasing rate. The percentage of employment in goods-producing industries will continue to decrease but at a decreasing rate. The percentage in service producing industries will begin stabilizing in 1980.

Note that this chart reflects the percentage of the total labor force in each sector, *not* the percentage of growth in total employment in each sector. Total employment in every sector is projected to increase, except in agriculture and mining, with the greatest increases occurring in government. Table 3-5 summarizes this expected increase in employment by each of the major sectors of the economy.

AGE AND SEX OF THE LABOR FORCE

The final structural characteristic of the labor force which we will examine is its age-sex composition. This characteristic significantly influences the way employers structure jobs and hire new employees. For example, if the labor force consists of a greater number of both younger and female workers than in the past, employers are likely to be more hesitant in structuring and hiring for higher level jobs with increased authority for decision making.

The general trend has been an increase in the percentage of the labor force who are young and female. While all sectors of the age-sex categories have increased, the greatest increases have occurred among men and women in the 20–34 age group. As indicated in Table 3-6, total percentage of the labor force comprised of women is expected to increase from 32.3 percent in 1960 to 38.7 percent in 1985. The percentage of men comprising the labor force is expected to fall 6.4 percent to 61.3 percent in 1985.

Also note that the median age for both sexes is expected to decrease from 39.8 in 1960 to 35.8 in 1985. The labor force participation rate for women has been increasing over the last two decades and is expected to continue to increase projected to 1990. More and more women are entering the labor force. Smaller families, higher levels of education, home labor-saving devices, and changing cultural stereo-types have all been contributing factors for higher work rates for women.

Chart 3-3 depicts actual and projected labor force participation rates for women by age group to 1990. Notice the huge increase (from 47 percent to 68 percent) of those in the 16–20 age group who are entering the labor force. Note also that even during prime child-bearing years (20-35), the participation rate has increased from about 36 percent to over 50 percent. The only age group where the participation rates have, and will likely continue to remain constant is in the post-55 age group.

CHART 3-2

PERCENTAGE DISTRIBUTION OF TOTAL EMPLOYMENT (counting jobs rather than workers) FOR SELECTED YEARS AND PROJECTED 1980 AND 1985

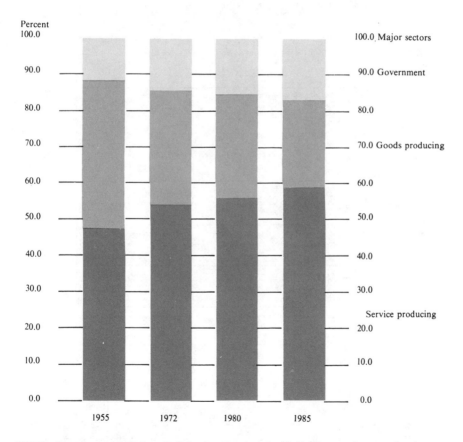

NOTE: Government includes all federal, state and local civilian employees. Goods producing includes agriculture, mining, construction, and manufacturing. Service producing includes transportation, communications, public utilities, trade, finance, insurance, and real estate, and other services.

Source: Ronald E. Kutscher, "The United States Economy in 1985: Projections of GNP, Income, Output and Employment," *Monthly Labor Review,* December 1973, p. 40.

TABLE 3-5

TOTAL EMPLOYMENT, BY MAJOR SECTOR, SELECTED YEARS 1955-72 AND PROJECTED TO 1980 AND 1985
(Thousands of jobs)

Sector	Actual				Projected		Average annual rate of change[1]					
	1955	1960	1968	1972	1980	1985	1955-68	1968-72	1968-85	1968-80	1972-80	1980-85
Total	65,745	68,732	80,926	85,597	101,576	107,609	1.6	1.4	1.7	1.9	2.2	1.2
Government	6,914	8,353	11,845	13,290	16,610	18,800	4.2	2.9	2.8	2.9	2.8	2.5
Total private	58,831	60,379	69,081	72,307	84,966	88,809	1.2	1.2	1.5	1.7	2.0	.9
Agriculture	6,434	5,398	3,816	3,450	2,300	1,900	-3.9	-2.5	-4.0	-4.1	-4.9	-3.7
Nonagriculture	52,397	54,990	65,265	68,857	82,666	86,909	1.7	1.4	1.7	2.0	2.3	1.0
Mining	832	748	640	645	655	632	-2.0	.2	-.1	-.2	-.4	-.7
Construction	3,577	3,654	4,038	4,352	4,908	5,184	.9	1.9	1.5	1.6	1.5	1.1
Manufacturing	17,309	17,197	20,138	19,281	22,923	23,499	1.2	-1.1	.9	1.1	2.2	.5
Durable	9,782	9,681	11,828	11,091	13,629	14,154	1.5	-1.6	1.1	1.2	2.6	.8
Nondurable	7,527	7,516	8,310	8,190	9,294	9,345	.8	-.4	.7	.9	1.6	.1
Transportation, communication, and public utilities	4,353	4,214	5,519	4,726	5,321	5,368	.3	1.1	1.0	1.4	1.5	.2
Transportation	2,918	2,824	2,868	2,842	3,250	3,266	-.1	-.2	.8	1.0	1.7	.1
Communication	832	844	986	1,150	1,300	1,312	1.3	3.9	1.7	2.3	1.5	.2
Public utilities	603	528	665	724	771	790	.8	2.1	1.0	1.2	.8	.5
Trade	13,201	14,177	16,655	18,432	21,695	22,381	1.8	2.6	1.8	2.2	2.1	.6
Wholesale trade	3,063	3,295	3,894	4,235	4,946	5,123	1.9	2.1	1.6	2.0	2.0	.7
Retail trade	10,138	10,882	12,761	14,197	16,749	17,258	1.8	2.7	1.8	2.3	2.1	.6
Finance, insurance and real estate	2,652	2,985	3,720	4,303	5,349	5,932	2.6	3.7	2.8	3.1	2.8	2.1
Other services	10,468	12,015	15,555	17,815	21,815	23,913	3.1	2.4	2.6	2.9	3.1	1.9

[1]Compound interest rate between terminal years.

Source: Ronald E. Kutscher, "The United States Economy in 1985: Projections of GNP, Income, Output and Employment," *Monthly Labor Review*, December 1973, p. 39.

TABLE 3-6

TOTAL LABOR FORCE, BY AGE AND SEX, ANNUAL AVERAGE 1960, 1972, AND PROJECTED TO 1980 AND 1985

Sex and age	Number (in thousands)				Percent distribution			
	1960	1972	1980	1985	1960	1972	1980	1985
BOTH SEXES								
Total, 16 years and over	72,142	88,991	101,809	107,716	100.0	100.0	100.0	100.0
16 to 19 years	5,246	8,367	8,337	7,165	7.3	9.4	8.2	6.7
20 to 23 years	22,749	32,463	42,223	44,758	31.5	36.5	41.5	41.6
35 to 54 years	31,562	33,689	35,165	39,463	43.7	37.9	34.5	36.6
55 years and over	12,585	14,472	16,084	16,084	17.4	16.3	15.8	15.2
Median age in years	39.8	37.2	35.2	25.8				
MEN								
Total, 16 years and over	48,870	55,671	62,590	66,017	67.7	62.6	61.5	61.3
16 to 19 years	3,184	4,791	4,668	3,962	4.4	5.4	4.6	3.7
20 to 34 years	16,019	20,601	26,375	27,892	22.2	23.1	25.9	25.9
35 to 54 years	20,974	21,116	21,759	24,361	29.1	23.7	21.4	22.6
55 years and over	8,692	9,163	9,788	9,798	12.0	10.3	9.6	9.1
WOMEN								
Total, 16 years and over	23,272	33,320	39,219	41,699	32.3	37.4	38.5	38.7
16 to 19 years	2,062	3,576	3,669	3,203	2.8	4.0	3.6	3.0
20 to 34 years	6,730	11,862	15,848	16,862	9.3	13.3	15.6	15.7
35 to 54 years	10,588	12,573	13,406	15,102	14.7	14.1	13.2	14.0
55 years and over	3,893	5,309	6,296	6,532	5.4	6.0	6.2	6.1

Source: For 1960 and 1972, U. S. Department of Labor, *1973 Manpower Report of the President*, table A-2; for 1980 and 1985, Denis F. Johnston, "The U. S. Labor Force: Projections to 1990," *Monthly Labor Review* July 1973, pp. 3-13.

CHART 3-3

LABOR FORCE PARTICIPATION RATES OF WOMEN, BY AGE, 1960, 1980, AND 1990
(Percent of total population in total labor force)

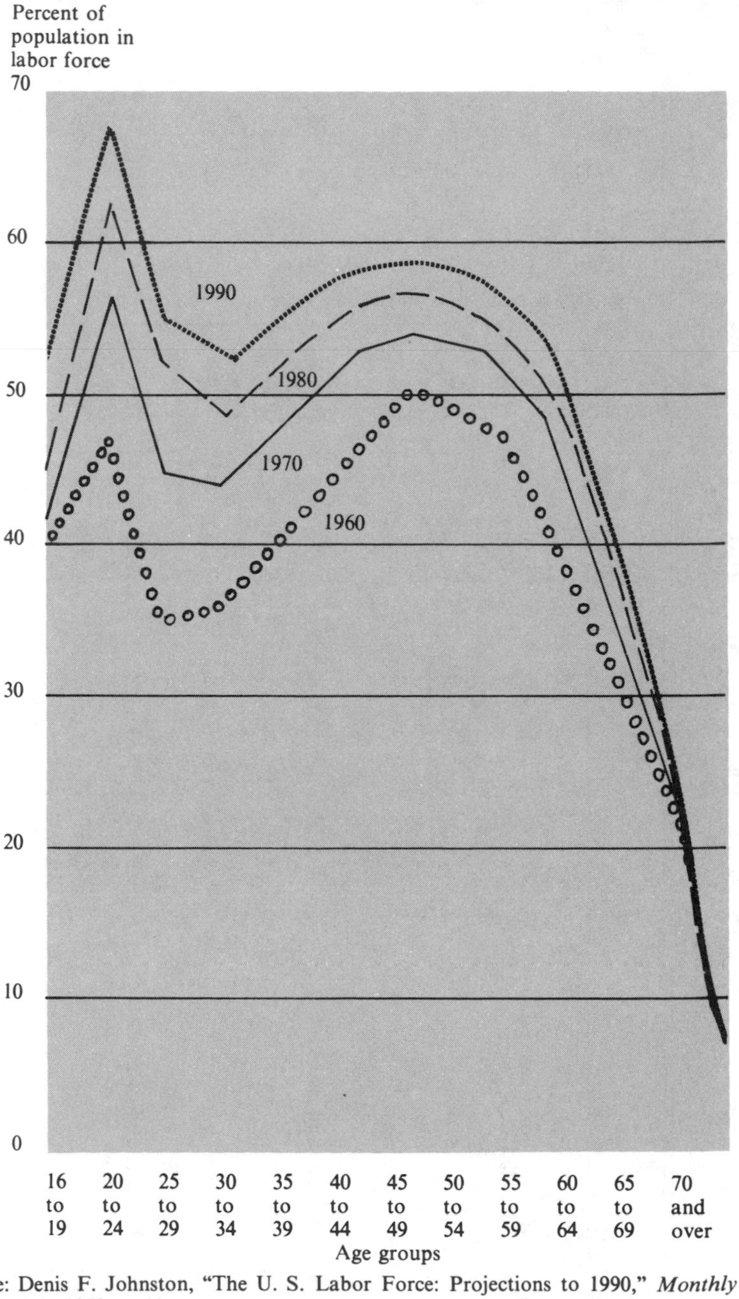

Source: Denis F. Johnston, "The U. S. Labor Force: Projections to 1990," *Monthly Labor Review,* July 1973, p. 11.

Chart 3-4 shows the age-sex profile of the total labor force from 1970–1990. Note that for both males and females the very great increase in individuals in the 25–44 age category by 1990. Note also the corresponding decrease in the 16 to 19 age group for both sexes. This bulge in the 24–44 age group reflects the movement of the post-World War II baby boom into and through the labor force. With a decrease in the birth rate, the younger

CHART 3-4

AGE-SEX PROFILE OF TOTAL LABOR FORCE, 1970 ACTUAL AND 1990 PROJECTED

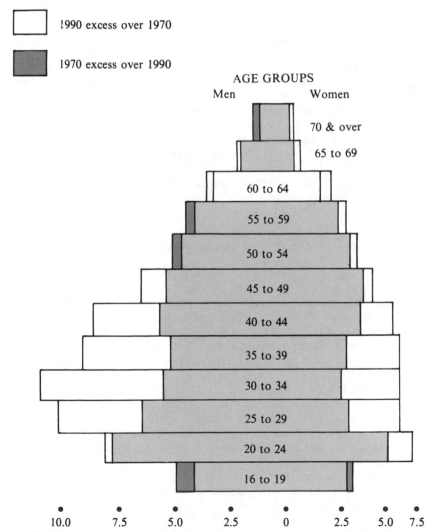

1990 excess over 1970

1970 excess over 1990

AGE GROUPS

Men   Women

70 & over

65 to 69

60 to 64

55 to 59

50 to 54

45 to 49

40 to 44

35 to 39

30 to 34

25 to 29

20 to 24

16 to 19

10.0   7.5   5.0   2.5   0   2.5   5.0   7.5

Source: Denis F. Johnston, "The U. S. Labor Force: Projections to 1990," *Monthly Labor Review,* July 1973, p. 10.

age groups (especially the 16 to 19 group) will be a smaller part of the labor force in 1990 than they were in 1970.

Thus, the labor force will likely continue to have a higher percentage of female and youth to 1990. However, by 1990, it is expected that the average age of the labor force will begin to increase as the post World War II baby boom grows older.

CONCLUSION

In this chapter we have attempted to briefly sketch some present and future parameters of the labor force. We have not attempted to provide an in-depth analysis of all major labor force or labor market trends. However, we have focused on those labor force constructs which have a major impact on human resource management decisions in the organization.

In general, we can say that for the next ten to fifteen years, we are likely to have a more highly educated, younger, female labor force, working in white collar occupations primarily in the government and service-producing section of the economy. Each individual organization in constructing its manpower plan and in designing its recruitment, selection, reward, and other manpower systems will need to account for these changes in the labor force section of the macro environment.

In the ensuing chapters, we will indicate how these changes in labor force constructs impenge on the various manpower decisions in the organization. In particular, the next chapter examines manpower planning systems in the organization with particular focus on changes in the labor market and the need to properly match people and jobs in the organization.

CASE 1
COMPUTER PROGRAMMER

Oscar Purdue is forty-four years old and has been with the computer center at a large research and development oriented Air Force Base since his graduation from college twenty-two years ago. Mr. Purdue's degree was in physics and his training, which was with an early computer that is no longer in use, is no longer a viable skill. About twelve years ago the computer center bought new computers which did the very work Purdue and the fellow members of his group had been trained to do. Rather than fire him, the Air Force offered Purdue the opportunity to learn the needed new skills. Faced with the option of trying to locate another job or continuing with the computer center, Purdue opted for the in-house training, since his friends were there, and his large family was established in the community. Although Purdue initially found the training confusing, he was able to master the new techniques by the end of the three months intensive in-house training.

Over the last few years the nature of the work at the computer center has changed; not through the introduction of a major new type of computer system, but through the gradual evolution and maturing of the computer industry. There are more and more "canned" programs—programmers no longer need to "re-invent the wheel." Time-sharing, video display terminals, on-line editing, and structured programming are only a few of the examples that have evolved over the last few years. The professionals at the computer center have to spend less time on programming, but much more time on analysis. Their job structure has also changed significantly in that they now have much more responsibility for the projects.

Mr. Purdue, however, has not kept up with these new developments. While he was content to continue the programming he had been retrained to do, the technology—and other programmers—passed him by. Over the years these programmers, having been excited by the new computer developments, learned the new techniques, either through self-study or taking (Air Force paid) courses at local universities. Other programmers who were either not interested in computer advances and/or did not want to take on the additional responsibilities have taken other jobs.

Purdue has been given the same opportunity as the others to update his knowledge—by self-study on the job or college courses. Since his job is not threatened at this time he, in effect, turns down the opportunity by consistently putting off the date to start his new training. He much prefers what he has been doing. He wants his job to be comfortable, and he resents and resists efforts to have him acquire new skills or take on new responsibilities. His motivation for learning the new skills is presently negligible, and the effectiveness of any training for him might prove to be negligible.

Mr. Purdue's greatest satisfaction from his job comes from the people he interacts with on a daily basis. Everyone likes Oscar Purdue, including his superiors. He is one of the few people within the organization that everyone can get along with. His peers enjoy his company so much that they have, in effect, "forgiven" his nonconformance with one of the main group norms, i. e., the work produced. He has no desire for promotion; he does not enjoy managing or sanctioning subordinates; and he has no intention of acquiring any more power or prestige. Purdue perceives that he is in a comfortable position and does not want anything or anyone to change his job structure. He derives great satisfaction from the people around him, his hobbies (at which he excels) and his family. Career achievement and increased status have never been goals he has concerned himself with reaching. He merely wants to spend a quiet, pleasurable day at the office and then be with the people and hobbies he enjoys. This is not to suggest that Mr. Purdue dislikes his job or does not care about what he does at work. Rather, Purdue derives most of his satisfaction from interaction with his wide circle of friends, and not from striving for power and success. He satisfactorily does the tasks given to him, but they are not the most important features in his world.

Questions

1. What is likely to occur in the future to affect Oscar Purdue's job?

2. Is Oscar Purdue a valued member of his work group?

3. Does this situation require any personnel decisions immediately? Explain your answer.

4. Is Purdue under-educated for his job? Over-educated?

CASE 2
MORE EDUCATION

George Davis has been employed by the Dressler Chemical Corporation of Boulder, Colorado, for almost fourteen years. When Mr. Davis came to Dressler he had a bachelor's degree in chemical engineering. As he advanced from the engineering trainee position where he was exposed to, and ultimately given increased responsibilities in, various related areas, he realized that he needed further training in chemical engineering. Thus, a couple of years after he started working at Dressler, Davis began taking graduate courses at a nearby university.

Dressler has continued a policy of paying the tuition for their employees if the courses selected served to enhance job performance. Davis took advantage of this opportunity and, enjoying his school work, eventually completed requirements for a master's degree. By this time, Davis was being asked to delve into areas of research for which his degree had trained him, and he was deriving a great deal of satisfaction from his job. He perceived he would have a chance for merit increases in salary and an opportunity for advancement within his company in future years.

A few years later, however, the tasks had become familiar and Davis was getting bored with his job. He remembered how he had enjoyed his experience in the master's program, and how intellectually stimulated and excited he became while learning new research techniques and theories. Davis therefore found himself back at the university as a PhD candidate working in the areas of chemistry that he found challenging. He assumed that his doctorate would enable him to advance to a position within Dressler that would allow him to devote considerable time to the areas of research which were meaningful to him and yet of potential long range benefit to the company. Although Davis found himself "stretching" beyond his job level, going to classes and working full-time was so physically and emotionally draining that the possibility of any undesirable consequences of his educational goals were filtered out of his consciousness. If did not occur to either the company or to Davis himself that he was becoming over-qualified for his present job and that Dressler's cutting back on research funding would eventually have an adverse affect on him.

In due course, Davis successfully completed his academic work, passed his preliminary examinations for the doctoral program, and wrote a solid dissertation from which he would be able to publish several papers. Davis experienced a great deal of satisfaction from achieving his educational goals and looked forward to a promotion at the Dressler Chemical Corporation.

His job was now mundane. There was no longer a challenge. The work was not stimulating. Davis had been taught to explore his mental capabilities for new and innovative ideas—to achieve higher goals in his work pursuits. The logical progression in this area would be promotion.

Weeks, then months, went by after Davis earned his doctorate and the anticipated promotion was not forthcoming. He continued in his old position; frustrated that he was not able to put his years of doctoral course work to good use. He felt even more frustrated knowing that he was not able to pursue his research nor work on his own as he had done for his doctorate, and as he had envisioned being able to do at Dressler's with a PhD. He felt very confined in what he now considered to be a narrow job structure in comparison with the much more unstructured research environment.

Davis was finally told that although he would be getting some salary increase, research funds were so tight that he would have to wait about a year before there would be an opening for his talents.

Frustrated and anxious, Mr. Davis waited out the year. During that year he continued in his present position, and, with one of his professors from graduate school, published a paper from his dissertation data. The year went by without any word about the desired job that he considered his skills and educational attainment had earned for him. Repeated requests for the promotion were sent back to Davis or to his immediate supervisors with various negative comments. For example, "at this particular time the promotion is undesirable for the company;" "there is no position now open in that area;" or "the company considers him too valuable in his current position to consider moving him to a research position." Davis perceived these "reasons" as "excuses" and finally acknowledged that he would be forced to continue in his present capacity for a long while or find another position outside the company.

As Davis began looking for other jobs he came to the realization that the changing structure of American industry was having a direct impact on him. Funds for basic research were being cut considerably, not only at Dressler, but also throughout private and governmental sectors. This was happening partly because of an economic recession and partly because of the explosion of basic research advances in the last decade that will take applied science and engineering years to catch up with and utilize in practical applications. Because they were not as involved as they used to be in research, many companies did not want to hire Davis since they would have had to pay him more (for basically the same work) than a person with a bachelor's or master's degree.

For a time, Davis toyed with the idea of seeking an academic position. However, university positions were scarce (due to decreases in research funds and student enrollment and increases in PhDs) and, without tenure, somewhat risky. He did not want to subject his growing family to the risk, nor the decrease in salary, that becoming an assistant professor would entail. Furthermore, the only positions available were outside the Boulder area, which would mean that his children would have to change school systems and find new friends, and that his wife would have to leave the rest of her family—all for an uncertain future.

Yet, he was keenly aware of the dissatisfaction with his job. He found that doing the work that demanded only master's degree qualifications frustrating and boring. Davis could not see any way to resolve the situation. Maybe the promotion would eventually materialize.

Questions

1. Were Davis' efforts wise?

2. Were Dressler's policies appropriate?

3. What modifications in Dressler's policies would you recommend?

4. What would you do now if you were Davis? Why?

STUDY AND DISCUSSION QUESTIONS

1. What affect did immigration have on the development of jobs in our industrial economy? Did immigration or technology cause job specialization?

2. What managerial style would you expect managers to adopt in managing a relatively unskilled, unsophisticated workforce made up of immigrants?

3. Which occupations are forecasted to grow and which to decline in the next fifteen years?

4. Why have so many women entered the labor force over the last twenty years? Will this trend continue?

5. Is there no longer a need for the unskilled or semi-skilled worker in today's economy?

6. Are today's workers "over-educated" for jobs of the future?

7. In what occupations is skill and knowledge obsolescence likely to be a major problem in the future and what should be done about it?

8. What are the implications for a society of the industrialization process when workers moved from farms to factories?

9. Can technical education substitute for general education in preparing people for the "world of work?"

10. Should some people be prohibited by government from completing high school or from going to college based upon an objective measurement of their potential skills and abilities?

ENDNOTES

1. Louis E. Davis, "The Design of Jobs," *Industrial Relations: A Journal of Economy and and Society,* Vol. 6, No. 2, p. 22.
2. U.S. Bureau of the Census, *Historical Statictics of the United States: Colonial Times to 1957* (Washington, D.C.: Superintendent of Documents, 1960), p. 140.
3. Ibid.

ADDITIONAL READING

Bloom, Gordon F. and Herbert R. Northrup. *Economics of Labor Relations,* 6th ed. Home-wood, Ill.: Richard D. Irwin, Inc. 1969.

Cartler, Allan M. and F. Ray Marshall. *Labor Economics: Wages, Employment, and Trade Unionism,* rev. ed. Homewood, Ill.: Richard D. Irwin, Inc. 1972.

Cohen, Sanford. *Labor in the United States,* 4th ed. Columbus: Charles E. Merrill, Inc., 1975.

Fleisher, Belton M. *Labor Economics: Theory and Evidence.* Englewood Cliffs, N. J.: Prentice-Hall, 1970.

Galbraith, John Kenneth. *Economics and The Public Purpose.* Houghton Mifflin Company, 1973.

Robinson, James W. and Roger W. Walker. *Labor Economics and Labor Relations.* New York: Ronald Press Co., 1973.

Reynolds, Lloyd G. *Labor Economics and Labor Relations,* 6th ed. Englewood Cliffs, N. J.: Prentice-Hall, Inc., 1974.

Williams, C. G. *Labor Economics.* New York: John Wiley and Sons, Inc., 1970.

JOBS, THEIR DESIGN AND EVALUATION

The preceding chapter outlined the occupational dimensions of the labor force. This chapter will discuss jobs in the micro-environment. Thus, we are focusing on the job design and evaluation square indicated in our model as shown in Figure 4-1. In a free economy the demand for labor, both type and amount, is the result of aggregate demand for goods and services and the decisions on the part of employers regarding *how* to produce for the market. It is often a tacit assumption that the mechanized nature of production processes determines the tasks, duties, and responsibilities that constitute jobs in the economy. This chapter examines this assumption, discusses the nature of job design in modern organizations, and reviews the theory and methods of job evaluation.

HISTORICAL DESIGN PRINCIPLES

The historical influence of early management theorists like F. W. Taylor, Mary Parker Follett, Henri Fayol, and Chester Barnard was as important to the nature of job design as the mechanical designs and innovations that constitute the industrial revolution of the nineteenth century. As writers, consultants, and practicing managers, these early theorists chronicled and preached a new industrial ethic. For example, Taylor's work emphasized what he considered to be scientific principles of management and argued that by applying these principles organizations could pay high wages and, at the same time, incur low unit production costs. Four succinct statements make up the essence of his ideas:

First: Develop a science for each element of a man's work, which replaces the old rule-of-thumb method.

Second: Scientifically select and then train, teach, and develop the workman, whereas in the past he chose his own work and trained himself as best he could.

Third: Heartily cooperate with the men so as to insure all of the work being done in accordance with the principles of the science which has been developed.

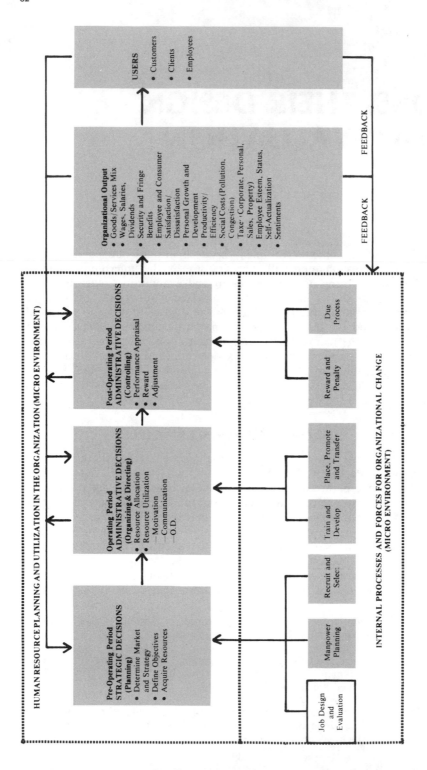

FIGURE 4-1   THE MICRO HUMAN RESOURCE SYSTEM

Fourth: There is an almost equal division of the work and the responsibility between the management and the workmen. The
management take over all work for which they are better fitted
than the workmen, while in the past almost all of the responsibility were thrown upon the men.[1]

Claude George summarizes Taylor's thought and explains that:

If nothing else, Taylor firmly planted the concept of research in place
of rule-of-thumb. And the newer management has continued to experiment and look for the new as a basic element in a sound managerial
approach. He also championed the use of standards in every phase of
management, always driving hard the need for standards of consistency
as a prelude to high standards of operation and product quality.

A third impact—for many years overlooked and neglected—was the
systematic planning that was necessary for any visible improvement.
For years, many individuals confused the mechanics with the system,
failing to see that these were only the evidences of the planning aspect
of his system. Taylor gave to management the collective concept of
control—control as a sensing mechanism to maintain established procedures, standards, conditions, and the like necessary for the effective
and total operation of the system.

Finally, Taylor introduced the principle of cooperation, pointing out that
only through mutual understanding and cooperation could the basic
needs and desires of both management and labor be met.[2]

Taylor's ideas were instrumental in creating more efficient organizations through the development of more systematic techniques for analyzing
tasks and creating jobs that were logically related, easily learned, with
accurately determined cost and output standards. In a sense Taylor was
the philosopher-king of what came to be known as the scientific management school of thought. If Taylor was the philosopher-king, Frank and
Lillian Gilbreth should be considered the policy ministers. The Gilbreths
were pioneers in the field of motion study and their efforts, ". . . laid the
entire foundation for our modern applications of job simplification,
meaningful work standards, and incentive wage plans."[3] This unique
husband and wife team was dedicated to the tasks of economy of effort.
Through their efforts, time and motion study became a precise way of
determining not only how to execute the tasks of a job, but went beyond
the job to determining relationships among tasks and among jobs. Their
efforts resulted in the widespread practical application of the tenets of
scientific management.

The principles of specialization and division of labor that formed the
basis of the revolution in work in the eighteenth century found expression
in the works of Taylor, the Gilbreths, and others and became a new ethic
of management in the United States. It allowed industrialists to divide
complex tasks into their simplest components, determine the "one best
way" to execute the simple tasks, quickly teach unskilled, uneducated
immigrants how to perform a few tasks efficiently, and through careful
coordination, manufacture technically sophisticated products at low unit

costs. The productivity of the worker was increased many-fold, not by increasing his skill but by reducing the skill required to perform a job efficiently. The worker's tasks were made simple and few, they were performed repetitively, and required little if any judgement on the part of the worker. Machines often paced the speed of work, and supervisors were close at hand to assure that workers conformed to the procedures established by management and to deal with anything that went awry.

Not only did the early theorists argue for job specialization at the worker level, but the principles of division of labor were extended to management. In Taylor's view, management's tasks were to plan, organize, and control the work of others. However the principles of scientific management required specialized staff functions in finance, marketing, engineering, personnel services, etc. Moreover, the coordination of these functions, along with operations, required at least a second level of management and often a third or fourth depending upon the size of the organization and the complexity of integrating these specialized functions to produce products or services efficiently. The requirements of the new industrial ethic of Taylor, et al. created the job of management that in a sense was independent of either the product of the organization or the processes of production. Managers were specialists in planning, organizing, and controlling.

The industrial revolution was born of both mechanical inventions and the ideas of Adam Smith, Frederick Taylor, the Gilbreths, and others. When we refer to industrial technology we mean not only the mechanical/electronic processes that underlie the modern economy, but we include the influential ideas and techniques of industrial production that determine the tasks, responsibilities, and duties that constitute jobs in the economy. In a real sense, the industrial revolution was simply a revolution of jobs; i.e., few new products or services were produced in the early stages, but, instead, the products and services of the eighteenth century were provided to more people at lower costs through more efficient production methods.

JOB DESIGN TODAY

A typical approach to job design in a modern organization is to consider the organization's objectives in terms of the tasks to be performed to produce goods and services in the type and amount needed by consumers in the marketplace. Although the process may more logically begin with a consideration by top-management concerning what tasks it wishes to delegate to subordinates and what tasks top-management wishes to reserve for itself, job design is easier to conceptualize if we begin at the bottom of a complex organization.

The simplest element of work is referred to as a *task,* i.e., sawing, lifting, pushing, drilling. A collection of tasks to be performed in some sequence or by some established set of rules, procedures, policies, or guidelines constitutes a *job*. Jobs include not only what one is expected to do, physically, but also what one is expected to accomplish (objectives), what authority one has, and the extent of one's responsibility. A job description is likely to be phrased in terms of duties and responsibilities that explicitly state or infer the tasks to be performed.

Figure 4-2 is an example of a typical job description that includes job specifications, i.e., the knowledge, ability, and skills required to carryout the assigned tasks and responsibilities. Note that there is some emphasis on decision-making abilities in this description. An individual occupying such a position would have responsibility for organizing his/her own work and the work of others and some supervisory responsibilities over a group of individuals performing routine clerical tasks. Work is typically classified as managerial or nonmanagerial, and line or staff work. Figure 4-3 illustrates how various jobs are classified using these two variables plus the level of complexity of the job. Managerial jobs are those with responsibility for planning, organizing, and controlling the work of others. Line jobs can be either managerial or nonmanagerial (or sometimes called operative jobs). Line operations or jobs are those jobs in a chain of command that are involved directly in the production or distribution of goods and services for the consuming public. In comparison, a staff job is a specialized function with responsibility to assist the line organization in performing its duties. These distinctions are not always clear in complex organizations; however, the managerial-nonmanagerial/line-staff dichotomies are important considerations in the design of jobs.

The complexity of jobs is related to the variety of tasks that make up a job and the technical requirements of the tasks. The more homogeneous the tasks to be performed and the lower the skill required to perform them, the less prestige and rewards typically accorded a job. The most prestigious jobs in an organization are typically those that are line-managerial in nature and require the ability to integrate many relatively technical functions or tasks in the discharge of job duties.

DEPARTMENT	WORKING TITLE OF POSITION	WORK LOCATION OF POSITION
School of Business-Management Dept.	Departmental Secretary	Management Office

Duties and Responsibilities:	% of Time
A. Receives telephone and personal callers and incoming mail. Answers routine and nonroutine correspondence, routes more technical correspondence to department chairman or other appropriate faculty member. Reviews all outgoing correspondence, for format, typographic, and grammatic accuracy, and conformance with procedural instructions. Transmits administrative decisions and refers questions to appropriate faculty members in the absence of the chairman.	30
B. Takes and transcribes dictation, from departmental faculty members, composes nonroutine letters, and types material dealing with technical subject matter.	10
C. Maintains chairman's calendar, schedules appointments and conferences without prior clearance, rearranges and reschedules as necessary to avoid overlap or conflict and sees that chairman is fully briefed prior to meeting.	5

FIGURE 4-2   POSITION DESCRIPTION

DEPARTMENT	WORKING TITLE	WORK LOCATION OF POSITION
School of Business-Management Dept.	OF POSITION	
	Departmental Secretary	Management Office

D. Makes travel arrangements for all faculty members including billeting and hotel reservations; prepares trip reports from brief notes.   1

E. May be required to attend meetings with chairman and monitor phone calls, preparing notes and summaries of conversations and commitments made.   5

F. Establishes and maintains files, records, and reports. Determines the need for and sets up chronological, subject matter, and faculty personnel files, screens for destruction or retirement of files.   10

G. Supervises a part-time clerical staff performing stenographic duties, preparing payrolls, assembling diverse reports, requisitioning supplies, and indexing and filing office records. Provides guidance, training, and technical direction to subordinate clerical personnel.   20

H. Approves routine bills for payment, checks expense accounts, and keeps a small set of departmental budget records.   2

I. Meets students inquiring about courses and academic matters, answers routine questions, but refers others to faculty members for counseling.   10

J. Gathers material from a variety of designated sources for articles or speeches and assembles material for consideration of faculty member.   1

K. Performs related work as required.   1

Essential Knowledge Abilities and Skills:

Incumbent must have:

Extensive knowledge of business English, spelling, and commercial arithmetic.

Thorough knowledge of modern office practices, procedures, and methods.

Thorough knowledge of modern office equipment and its application to complex work problems.

Some knowledge of the principles and practices of bookkeeping.

High degree of skill and ability to take and transcribe dictation of a complex and technical nature and to type from rough draft or plain copy at a working rate of speed.

Ability to keep involved or complex clerical records and to prepare accurate reports from statistical or accounting information pertaining to operational problems.

Ability to make minor decisions in accordance with laws, rules, and regulations to apply departmental policies to daily work problems,

FIGURE 4-2 POSITION DESCRIPTION (continued)

DEPARTMENT School of Business- Management Dept.	WORKING TITLE OF POSITION Departmental Secretary	WORK LOCATION OF POSITION Management Office

and to conduct correspondence on routine and nonroutine matters following general instructions and without review.

Ability to organize, lay out, assign, and review the work of a moderately-sized group of employees engaged in routine or involved stenographic or general clerical duties.

Ability to understand and follow complex oral and written directions.

High degree of ability to maintain harmonious working relationships with other employees, faculty members, students, and the general public.

Other Significant Facts:

Incumbent prepares and safeguards confidential information such as examinations, personnel files, student records, and personal recommendations. Therefore, it is *mandatory* that the incumbent be a person who exercises discretion and high standards of honesty and integrity.

Qualifications:

Two years of clerical experience which includes stenographic work. Completion of one academic year of business school or college with course work in secretarial practices may be substituted for one year of the required experience.

Other college training may be substituted on the basis of one year of college for six months of the required experience.

FIGURE 4-2   POSITION DESCRIPTION (continued)

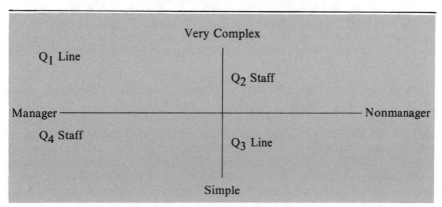

FIGURE 4-3

JOB-DESIGN FACTORS

CRITICISM OF INDUSTRIAL JOBS

As with all revolutions, the job revolution has its persistent critics. The early industrialization of England and Europe resulted in a debate that rages yet. The purpose of this section is to assess the results of the job revolution from the vantage point of modern society, a hundred years since the United States embarked on a revolution that has contributed to unparalleled material well-being. It has been argued by intellectuals and political polls that industrialization in the eighteenth century was a brutalizing force that created alien and intolerable conditions for workers who were lured or forced out of a rural life of peace and natural harmony, not for their own benefits, but to create surplus profits for their capitalist employers. Marx predicted that the growing working class would soon rebel and overthrow the capitalist masters. Others predicted a rapid moral degeneracy would befall society, blamed most of society's ills on technology and industrialization, and longed for a return to a romanticized past of pastoral manors.

Even the obvious benefits to the workers that resulted in this high standard of material well-being—longer-healthier life spans, and freedom of opportunity—has not quieted the critics. Fritz Pappenheim in the *Alienation of Modern Man* summarizes the critics' views:

> Man can no longer express himself in his work. The increasing mechanization of life engenders a calculating outlook toward nature and society and dissolves the individual's bond of union with them. The world of machines follows its own course and escapes man's direction. These indictments culminate in the accusation that man in the technological age has become alienated from his work, from himself, and from the reality of society and nature.

> The satisfaction which most of us find in our work is not inherent in the occupational activities which we have to carry out; it is found primarily in the pay envelope which is handed to us as the equivalent for the number of hours put in. Thus work is not done for its own sake but for an extrinsic end. Work of this kind requires a society in which man has learned to differentiate between means and ends, to avail himself of means which have no inner relationship to his life and its goals and which he chooses to use because he has figured out the advantages they are likely to yield.[4]

In recent years the unions, management theorists, consultants, and the federal government have expressed similar concern over the nature of jobs in the economy. Their criticism is two-fold: first, there is a belief that jobs are providing less and less satisfaction to workers than in the past and may even be a major cause of what some believe to be a growing problem of worker alienation; and secondly, they are concerned that jobs in the modern economy fail to motivate workers to high levels of productivity. Out of these concerns have grown many studies of job satisfaction and worker motivation as well as experiments in the redesign of jobs. The following section reviews some recent research and organizational experiments to increase both worker satisfaction and productivity through job redesign.

JOB REDESIGN

The term job redesign is rather imprecise in meaning and has several connotations. George Strauss defines it as a ". . . term covering efforts to restructure jobs so as to reduce dissatisfaction and increase productivity."[5] As he points out in a recent review the concepts are not new to the 1970s but ". . . were prescribed by personnel books as early as the 1950s.[6] The term covers at least the following concepts: job rotation, job enlargement, job enrichment, and feedback mechanisms—terms which are discussed in greater detail later in the chapter. Moreover, they all draw intellectual support from the theoretical work on motivation by such writers as Douglas McGregor, Abraham Maslow, and Frederick Herzberg. If one judges by the frequency of the citations in the organizational behavior literature and the emphasis given the theories of these three humanistic psychologists in management textbooks, it appears that they have fathered the resurgence of interest in job redesign.

Management theorists in the early part of the twentieth century advocated a separation of *doing* from the task of *deciding*. Where the principles of scientific management were fully developed, the workers' responsibilities were to carry out rather simple, repetitious tasks that were planned, organized, and controlled by managers. McGregor objected to these principles because, in his view, they were based upon "wrong-headed" assumptions about the nature of workers that are at best only partially true. He states that the traditional view of direction and control in organization is based upon three assumptions:

1. The average human being has an inherent dislike of work and will avoid it if he can.
2. Because of this human characteristic of dislike of work, most people must be coerced, controlled, directed, threatened with punishment to get them to put forth adequate effort toward the achievement of organizational objectives.
3. The average human being prefers to be directed, wishes to avoid responsibility, has relatively little ambition, and wants security above all.[7]

These assumptions are referred to as *Theory X* and form the basis for the design of jobs, wage and incentive systems, and methods of supervision in organizations. Theory X assumptions lead to reliance on "carrot and stick" approaches to motivation and to jobs and rewards that appeal only to the lower order needs of man. Maslow, in agreement with McGregor, argues that man's needs are *hierarchical* as depicted in Figure 4-4 and most jobs in the modern economy tend to satisfy the lower order physiological needs, the need for security, and, to a lesser extent, the need for belongingness. The problem, as Maslow points out, is that these needs are rather routinely satisfied without much effort on the part of the worker in an industrialized society and therefore are less important determinants of behavior. As Maslow observed, the satisfied need does not motivate. If you wish to increase worker motivation, he argues, jobs, wage and incentive systems, and supervisory practices must appeal to these higher order needs. If workers appear to conform to the assumptions of Theory X, it is because their true nature has been inhibited by the practices of management that have become self-fullfilling prophecies.

Maslow's Hierarchy of Needs[a]	Herzberg's Motivators & Hygiene factors[b]	McGregor's Theories X and Y[c]
Physiological Needs Safety Needs	Hygiene: Company Policies Supervision, Supervisor Relations, Working Conditions, Personal Life	Theory X
Need to Belong Esteem Needs Self-Actualization	Motivators: Recognition, Achievement, Advancement, Responsibility	Theory Y

FIGURE 4-4

[a]See A.H. Maslow, *Motivation and Personality* (New York: Harper and Bros., 1954).

[b]See F. Herzberg, et. al., *The Motivation to Work* (New York: John Wiley and Sons, Inc. 1959). Hygiene factors refer to maintenance factors expected by employees on the job and required to avoid dissatisfaction.

[c]See D. McGregor, *The Human Side of Enterprise* (New York: McGraw-Hill Book Co., Inc., 1960).

The more correct assumptions McGregor labels *Theory Y* and he believes that if management designed jobs and incentive systems based upon them, the result would be higher productivity and a more satisfied worker who could fulfill through work both his lower order needs *and* his higher order needs. Man's nature, if not inhibited by management practices, will lead workers to conform to the assumptions of Theory Y listed:

1. The expenditure of physical and mental effort in work is as natural as play or rest. The average human being does not inherently dislike work. Depending upon controllable conditions, work may be a source of satisfaction or a source of punishment.
2. External control and the threat of punishment are not the only means for bringing about effort toward organizational objectives. Man will exercise self-direction and self-control in the service of objectives to which he is committed.
3. Commitment to objectives is a function of the rewards associated with their achievement. The most significant of such rewards, e.g., the satisfaction of ego and self-actualization needs, can be direct products of effort directed toward organizational objectives.
4. The average human being learns, under proper conditions, not only to accept but to seek responsibility. Lack of ambition, and emphasis on security are generally consequences of experience, not inherent human characteristics.
5. The capacity to exercise a relatively high degree of imagination, ingenuity, and creativity in the solution of organizational problems is widely, not narrowly, distributed in the population.
6. Under the conditions of modern industrial life, the intellectual potentialities of the average human being are only partially utilized.[8]

The theoretical concepts of Maslow and McGregor are tied more specifically to job design by Herzberg. Figure 4-4 lists the job factors that Herzberg's research identified as motivators. If a job provides significant responsibility, opportunity for advancement, recognition, and achievement, it will motivate the worker to high levels of performance and serve as a source of satisfaction to employees. However a job that provides the incentives based solely upon the hygiene factors will not lead to job satisfaction or high levels of performance but may be sources of dissatisfaction to workers. The conclusion supported by these three humanists is that jobs must be redesigned by adding more "motivators" that satisfy higher order needs, and that management should adopt Theory Y assumptions as the basis for management practices.

Following their lead, industry has experimented with redesigning jobs. Job rotation and job enlargement were among the earliest ideas developed to create more satisfying jobs and, hopefully, increase employee motivation. Job rotation permits workers to periodically switch to other jobs. The assumption is that frequent job changes might reduce the boredom associated with the repetitive nature of many jobs and add variety to the employees' work life. This, in a strict sense, is not a redesign of jobs, but a rather simple measure to overcome some of the problems associated with specialized, simplified work, especially assembly line jobs. Job enlargement, on the other hand, does constitute job redesign inasmuch as it adds tasks to the job. Where a job might be composed of three simple tasks, the enlarged job might incorporate nine tasks, by combining the operations of the job with others. Job enlargement increases the variety of tasks, reduces specialization, and sometimes increases the skills necessary to perform the jobs.

Job enrichment differs from job enlargement because it often includes adding "management" functions to the job. One form of enrichment is to create work teams that have the responsibility for planning, organizing, and controlling their own efforts. The tasks of making work assignments, scheduling output, establishing output standards, inspecting for quality, even hiring and disciplinary responsibilities are assigned to a group. Members are jointly responsible for output, and they have much wider discretion than previously in determining how to accomplish their tasks. Individual jobs may be enriched, as well, without creating work teams. The enrichment process in Herzberg's view is anything that increases the number and amount of motivators in a job. This includes task redesign, adding of responsibilities, increasing the skill content of the job, and/or reorganizing the reward system in the organization. Some of the more well-known experiments discussed below will illustrate the variety of ways organizations have sought to enrich jobs.

American Telephone and Telegraph

The American Telephone and Telegraph Company was an early advocate of job enrichment and other innovative personnel programs. In the mid-1960s, AT&T undertook nineteen field experiences designed around the following strategy:[9]

1. Work "modules" were changed, i.e., tasks and responsibilities of several jobs were combined to form a new job. The new jobs were created to ". . . give each employee a natural area of responsibility . . ." for a customer outside of the business, a client inside the business, or tasks where an individual produced complete items (e.g. a telephone book or a section of a book).
2. Control over the work was handed to the employee by the supervisor as he became ready to assume what were formerly supervisory functions.
3. Feedback concerning results of work efforts was given directly to the worker, not through supervisors.
4. Job "nesting" was brought about by bringing several jobs in close physical proximity to each other to encourage teamwork, and communication among job holders.

This strategy is the heart of the efforts to enrich jobs in several types of processes at AT&T including the production of telephone books, telephone installation and repair, and customer service work. The results reported by AT&T indicate that job satisfaction has increased, turnover and absenteeism have declined, and, in some instances, productivity has increased. Their conclusion is that:[10]

1. Enriching jobs pays off.
2. Job enrichment requires a big change in managerial style (moving decision – making downward).
3. It is important not to neglect "maintenance" factors (e.g. physical layout, pay, etc.).
4. Nesting into mini-groups improves morale and facilitates work.
5. Unions welcome [this] kind of effort.
6. New technology . . . should enable us to break free of old work arrangements.

Texas Instruments

Like AT&T, Texas Instruments, Inc. (T.I.) has been an innovator in the management of human resources.[11] In 1967, a T.I. manufacturing plant in Dallas was contracting with outside firms for janitorial services. The level of service was considered unacceptable and, in an effort to improve the cleanliness of the site, the responsibilities were assigned to an in-plant department. The following strategy was followed:

1. Janitorial wages were increased to the industry average.
2. Improved cleaning technology and equipment were sought.
3. Improved selection and training of workers programs were implemented.
4. Jobs were redesigned to increase the amount of planning and control at the worker's level.
5. Supervisors were trained in developing teamwork and using Theory Y leadership styles.

Both supervisors and workers were carefully selected for the experiments. Work teams were established and workers engaged in reorganizing the tasks and recommending changes in equipment and supplies. They established their own schedules and were taught and given the responsibility of measuring their own performance.

Texas Instrument reports that the cleanliness level of the site increased, the number of workers needed declined by approximately 40 percent, quarterly turnover dropped from 100 percent to less than 10 percent, and an annual cost saving of $103,000 was realized. These improvements were probably caused to some extent by the higher salaries and better equipment, but there is little doubt that increased responsibility and job enrichment also influenced better performance.

Sweden

Among the most publicized job redesign efforts are those taking place in Sweden in the auto industry. Assembly-line jobs in the auto industry have always represented the epitomy of boring, repetitious, mindless, dissatisfying work. But on the other hand, the economies of assembly-line technology remain obvious; and any thought of a fundamental change has been easily set aside by cost considerations. The widely publicized "success" of efforts at Volvo and Saab has fired the imagination of many of the critics who see the Detroit automakers as the biggest symbol of what's wrong with work today. At Saab and Volvo, production teams have been formed in a number of plants for some operations, but the experiments are not yet widespread. Dowling reports on these and emphasizes that the major impetus to change arose out of a concern over very high turnover and absenteeism rates. At Saab "employee turnover was running around 45 percent annually, and in the auto assembly plant, 70 percent. Absenteeism was also extraordinary—close to 20 percent."[12] Similar problems existed at Volvo. The major strategy at both plants was:

1. Combine some assembly line stations under the responsibility of work teams.
2. Allow team members to divide the tasks among themselves.
3. Allow team members to determine the teams' work pace and work breaks within the production goals required.

The results of these two experiments, Dowling reports, have been less than hoped for, were not dramatic, and, at Saab, turnover worsened. Job satisfaction may have increased for those workers who chose to be involved in the new teams, and there appears to be no economic loss as a result of the redesign; however, there was little evidence to support increased levels of productivity.

A CRITIQUE OF JOB REDESIGN

Is job redesign the answer to the many ills that beset our workforce? As a matter of policy in 1968, the federal government articulated a new thrust concerning the labor force. The *Manpower Report of the President* that year stated that:

The goals and functions of employment should go beyond the avoidance of poverty, insecurity, and illness and purposively and progressively advance worker well-being in keeping with the contnuously rising aspirations and expectations throughout our society[13]

The problem, as the advocates of job enrichment see it, is that society has changed greatly, but work technology has not. They point out that the labor force is younger, better educated, less materialistic, more mobile, and expect more from work than economic security.[14] Furthermore, they argue it makes good economic sense to consider changing work technology. It has long been assumed that for efficiency's sake, job content must be determined by the technological processes best suited for the product. In other words, the worker's tasks are determined by technical relationships that are somehow immutable. The advocates of job redesign argue that production technology is variable, and efficiency requires that it be selected to suit the work force as well as the social conditions of work.[15] Others are concerned that we are undermining our society unless we undertake widespread job redesign. Walton believes that:

> Employee alienation affects productivity and reflects social costs incurred in the workplace. Increasingly, blue- and white-collar employees and, to some extent, middle managers tend to dislike their jobs and resent their bosses. Workers tend to rebel against their union leaders. They are becoming less concerned about the quality of the product of their labor and more angered about the quality of the context in which they labor.[16]

It is not clear that job redesign is the answer to the personal and social ills that concern federal policy makers, social critics, and managers alike. Nor is there a clear case to advocate job redesign in the interest of economic efficiency. Some research supports the notion that job redesign works well only with certain types of workers. Blood and Hulin found that rural workers who embraced the middle-class ethic of "working hard to try to get ahead" were more likely to experience an increase in job satisfaction than urban workers as a result of job enrichment.[17] They conclude that alienation exists because urban workers have not been socialized to middle-class work values. Others argue that the few successful experiments have been poorly designed and the benefits short-lived. Moreover, they point out that, without question, technology, especially its hardware, is far and away the most important factor in job design.[18] But most important in the United States, workers are more interested in the standard of living than in the quality of life at work.[19] Salary, job security, fair supervision, safe working conditions, and other "hygiene" factors are likely to bring more and lasting satisfaction than attempting to improve the intrinsic nature of jobs.

Where does this leave us? Strauss summarizes the middleground:

> By and large, it is fair to conclude that most blue-collar workers—and perhaps many white-collar workers as well—(1) would prefer some increase in challenge and autonomy in their jobs, or would learn to like these if they had them, but (2) are not prepared to give up much in the way of material benefits, at least at the moment, to obtain challenge and autonomy; nor (3) would they give higher priority to challenge and autonomy than to various hygienes such as higher pay, safety, flextime, voluntary overtime, and the like.[20]

While we wish to increase job satisfaction, generalizations from limited experiments to date do not support the need for widespread j redesign. This is particularly so when one considers some increased costs (training, equipment, etc.) often associated with job enrichment. However, the positive results of some organizations encourages us to carefully consider whether, on balance for some jobs, both worker satisfaction and economic efficiency might be improved through job redesign. That efforts should continue is unquestionable, but as with all management problems, panaceas are seldom found.

JOB ANALYSIS AND EVALUATION

In the absence of any clear-cut verdict on the increased motivation and productivity through job redesign, organizations are still very much concerned with various extrinsic factors associated with jobs. Thus traditional manpower planning has focused on systematic procedures for defining jobs, specifying the skills, abilities, and aptitudes required by jobs, and establishing the rate of compensation for jobs. This process is known as job analysis and evaluation. "Job analysis is the process of gathering information about jobs: specifically, what the worker does; how he gets it done; why he does it; skill, education, and training required; relationships to other jobs; physical demands; and environmental conditions."[21]

A survey of 900 firms in the United States in 1968 found that 75 percent have some type of job analysis program, and many without them were considering one for the future.[22] The most frequent uses of the information by these firms that have job analysis appears in Table 4-1:

TABLE 4-1

MAJOR USES OF JOB ANALYSIS INFORMATION

	Programs for Salary-Rated	Programs for Hourly-Rated
Job Evaluation	98%	95%
Recruiting and Placing	95	92
Conducting Labor and Personnel Relations	83	79
Utilizing Personnel	72	67
Training	61	63

Source: Jean J. Jones, Jr. and Thomas A. Decoths, "Job Analysis: National Survey Findings," *Personnel Journal* Vol. 49, No. 10. Reprinted with permission, Copyright May 1974.

The establishment of wage rates and recruiting and placement needs are usually the most compelling reason to undertake a systematic program of job analysis. Table 4-1 describes the ways in which job analysis programs are used for both salary and hourly rated jobs among the 900 firms. This survey also revealed that interviews with workers and supervisors, direct observation of jobs being performed, and analysis of old job descriptions are the most frequently used methods of analysis.

Systematic procedures for developing job information should form the basis for both job redesign and manpower planning. Typically, a job analysis program will involve the following:

Job descriptions—which describe the tasks, duties, and responsibilities of the position
Job specifications—which describe the human skills, abilities, and aptitudes required of job holders.
Performance standards—which set forth the expected level and quality of performance expected of job holders.
Job evaluations—which establishes compensation rates for positions.

Over the years, the emphasis in organizations has been on job evaluation techniques which tend to determine both the form and substance of job descriptions, job specifications, and performance standards. Four basic approaches to job evaluation have come to be recognized as acceptable techniques of evaluation: the ranking method, the classification method, the factor comparison method, and the point method. While all of these methods require that the other aspects of job analysis be undertaken, written descriptions, specifications, and performance standards must be consistent with the chosen method of evaluation. A brief description of each method follows; however, a more detailed description of establishing wage rates will be left to Chapter 8.

The Job Ranking Method

As the name implies, using this method jobs in the organization are ranked in order of importance. The process may begin with description of all jobs to be ranked, and the analyst or a committee proceeds to make an overall assessment of how important each job is relative to each other. No attempt may be made to specify the basis for ranking and may consist of simply "the judgments" of the analysts.

This method, although simple and inexpensive to undertake, has serious limitations for other than very small organizations. First, it is not a technique that provides much useful information for manpower planning or job redesign. Since the factors used in the evaluation are not overtly identified, there is no basis for determining what should be changed in a job redesign program, or, what are the factors (ability, aptitude, skills) most important in selecting, placing, or training employees; nor will it permit accurate determination of relative wage rates. The results of the ranking method make a judgment about the relative position of a job in an organization, but do not determine how far apart jobs are on a scale. For example: a small tool and die shop may have the following ranking; the president/owner, the operations manager, the job of master tool-and-die maker, the job of journeyman, the job of apprentice tool-and-die maker, the job of office assistant, and the job of janitor. Is the difference in importance between operations manager and master the same as between journeyman and apprentice? The question is not answered by the ranking method in any systematic way.

Other, and perhaps more important, limitations of the method are that it provides no basis for explaining one's judgment to job holders, and the results are soon made obsolete even in the small firm if many new jobs are created.

The Job Classification Method

Job classification is a widely used method of evaluation, especially in public employment. The most widely known classification system is the one established in 1923 by the federal government for civil service employees. This system, known as the General Schedule, covers nearly all white collar jobs: professional, administrative, scientific, and clerical. There are eighteen classifications and a related pay schedule. Within each classification, there are steps that have incremental pay rates that increase salaries for those who remain in the classification, and merit increased compensation through performance and longevity of service. Jobs are classified on the basis of four broad criteria: duties of the job (tasks to be performed), responsibilities of the position (people, budgets, or machinery), qualifications required of job incumbents, and the impact the person can have on the job.[23] Other factors typically used to classify jobs in industry are whether the job has supervisory responsibilities, the nature of the work environment, and the amount of judgment required. Classifications typically made among positions in private industry are executives, supervisors, professionals, clerical workers, and operative jobs. Within these classes, jobs may be further evaluated using additional classification variables; e.g., policy-making, administrative, skilled, semi-skilled, or another method of evaluation, such as a point method, is often utilized.

Job classification is widely used in organizations and has the advantages of being easy and quick to install and being based upon readily understood differences among jobs. The major disadvantages are that job evaluators are called on to rate the "whole" job and are ". . . apt to be influenced by such factors as present (salary) rate, quality of persons on the job, and prestige value",[24] and some jobs may fall into two or more classifications. Moreover, in large diverse organizations there is a tendency to increase the number of classifications as new jobs are created and, thus, the system becomes unwieldy.

The Point Method

The point system assigns numerical values to job characteristics to reduce jobs to a single basis for comparison. There are many versions of this approach to job evaluation, but nearly all follow similar rating procedures. As a first step, the analyst must establish a number of factors that are common to the jobs being evaluated. A classification of factors into skill, effort, responsibility, and working conditions is common. Table 4-2 is illustrative of this classification.

Once the factors have been chosen, total points must be allocated to each of the factors. The allocation of points to the factors is usually arrived at by an evaluation committee or by a consensus of opinions among a number of managers in the organization. Degrees are then established and defined, and points are assigned to each of the factors. For example, in

Table 4-2 the first degree *supervision of others* might be defined as "having some supervisory responsibility, but only as a minor part of the job;" the second degree of the factor might be defined as "supervision of operative employees as a major part of job responsibility; the third degree might be defined as "supervising first level supervisor as a major part of the job responsibility," etc.

For each factor, each degree is defined prior to the evaluation of jobs. If job descriptions are not written in terms of the factors selected, existing jobs must be described using the list of factors. Once this has been accomplished, each job is evaluated as to the degree of each factor required by the position and assigned points. The total accumulated points determine the basis for setting the wage rate for each job.

TABLE 4-2

POINT ALLOCATION TO JOB FACTORS

Factor	Total Points	1st Degree	2nd Degree	3rd Degree	4th Degree	5th Degree
Skill	300					
1. Education	125	25	50	75	100	125
2. Experience	70	14	28	42	56	70
3. Judgment	70	14	28	42	56	70
4. Physical Dexterity	35	7	14	21	28	35
Effort	250					
1. Mental Effort	150	30	60	90	120	150
2. Physical Effort	100	20	40	60	80	100
Responsibility	200					
1. Supervision of Others	70	6	28	42	56	70
2. Safety of Others	50	10	20	30	40	50
3. Output Quality	30	6	12	18	24	30
4. Materials	25	5	10	15	20	25
5. Equipment	25	5	10	15	20	25
Working Conditions	100					
1. Hazardous	70	14	28	42	56	70
2. Disagreeable	30	6	12	18	24	30

The advantages of a point system are that it measures the differences between jobs using well defined factors that tend to increase the validity and consistency of judgments among jobs. Secondly, since the present wage rates are not a consideration during the evaluation, the chance of them biasing the rater's judgment is reduced. Thirdly, it can accommodate both small and large organizations, and new jobs are easily integrated into the system without requiring a reevaluation of existing jobs. Finally, the pricing of jobs is made easier by converting points to dollars, either by the straight line conversion of a fixed dollar-to-point ratio or by an increasing dollar-to-point ratio.

The disadvantages often cited are that it requires well-trained analysts to construct the system and evaluate jobs, and it is difficult to determine the proper weights to be assigned each factor. Furthermore, it may give the illusion of finiteness. Despite these disadvantages, point systems are widely used and preferred over ranking or simple classification systems.

The Factor Comparison Method

A more recent method of job evaluation was developed by Eugene J. Benge, Samuel L. H. Burk, and Edward N. Hay.[25] It is similar to the point method but relies on the evaluation of *key jobs*. The concept of key jobs requires that job analysts select jobs from all levels representative of all departments to be included in the evaluation. Benge recommends that the following factors should be the basis of evaluation for hourly rated jobs:

1. Mental requirements
2. Skill requirements
3. Physical requirements
4. Responsibilities
5. Working conditions

For supervisory, technical, or clerical jobs he suggests these factors:

1. Mental requirements
2. Skill requirements (as related to experience)
3. Physical factors (both physical requirements and working conditions)
4. Responsibility for supervision
5. Other responsibilities[26]

Each of these factors must be defined, as with the point method, and the key jobs analyzed using the agreed-upon definitions. The next step is to rank the key jobs one factor at a time. The present wage rate on each key job is assumed to be a correct rate, and a portion of the wage rate is allocated to each of the factors. In Table 4-3, jobs A-D are key jobs and their factors have been "priced." The final step is to compare all jobs, factor by factor, to the key jobs. The pricing of all jobs is based upon the "prices" established on the key jobs.

TABLE 4-3

DOLLAR ALLOCATION TO JOB FACTORS

Job	Hourly Wage Rate	Mental Require- ments	Skill Require- ments	Physical Require- ments	Responsi- bilities	Working Conditions
A	$5.85	$2.35	$1.85	$.50	$.25	$.90
B	5.25	2.00	1.50	.50	.75	.50
C	4.75	1.50	1.50	.75	.50	.50
D	4.15	1.15	1.25	.40	.60	.75

For example, if the analyst determines that the mental requirements for job X are similar to job A in Table 4-3 then $2.35 is allocated to job X for this factor (see Figure 4-5). Furthermore job X requires skill similar to key job B, but physical requirements, responsibilities, and working conditions are most like key job C, then the hourly wage rate for job X is $5.60.

The advantages of the factor comparison method are similar to those of the point method; however it is argued that once the system has been set-up, highly trained specialists are not needed to evaluate new jobs, and companies can tailor the method to fit their particular needs.[27] Moreover, it is relatively easy to up-date the wage structure by periodic wage surveys including only key jobs in the survey.

The major criticisms of the method are that it requires considerable time and expense to construct, and selecting representative key jobs is always a problem. Nevertheless, the method has been adopted widely and, in a modified form known as the "Hay Plan" for job evaluation, is gaining many adherents and may become the most frequently used method in use. This approach will be explained in Chapter 8.

Mental Requirements	$2.35
Skill Requirements	1.50
Physical Requirements	.75
Responsibilities	.50
Working Condition	.50
Hourly Wage Rate	$5.60

FIGURE 4-5

ANALYSIS OF JOB X

CONCLUSION

The efficient use of human resources requires that each organization be responsive to the need for improving not only economic output, but also output that accrues to workers and society at large, i.e., job satisfaction. Critics of industrial jobs have been concerned that the worker is becoming increasingly alienated because jobs in our modern economy are not, on the whole, intrinsically motivating. These criticisms began as far back as the eighteenth Century and remain a concern in modern times. There is evidence that since the 1950s, intellectuals, managers, and government officials alike have become increasingly concerned about worker satisfaction and the design of jobs. This concern has resulted in a small number of experiments to redesign jobs to increase job satisfaction, reduce employee turnover, and absenteeism. The results of these experiments are mixed and do not provide a convincing case for undertaking widespread efforts to redesign jobs. The problem of increasing worker satisfaction may be better met by the traditional routes of improving pay and working conditions, because workers may be more concerned with their standard of living than the quality of their working lives, although the evidence on this is also inconclusive.

Even though the results of job redesign efforts have been less than hoped for, experimentation with jobs is still justified. The effective management of jobs requires a systematic procedure for analyzing jobs and establishing equitable rates of compensation. Although job ranking and classification systems can be used successfully in some organizations, the more sophisticated point or factor-comparison methods are preferable, not only for establishing wage rates, but for providing a job information system that is useful to the personnel functions of manpower planning, personnel recruitment, selection, training, and organizational development.

CASE 1
RADIO STATION WRWR

Mr. Smith is the student program director of college radio station WRWR. The station is a student-run organization, and all work is done on a voluntary basis.

It is difficult for Smith to find students to help program during the weekends. So as not to burden a few individuals with weekend shifts, Smith decided to set up a rotation schedule for the weekends. This meant that each programmer would receive two four-hour shifts per term. It was set up so that the weekends the individual would have to work, were weeks apart.

Smith made the weekend schedule far in advance, and each member of the staff was issued a copy. It was clearly set up so that each individual could understand how the rotation would work. Smith also made it a point to explain that each programmer was responsible for his assigned shift, and, if he could not be present, it was his duty to find a replacement.

The weekend shifts dealt with playing pre-recorded tapes and giving required call letters for identification whenever necessary. The programmer had very little to do when he was on duty, and as a result, the programmers thought it was a waste of time.

Around the middle of the term, Smith started receiving complaints from the programmers about how uninteresting the weekend shifts were. Smith replied, "Well, someone has to do them, even if they are boring." Soon after these complaints, Smith began to receive calls from programmers who explained that they would be unable to work their assigned shift. Smith, wanting to keep peace, said he would find someone else to do the rotation. This occured increasingly, and Smith became upset. He began to put the responsibility back on the individual to find a replacement. Soon after, people started not showing up for their assigned shifts.

Questions
1. Explain how this job might be "redesigned" to solve the problems of staffing?

2. Are there solutions, other than job redesign, that might solve Smith's problems? Explain your reasoning carefully.

CASE 2
BALLENGER BAG COMPANY

Ballenger Bag Company is a manufacturer of multiwall paper bags. The plant is located in a large metropolitan area, and wage rates are substantially lower than those of other industries, while fringe benefits are comparable.

A problem has recently occured in the Pasted Ending department (PE) where the final product is made and inspected before shipment. The PE department consists of three machines each of which folds the top and bottom and applies adhesive to produce a finished paper bag. Each machine can make four to five thousand bags per hour, but recently have averaged only two to three thousand.

Each machine in the department has a two person crew (traditionally male) consisting of the operator and the helper. Becoming a good helper takes from six to twelve months, and an operator may require one to three years of on-the-job training to become proficient. (The operator position is the highest paid in the department.)

In addition to this crew, each machine is assigned an inspector (traditionally female) to check the final quality of the bags as they leave the machine. The inspector has the authority to shut the machine off if the operator does not respond to her requests. (The inspector is the lowest paid position in the department.)

The position descriptions are:

Operator—Is responsible for the quantity and quality of production, trains and directs helper in the set-up and operation of the machine.

Helper—Assists operator with set-up and operation of the machine, secures needed supplies for the shift, prepares production records and reports scrap loss, helps reclaim rejected bags.

Inspector—Responsible for quality of production, reclaims rejected bags, directs operators' attention to any defects in quality.

There is a department foreman in charge on each of three shifts, who in turn reports to the shift superintendent.

This department has historically enjoyed good productivity until the departure of two experienced operators and one inspector about one year ago. Since their departure, productivity has declined to levels previously mentioned, and other problems have been growing steadily. The PE department has experienced a thirty percent higher turnover rate than other departments, quality complaints have increased, and employee morale is noticably low. The foremen have begun "cracking down" to reverse the undesirable trends, with little result. The everpresent conflict between operator and inspector is growing intolerable.

Questions
1. Explain how this situation might have resulted from the principle of division of labor.

2. How would you redesign this job to eliminate the problems of turnover, low productivity, and increasing quality control problems?

STUDY AND DISCUSSION QUESTIONS

1. Are the lowest-level manufacturing jobs in an organization just as important as top-level managerial jobs?

2. How are Maslow's Need Hierarchy, Herzberg's Hygiene (maintenance), and Motivators and McGregor's Theory X and Y all inter-related?

3. What seems to be the greatest costs and benefits of job redesign and enrichment programs?

4. Do all people want challenging jobs with lots of responsibility?

5. Do you think the size or type of industry of an organization affects the success of job enrichment and redesign efforts?

6. Distinguish between job design, job evaluation, job enrichment, and job enlargement.

7. As you see it, what is the greatest disadvantage to job evaluation methods in use today?

8. In view of the current emphasis on Management by Objectives (MBO) and goal attainment based upon performance and results of people, of what use are job descriptions which are simply lists of activities to be performed? Aren't we concerned with the results of this activity?

9. Is today's average worker alienated? Would it depend on his industry, occupation, and educational background?

10. Should all boring, routine, nonchallenging jobs on the assembly line be "automated out of existance?"

11. Do you think money really does not motivate and is simply a maintenance or hygiene factor? Does it matter as to the amount of money?

12. Do most workers really conform to the assumptions of Theory Y as stated by McGregor?

ENDNOTES

1. Fredrick W. Taylor, *Principles of Scientific Management* (New York: Harper & Bros., 1911), pp. 36-37.
2. Claude S. George, Jr. *The History of Management Thought* (Englewood Cliffs, N. J.: Prentice-Hall, Inc. 1968), p. 94.
3. Ibid., pp. 96-97.
4. Fritz Pappenheim, *The Alienation of Modern Man: An Interpretation Based on Marx and Tonnies* (New York: Modern Reader Paperbacks, 1959), pp. 43 & 71.
5. George Strauss, et al. (ed.), *Organizational Behavior and Issues* (Madison, Wisconsin: Industrial Relations Research Assn., 1974) p. 38.
6. Ibid., p. 39
7. Douglas McGregor, *The Human Side of Enterprise* (New York: McGraw-Hill Book Company, Inc., 1970), pp. 33-34.
8. Ibid., pp. 47-48.
9. For a more comprehensive discussion see: Robert N. Ford, "Job Enrichment Lessons From AT&T," *Harvard Business Review*, January-February 1973, pp. 96-106.
10. Ibid., pp. 105-106.

11. See Earl D. Weed, Jr., "Job Enrichment 'Cleans Up' at Texas Instruments" in John R. Maher, *New Perspectives in Job Enrichment* (New York: Van Nostrand Reinhold Co., 1971), pp. 55-77.

12. For a more complete discussion see: William F. Dowling, "Job Redesign on the Assembly Line: Farewell to Blue-Collar Blues?" *Organizational Dynamics,* Autumn 1973, pp. 51-67.

13. U.S. Department of Labor, *Manpower Report of the President* (Washington, D.C.: U.S. Government Printing Office, 1968), p. 47.

14. Judson Goodings, "Blue-collar Blues on the Assembly Line," *Fortune,* July 1970 pp. 69-71.

15. Louis Davis, "The Design of Jobs," *Industrial Relations,* Vol. 6, No. 1, pp. 21-45.

16. Richard E. Walton, "How to Counter Alienation in the Plant," *Harvard Business Review,* November-December 1972, p. 71.

17. Milton R. Blood and Charles L. Hulin, "Alienation, Environmental Characteristics, and Worker Responses," *Journal of Applied Psychology,* Vol. 51, No. 3, p. 285.

18. Sar A. Levitan and William B. Johnson, "Job Redesign, Reform, Enrichment-Exploring the Limitations," *Monthly Labor Review,* July 1973, p. 36.

19. Ibid., p. 39.

20. Strauss, op. cit., p. 49.

21. Jean J. Jones, Jr. and Thomas A. Decoths, "Job Analysis: National Survey Findings," *Personnel Journal,* Vol. 49, No. 10, p. 805. Copyright May 1974.

22. Ibid.

23. U.S. Civil Service Commission, *Classification Principles and Policies,* Personnel Management Series, No. 16 (Washington, D.C.: U.S. Government Printing Office, 1963), pp. 29-33.

24. Jay L. Otis and Richard H. Leukart, *Job Evaluation: A Basis for Sound Wage Administration* (Englewood Cliffs, N.J.: Prentice-Hall, Inc., 1954), pp. 70-71.

25. For an elaborate example of this method see Eugene J. Benge, "Using Factor Methods to Measure Jobs" in Milton L. Rock, *Handbook of Wage and Salary Administration* (New York: McGraw-Hill Book Company, Inc., 1972), pp. 2-42 to 2-55.

26. Ibid., p. 2-43.

27. Herbert G. Zollitsch and Adolph Langsner, *Wage and Salary Administration* (Cincinnati: South-Western Publishing Co., 1970), p. 184.

ADDITIONAL READING

Bass, Bernard M. and Gerald V. Barrett. *Man, Work, and Organizations.* Boston Allyn and Bacon, Inc., 1972.

Bendix, Reinhard. *Work and Authority in Industry.* New York: Harper and Row, 1963.

Dalton, Gene W. and Paul R. Lawrence (eds.) *Motivation and Control in Organizations.* Homewood, Ill.: Irwin-Dorsey, 1971.

Davis, Keith. *Human Behavior at Work,* 4th ed. New York: McGraw-Hill Book Co., 1972.

Dubin, Robert. *Human Relations in Administration.* 3rd ed. Englewood Cliffs, N. J.: Prentice Hall, 1968.

Dunn, J. D. and Frank M. Rachel. *Wage and Salary Administration: Total Compensation Systems.* New York: McGraw Hill Book Co., 1971.

Hersey, Paul and Kenneth H. Blanchard. *Management of Organizational Behavior. Utilizing Human Resources,* 2nd ed. Englewood Cliffs, N. J.: Prentice-Hall 1972.

McNaul, James P., H. Randolph Bobbitt, Robert H. Breinholt and Robert H. Doktor. *Organizational Behavior: Understanding and Prediction.* Englewood Cliffs, N. J.: Prentice-Hall, 1974.

Maker, John R. (ed.) *New Perspectives in Job Environment.* New York: Van Nostrand Reinhold Co., 1971.

Sanford, Aubrey C. *Human Relations: Theory and Practice,* Columbus: Charles E. Merrill Publishing Co., 1973.

Sutermeister, Robert A., ed. *People and Productivity,* 2nd ed. New York: McGraw-Hill, 1969

Whyte, William F. *Organizational Behavior: Theory and Application.* Homeward, Ill.: Irwin-Dorsey, 1969.

5

MANPOWER PLANNING SYSTEMS

This chapter outlines approaches that organizations use to effectively match jobs with people. The focus is on the planning process concerned with the acquisition and effective utilization of human resources in the organization. We are especially concerned with the job-person relationship, i.e., with manpower plans that match jobs with people as well as match people with jobs. As we discussed in the previous chapter, the traditional approach of matching people with jobs differs in a subtle manner from the approach of matching jobs with people. With the former, the emphasis is on engineering people to fit available jobs, and the manpower plan emphasizes finding the right person with the right qualifications for the job. On the other hand, when one is concerned with matching jobs with people, the emphasis in the manpower plan subtly changes to one of engineering jobs to fit available human resources.

This latter approach does not ignore the need to find human resources with the right qualifications to fit the job. Rather it also allows for the desirability, and sometimes necessity, of redesigning jobs to fit the available human resources of a changing technological society.

THE NATURE OF MANPOWER PLANNING

Manpower planning is the process of making decisions regarding the acquisition and utilization of human resources. As such, it is part of the strategic decision-making process outlined in the human resources model presented in Chapter 2. That portion of Figure 5-1 heavily outlined is directly concerned with the manpower planning process. In particular, the manpower plan focuses on an analysis of the organization's objectives and the plan for acquiring resources to meet these objectives. The organization's objectives and the resource acquisition process are analyzed in terms of the role that human resources plan in achieving organizational goals.

HUMAN RESOURCE PLANNING AND UTILIZATION IN THE ORGANIZATION

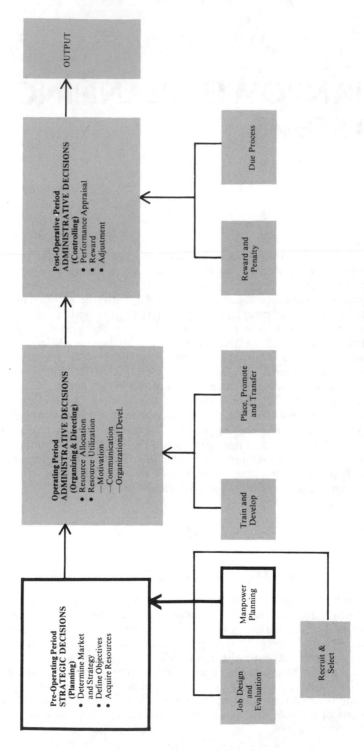

FIGURE 5-1   MANPOWER PLANNING IN THE RESOURCE MODEL

PLANNING

Planning is often considered "formal decision making" in the sense that it involves ". . . deciding in advance what to do, how to do it and who is to do it."[1] It involves a determination of objectives to be accomplished at some future date, an assessment of whether existing organizational policies, programs, and procedures are sufficient to accomplish the objectives, a review of alternative approaches to accomplishing objectives, and the organization of resources to implement the alternative(s) chosen.

Strategic planning is the process of allocating resources into new areas whether they be in new product markets, geographical areas, or into new production processes in an effort to more effectively accomplish the goals of the organization. Strategic decisions in organizations are made on a continuous basis, sometimes systematically using sophisticated planning techniques, and sometimes without much involvement in formal processes. The emphasis of this chapter is on the need for a systematic approach to manpower planning and a general model of a manpower plan.

A narrower definition of planning focuses simply on the "how to do" and "when to do" portion of the objectives. Here, laying out a course of action to be followed is considered planning. It is assumed objectives have been identified in a previous step and that making task assignments to accomplish the plan will occur in a later step.

For our purposes, we will use the broader definition of planning since we are concerned with insuring that a given plan is objective oriented— that it does indeed focus on the accomplishment of a given goal or end result and that some time sequencing in carrying out the plan is specified. However, we will not be as concerned with making specific task assignments to carry out the plan.

Manpower planning is the sum total of the plans formulated for the recruiting, screening, compensation, training, job structure, promotion, and work rules of an organization's human resources.[2] It ". . . is a process designed to translate the corporate or institutional plans and objectives into future quantitative and qualitative manpower requirements, together with plans to fulfill those requirements over both the shorter and longer terms, through manpower utilization, human resource development, employment and recruiting, and manpower information systems."[3]

The emphasis in this definition is on structuring plans to carry out what are considered to be the traditional personnel management functions of hiring, training, compensation, and promotion. Thus, manpower planning is a pervasive function in that it involves planning for the operation of other areas of human resource management as indicated in the portion of the human resource model presented in Figure 5-1.

MACRO-MICRO DISTINCTION

Manpower planning is done on a national level primarily by the federal government aided by the states. This type of planning has a different focus from the manpower planning done by an individual organization. National manpower planning, or *macro* manpower planning, involves the specification of national manpower objectives and programs for their accomplishment. It usually involves federal agencies, such as the Department of Labor, particularly, the Employment and Training Administration, and certain agencies within the Department of Health, Education and Welfare. However, other national organizations, such as the Brookings Institution, are also involved in macro manpower planning activities.

Manpower plans at the national level change as the priorities of a particular Congress and/or administration change. For example, under Presidents Kennedy and Johnson a great deal of effort and funds were spent to develop manpower plans to deal with specific manpower problems. Programs were established for remedial education and skill training, mobility benefits, equal employment opportunity, and labor market information systems. Most of these programs in this period were directed at improving the employment relationship of minorities and disadvantaged groups in keeping with the philosophy of the New Frontier of the Kennedy administration and the Great Society Program of the Johnson administration.

However, during the Nixon administration manpower priorities changed. Increased emphasis was given to improving the employment situation of veterans and in improving the already existing federal offices, such as the federal–state Bureaus of Employment, to help all levels of manpower. The emphasis on programs for the disadvantaged and minorities was reduced.

The Nixon administration also decentralized the national manpower planning effort by establishing regional offices throughout the nation and, through the revenue sharing program, by asking each state to handle the manpower planning function for the state. Even though the decentralization process has achieved only limited success, the responsibility for national manpower planning has shifted from a centralized federal government in Washington to decentralized regional manpower offices and individual state governments.

Micro manpower planning involves the planning an organization does for the acquisition and utilization of its manpower. As seen in our definition of manpower planning, this is the focus we use in our book. However, this does not mean that macro manpower planning, whether it be done solely by the federal government or jointly by the federal government and the states, has an insignificant impact on micro manpower planning. For example, when federal programs were established to improve the employment opportunities for the so called "hard-core" unemployed, individual organizations were asked to commit extra resources and to develop manpower plans that included programs for recruiting, training, and employing these individuals.

Often federal programs will stimulate an organization to do manpower planning that did little if any manpower planning in the past. For example, federal law and programs dealing with equal employment opportunity and affirmative action caused many organizations to review their present manpower planning process. The thurst of affirmative action planning involves the development of an organizational plan to recruit, train, and employ more members of minorities and women than are presently employed by the organization. As organizations review the number of employees presently employed in various positions and develop plans to replace these employees to ensure that minorities are being recruited, they usually end up doing a comprehensive review of their total manpower planning system.

For example, an organization may decide to set up a skills bank or skills inventory of all minority and women employees currently employed to insure that they will be considered for future promotion when positions become vacant. As they begin setting up such a skills bank for minorities, they soon realize that this would be a good idea for all employees, whether white or black, male or female. Thus, they are on the way to developing a complete manpower or human resource information system for all employees, which is a critical aspect of manpower planning.

Therefore, the macro manpower planning done on the national level affects the micro manpower planning done by an individual organization. However, there are other aspects of the macro environment, besides national manpower planning, which also affect, in a major way, the micro manpower planning function.

THE MACRO ENVIRONMENT OF MANPOWER PLANNING

In the human resources model presented in Chapter 2, we identified some major components of an organization's macro environment. These are the cultural values and norms, social institutions, legal environment, product/service demand, technology, and human resource mix. Each of these components has an impact on the manpower planning system of an organization.

PRODUCT/SERVICE DEMAND MIX

Forecasted demand for an organization's product/service serves as the primary basis for an organization's manpower plan. As demand for an organization's product or service increases substantially, people are added to the organization, usually at all occupational levels. As demand decreases, people are usually laid off or discharged at all levels, even though individuals at lower occupational levels are usually released first.

Since most organizations have an objective of growth, and since national economic policy is one of growth, the predominant influence of product/service demand forecasts is one of providing additional manpower for the organization as it grows. Therefore, one function of the manpower plan is to ensure that the desired number of people with appropriate skills and abilities are available for appropriate jobs and occupations in the organization as the demand for the organization's product/service increases.

However, the manpower plan must also make provision for organizational manpower decisions for periods of retrenchment, such as during an economic recession. Some organizations, for example, lay off unskilled workers first during a recession rather than skilled, professional, or managerial employees. The rationale here is that the unskilled employee is the easiest to replace during an economic growth period. Other organizations tend to lay off employees regardless of skill (even managerial employees) during a downturn in activity. Aerospace and defense contractors, for example, typically lay off highly skilled supervisors, engineers, and technicians along with unskilled and semi-skilled employees during a business downturn.

Still other organizations will reduce the work hours of all employees rather than lay off anyone during a recession. For example, many organizations in Japan will go to a reduced work-week and a cut in wages and salary for all employees, including managers, rather than to lay people off during a business downturn. This reflects the paternalistic managerial philosophy of many Japanese organizations.

Governmental agencies typically reduce budgets for the next fiscal year and rely on normal attrition to reduce the workforce rather than laying off people during periods of economic downturn. As people retire or quit they are not replaced until economic conditions improve.

Whatever the particular policy of an organization during periods of economic recession, it needs to be clearly spelled out and implemented in making manpower decisions. Going through the process of formulating a manpower plan that thoroughly considers the effects of economic recession as well as economic growth often provides many unnoticed opportunities for an organization.

For example, some organizations actually add people in certain highly skilled occupational positions during a recession, for it is during this time that an organization can bring on board skilled people who aren't available during normal business activity except at a very high salary premium. Some companies hired skilled engineers rather than laying them off during the 1973-74 recession because they had a wide supply to choose from and did not have to pay a premium. Assuming these engineering skills would be needed when the economy picked up, these companies made a wise choice since they obtained skilled manpower at lower salaries than during normal periods. Some colleges and universities also followed this policy during the 1973-74 recession to attract top faculty who would otherwise not be available at the salary these colleges could offer.

Thus, one major function of the manpower plan is to provide an orderly system to add employees to the organization during periods of economic growth and to specify procedures to be followed during periods of economic recession or organizational retrenchment. A good manpower plan allows organizations to smooth out the hiring process so that variations in hiring are not widely divergent from year to year, depending upon market conditions. Organizations without a good manpower plan often find that they hire large numbers of employees one year only to lay them all off the following year.

The key to an effective manpower plan that recognizes the effect of economic conditions is adequate forecasting of these conditions as well as the organization's product/service mix as economic conditions change. An organization should not be at the mercy of economic conditions, but should forecast and develop well-conceived manpower plans in advance of changing conditions.

CHANGING TECHNOLOGY

Technological changes have a profound impact on an organization's manpower plan. As technology changes, the skills required in particular occupations change. New occupations are created, and old ones cease to exist. The trend over the last fifty years has been to upgrade the skills required in most jobs in our economy. Many of the unskilled jobs, particularly those involving heavy labor, have been eliminated. Labor demand in some skilled occupations has also been eliminated or significantly reduced. We are all familiar with the plight of the blacksmith.

The composition of many skilled jobs changes as technology changes. Often the skill components are broken down into separate jobs, which can be performed by semi-skilled workers. For example, the introduction of a highly automated assembly line into the typical manufacturing operations of a company in the 1950s often broke up skilled jobs into several separate jobs requiring lesser skills. These jobs would be routinely performed by workers during the course of a normal day's work on the assembly lines and many became boring because of their repetitiveness.

Another aspect of a technological change is that, while it often eliminates unskilled jobs involving physical labor, it may create semi-skilled jobs requiring repetitive mental and manual labor. The modern auto assembly line has many examples of these.

Changing technology also requires organizations to plan for changes in locating sources of manpower to insure that supplies of needed manpower will be recruited. For example, the introduction of electronic data processing into an organization often requires the organization to recruit skilled computer technicians from technical schools in which they may not have recruited previously.

A technological change often means the organization's own training program must be revised to insure that people with skills needed in the future will be available. Thus, plans have to be made that: (1) forecast future technological change and the skill needs they will create, (2) determine classroom and on-the-job training programs to fill the needs, and (3) prepare instructors, instructional material, and facilities for the training. For many significant technological changes, such as the introduction of electronic data processing, an organization may choose to do little of its own internal training but rely on formal schooling. Any internal training becomes an orientation to show how the organization uses the EDP system.

HUMAN RESOURCE SKILL/EDUCATIONAL MIX

The changing skill/educational mix of the human resource supply and changing technology are closely related. As technology changes to require different skills and abilities, people attempt to change their ability/skill mix to gain skills required in jobs. This matching of the skill requirements of jobs with the skills of people in the work force has been the underlying thrust of federal manpower policy. Training and development programs sponsored by the government were established to ensure that people, particularly the disadvantaged and minorities, would be able to secure the needed skills to compete effectively in the labor market.

The tremendous growth in secondary and two year post-secondary vocational and technical schools since 1962 was a result of federal manpower planning, which indicated a need for formal classroom training to provide the skilled work force needed in today's highly technological society. Many regions of the country now have area vocational schools, and many students who might have not gone to college, now receive two years of post-secondary technical training in such fields as electronics, computer technology, aviation technology, automotive mechanics, and the applied medical fields.

When the human resource educational/skill mix differs significantly from the skills required by employers, manpower shortages develop. Employers have jobs open but cannot find people with the skills demanded. Many people want jobs but are not hired because they do not have needed skills. This mismatch between job skill requirements and the skills of the labor force can have a serious negative impact on the economy of a society. For example, in the late 1960s, we had a national unemployment rate under 4.0 percent for 1968 and 1969, a very low rate for the U.S. Employers had many job openings but were not able to find qualified employees. Yet in certain sections of the country, unemployment was very high. People wanted jobs but did not have the necessary skills. In several of our northern inner cities, the unemployment rate approached 50 percent, yet employers in these same cities could not find qualified employees to fill their job openings.

This human resource dislocation had an effect on inflation, since employers tended to bid the wage rate up for what few workers were available, and was also a contributing factor to the inner-city riots during this period since so many were without jobs in such a prosperous period of American history. The federal government reacted to this situation with several programs to hire the "hard-core unemployed" or hard-to-employ persons. The essence of these programs was to provide this disadvantaged group with remedial education and training, through joint federal-private business action, in the skills necessary for many entry level jobs in industry.

Even though some groups have not acquired needed skills to effectively compete for jobs in a highly technological labor market, the vast majority of the U.S. labor force has acquired such skills. In fact the average formal educational level now exceeds a high school education.[4]

The types of skills brought to the labor market by the labor force today are much more sophisticated than they were in the early 1960s. For example, various new engineering, computer, and medical technician jobs require much higher skills than previously required in these fields. Even the automotive mechanic of the 70s must be more highly skilled than his counterpart in the 60s because of the more sophisticated design of automobile engines and related auto systems, and because of the tremendous variety in automotive models within a given manufacturer's line.

Thus, any manpower plan must assess the human resource educational/skill level of the labor market from which it draws, predict future changes in this mix, assess the effect of federal manpower programs, and then plan recruiting, training, and job design systems that take maximum advantage of the forecasted educational/skill mix. An effective manpower plan requires a careful and accurate assessment of the present and forecasted skills of an organization's potential employees.

CULTURAL VALUES, NORMS, AND SOCIAL INSTITUTIONS

Many employers today are asking themselves what happened to the old-fashioned belief in hard work. This concern is but a symptom of a more general concern many people have regarding the nature of fundamental values which have supposedly been held by the work force in the U.S. society. Many people believe these values are changing. Others believe that present values are merely being redefined and arranged in a different priority.

Perhaps societal values toward work are not changing, but norms certainly are. Values are basic beliefs which give stability to society and are slow to change. Norms are guides to behavior. They manifest or represent values. Values tend to be hard to define, norms are more specific. For example, at one time the value of hard work was manifested through the norm of heavy physical labor. Today, hard work often means mental pressure and long hours, but not necessarily physical labor.

The conventional wisdom is that today's employees, particularly younger employees, seem to want jobs that are challenging, personally rewarding, and have opportunities for personal and professional growth. Work is not a necessary evil or something to be avoided, but rather an integral part of life, to be enjoyed to the greatest extent possible.

In addition, many people, particularly youth, desire to balance the goals associated with career development with other "life-space" goals such as family life, recreation, church affairs, and civic responsibilities. Long hours of a "work-aholic" may not be personally acceptable if they interfere with goals in other areas of one's life.

These changing norms regarding work mean that organizations should examine job enrichment techniques to determine their applicability. It also means that employers should consider these changes in developing manpower plans. Today's employees expect employing organizations and other social institutions to be more responsive to the demands made upon them by the organization's various membership groups.

CHANGING LEGAL ENVIRONMENT AND MANPOWER PLANNING

The greatest changes in the legal environment have occurred because of legislation and executive orders instituted by the federal government. In particular, the most significant changes have been in equal employment opportunity and affirmative action, occupational safety and health, government involvement in managing the economy to minimize inflation and unemployment and maximize economic growth, and more comprehensive coverage of wage and hour legislation. (These issues are discussed in Chapter 10.)

At the state level, laws have been passed by many states to legalize collective bargaining in public employment. This means that unions and collective bargaining procedures are becoming increasingly more common in state, city, and county units.

These changes in the legal environment are an extension of a trend begun in the 1930s to give employees more rights, and hence more power, in dealing with employers. From the Federal Wage and Hour law and the Wagner Act, which legalized unions in the private sector in the thirties, to Title VII of the 1964 Civil Rights Act, and the 1970 Occupational Safety and Health Act, employer action toward employees has become increasingly more constrained. No longer can an employer hire only white males, pay them what he wishes, and work them in an unsafe environment. He must now abide by equal employment regulations, pay at least the minimum wage and time and one-half for overtime, and meet the minimum safety requirements in his operations as specified by the Occupational Safety and Health Act.

Why has such legislation been passed to regulate employer treatment of employees? The primary reason is because the operation of the labor market did not regulate such behavior. The economic power of today's large employers in the labor market would far exceed the power of the individual worker in the absence of protective legislation. If the market did effectively regulate these practices, how could we have ever had women and children working twelve to fourteen hours per day seven days a week for a subsistance wage under sweat-shop conditions? These conditions were all too common at the turn of the century in our factories.

The role of government is to pass laws to achieve the public good. When the public good outweighs private property rights, government will pass laws to constrain these rights. Witness zoning laws, laws against prostitution and drugs, anti-monopoly laws as well as federal and state regulation of various industries such as airlines, railroads, transmission lines, utilities, and communications. In each case, it is believed that the public good would not be served in the absence of such regulations.

The same argument holds with legislation which affects the employer-employee relationship. The effect of the changing legal environment has been to improve wages, working conditions, and terms and conditions of employment for the average employee, thus leading to the accomplishment of the public good. Employer manpower plans have changed over time to be in conformity with the legislation and will continue to change as additional legislation is passed.

DESIGNING A HUMAN RESOURCE INFORMATION SYSTEM—MANPOWER PLANNING IN THE FIRM

Our discussion thus far has been concerned with the macro aspects of manpower planning. Macro manpower planning sets the environment for micro manpower planning in the organization. The objective of the internal manpower planning process for an organization is to insure that adequate manpower with the desired skills and abilities are available when and where they are needed.

The manpower planning process is a major component of an organization's *human resource information system*. The concept of the human resource information system developed as a result of the work by Likert, Brummet, Pyle, Flamholtz, and others at the University of Michigan in the late 1960s.[5] A major portion of a human resource information system is the system of human resource accounting. *Human Resource Accounting* is an attempt to assign a dollar value to an organization's human resources. Such components as the amounts an organization has invested in its human resources through training and development, hiring and replacement costs, employee salaries, and turnover costs are usually used to compute the worth of an organization's human resources.

Human resource accounting systems today have evolved to the point of ". . . identifying, measuring, and communicating information about human resources in order to facilitate effective management within an organization."[6] Management requires information regarding resource acquisition, development, maintenance, and utilization.[7]

Thus, today's human resource accounting system is in actuality a part of the total human resource information system. Not only are the human resources assigned a value for accounting purposes, but other information concerning human resources is gathered, coded, analyzed, stored, and disseminated to managers. This information includes the following components:

1. Demographic information: age, sex, race, educational levels, marital status
2. Skills and abilities
3. Aspiration levels
4. Performance appraisals
5. Company sponsored training programs or other training and education completed since employed
6. Past work assignments and job title before and since being hired
7. Special notations (awards, etc.)

Most organizations gather some or even all of these informational components, but few have developed a total information system that updates this information and makes it available to appropriate managers in a comprehensive fashion. Simply relying on the traditional personnel records system for gathering, analyzing, storing, and distributing information on an organization's human resources will not produce the quality and quantity of human resource information needed for a comprehensive manpower plan.

CONSTRUCTING A MANPOWER PLAN

The first step in constructing a manpower plan is to determine the organization's growth and market objectives. These objectives serve as the foundation for estimating the forecasted demand for human resources in the organization. These objectives may be expressed in terms of sales, market share, return on investment, development of new products and services, and development of new markets. These objectives ought to be expressed in terms of some time frame or *planning* horizon—the length of time over which the objectives and the plan for accomplishing them will occur.

The planning horizon for many organizations seldom exceeds fifteen years and is often expressed in terms of short-range, intermediate-range, and long-range periods. As a rule of thumb, short-range is a horizon of one year or less, intermediate-range of two to six years, and long-range of seven to fifteen years. Often the long-range objectives are quite general, and the intermediate and short-range objectives much more specific. This specificity is especially true of short-range or *operational* objectives.

Procedures for specifying objectives and the means for their accomplishment generally fall under the heading of *Management by Objectives (MBO)* in the management literature.[8] The determination of sound, long-range, intermediate-range, short-range organizational and associated departmental objectives is essential for an effective manpower plan, and the management by objectives technique is very effective for developing and specifying objectives.

Once the organization's objectives are specified, communicated and understood by all affected, then the personnel or manpower planning unit should specify their objectives with regard to human resource utilization in the organization. In developing these objectives, specific policies need to be formulated which address the following questions:

1. Shall we attempt to fill positions from within or by hiring individuals from the labor market? More specifically:
   a. What do we hope to accomplish from promotion from within and why?
   b. What jobs shall we fill by promotion?
   c. Does our organization have the needed skills and, if not, can our people be trained and developed for these jobs?
   d. What types of skills exist in our relevant labor market, and can we effectively recruit and attract people from this market?
   e. What effect will bringing in people from the outside have on our presently employed people?
2. Can we meet our commitments to affirmative action and equal employment opportunity?
3. How do our training and development objectives interface with our manpower planning objectives?
4. What union constraints do we face in manpower planning, and what policies should we develop to effectively handle these constraints?
5. What is our policy toward providing everyone in the organization with a meaningful, challenging job (job enrichment)? Will we continue to have some boring, routine jobs or should we be eliminating them?

The third step in the process is to estimate the skills and number of people required for the organization by occupational category for the planning horizon. Occupational skills change over time. Therefore, it is important at this stage that an organization have a complete, current listing of all occupational categories in the organization with explanatory job descriptions which specify the duties, skills, and qualifications required for each job. It should also attempt to forecast future changes in the duties, skills, and qualifications for these positions based on changes in technological requirements and the aspiration levels of individuals in the organization and the external labor market.

Fourth, the planner should estimate the manpower shortage or surplus for each occupational and job category and should determine what it plans to do about any estimated surplus or shortage in view of the human resource utilization objectives. Figure 5-2 presents a procedure that is useful in estimating a given surplus or shortage for a particular occupation or job category.

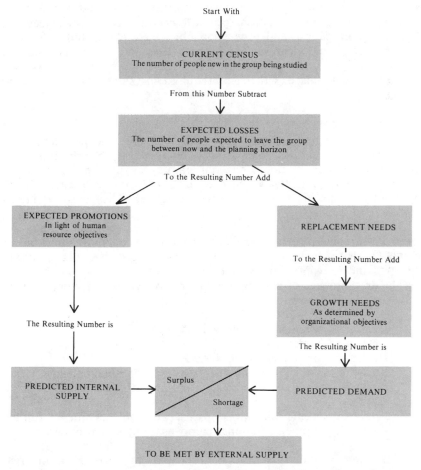

FIGURE 5-2   A PROCEDURE FOR ESTIMATING MANPOWER SHORTAGE OR SURPLUS FOR A JOB OR OCCUPATIONAL CATEGORY

Source: Albert N. Navas, K. M. Rowland, and E. G. Williams, *Managerial Manpower Forecasting and Planning,* (American Society for Personnel Administration, Research Report, 1965) as reprinted in Dale Yoder, *Personnel Management and Industrial Relations,* 6th ed. (Englewood Cliffs, Prentice-Hall, 1970), p. 176.

Note that this procedure ties in consideration of human resources objectives in filling jobs from within via internal promotions and organizational growth objectives.

If a surplus is predicted for an occupational category, the human resource planner needs to determine if these individuals will be discharged, temporarily laid off, transferred without any training, provided with training and then transferred, or provided with a cash bonus for quitting.[9] These decisions will probably be determined by the organization's overall human resource objectives for training and development.

If a shortage is predicted, then the organization must resort to the external labor market if it expects to fill the resulting job vacancies. This decision may cause the organization to review its human resource objectives with regard to hiring in the external market vis-á-vis other objectives.

The final step is to establish specific recruiting, selection, placement, training, compensation, and promotion objectives, plans, and policies to meet the estimated vacancies. The procedures and other information regarding each of these specific areas is discussed in later chapters.

Figure 5-3 summarizes the steps required in the manpower planning process.

CONCLUSION

Manpower planning should be a comprehensive and pervasive function in an organization. Manpower plans need to be developed for managerial as well as nonmanagerial employees of the organization. Effective plans are directly tied to organizational product/service/growth objectives and specific human resource objectives. They exist to implement these objectives.

They are shaped by national macro manpower objectives and programs. But the micro manpower plans developed by each organization are unique to that organization and ought to reflect that organization's objectives and relevant labor market.

The development of a manpower plan involves the accomplishment of the six following steps:

1. Determine organizational growth objectives
2. Determine human resource objectives
3. Determine job structure and design
4. Estimate future skill requirements by occupational category
5. Estimate manpower shortage or surplus for each occupational category
6. Establish specific objectives, plans, and policies for recruiting, selection, placement, training, compensation, and promotion

Manpower planning is part of the total planning process of an organization. It involves the specification of plans for more specific human resource areas. Each of these areas serves as topics for examination in the remainder of this book. The next chapter examines the development and implementation of effective recruitment and selection systems in the organization—a major portion of an effective manpower plan and of a comprehensive human resource system.

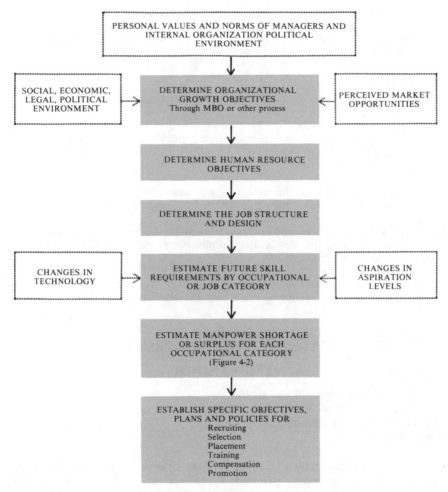

FIGURE 5-3   A PROCEDURE FOR CONSTRUCTING A MANPOWER PLAN

CASE 1
GOOD MONEY AFTER BAD

A quote recently made by a politician:

> The problem with most of these do-gooder liberals is that they have their heads in the clouds. Our manpower problems don't have easy solutions. They are very complex problems. We've had almost two decades of Great Society and New Federalism programs and we've still got the problems. The unemployment rate is sky-high and has been. Unemployment rates among minorities, especially teenagers, are deplorable.
>
> Let's face it, the federal government should not be in the manpower business. All of the federal dollars and programs have failed to solve

the problems. All we are doing is throwing good money after bad. I say let's let free enterprise work. Let's pass laws that encourage business to hire. Let's get government off the back of business and let's get people back to work. That's how we'll solve our manpower problems.

Questions
1. Do you believe this person adequately understands macro manpower planning?

2. What is the role of the federal government vis-à-vis that of private industry in macro manpower planning? Is this role adequately reflected in the statement?

3. What criteria should be used to judge macro manpower planning? Should the unemployment rate be used as suggested here?

4. How has federal manpower policy changed as the administrations changed from the democratic administration of Kennedy to the present administration?

5. How does macro manpower planning done by government affect micro manpower planning done by organizations?

CASE 2
SEMINOLE STATE UNIVERSITY
MEMORANDUM

To: Division and Department Heads
From: C. C. Johnson, Personnel
Subject: Manpower Planning
Date: April 1, 1978

The personnel department of Seminole State University is going to undertake a manpower planning program for all career staff positions at the University. During the next three months please see to it that all managers in your unit develop a manpower plan for the positions immediately under them. This plan should:

1. Predict future turnover in positions
2. Indicate resources in the University and community to fill vacant positions
3. Specify short term and long term manpower goals
4. Specify any training needed for the individual in order to fill positions

I know each of you will help in this effort. All manpower plans should be turned in to me by July 1, 1978. Thank you for your cooperation.

Questions
1. From this memo, how would you judge the managerial approach at Seminole State?

2. How successful do you believe Johnson will be in implementing this program?

3. Are there some important steps left out of the components of the manpower plan he suggests?

4. If you were a Division or Department Head, how would you react to this memo?

5. If you were a career staff person, how would you react to this once you found out about it?

CASE 3
STATE PLANNING

Analyze this statement made recently by a high level administrator of a large state agency:

Manpower planning is very important. I know business spends much time and effort in developing manpower plans and in providing the needed training. But we just can't do this in government. Our turnover is just too high. Why, over the last three years our turnover has averaged 65 percent per year in some of our units. It's impossible to plan with that high of a turnover rate and with such a low wage rate for our employees.

Besides that, our managers are so overworked now, they don't have time to spend working on manpower plans. It takes a lot of time to work out a good plan.

Finally, where will we get the money to do this planning and to do the recruiting and record keeping required? There's just no money in the legislature for our basic activities let alone for this stuff. The legislature just views this as a frill.

Questions
1. How would you cope with this situation if you were a manager employed with this agency? Does this statement mean individual managers have no responsibility to plan? What is the personnel unit's responsibility for manpower planning?

2. Are the agruments presented in this case valid? How might each of them be rebutted?

3. Do you believe that state government is really interested in any type of planning, let alone manpower planning. Why or why not? Are they interested in developing human resources?

CASE 4
LIVE OAK TELEPHONE COMPANY

Live Oak Telephone Company is located in a rapidly growing section of Central Florida. For the 1971-73 period, revenues increased 56 percent, profits 28 percent, and total investment in plant and equipment 38 percent. Also during this time employment increased 15 percent. The company was able to achieve its high growth levels without a commensurate increase in employment by heavy use of overtime. For example, it was not uncommon for an installer-repairman to work twenty hours of overtime a week and to work seven out of eight Saturdays. The company reasoned that the boom would eventually bust as so often happened in other parts of the state that there was no need to add a large number of permanent employees.

Their logic seems to have been justified since during the 1974-76 period, the boom turned to bust. Not only was overtime almost completely eliminated, but about 10 percent of the work force was laid off one time or another for short periods during this time. However, business was once again picking up at the start of 1977, and the company planned on following the same strategy.

Questions

1. What factors should be considered by an organization when determining if permanent employees should be added or more overtime worked by present employees?

2. Evaluate the strategy used by Live Oak Telephone Company? What are its advantages and disadvantages?

3. Should Live Oak continue with the same strategy in the 1977-1980 period? Beyond this time? What are the implications of your answer?

4. To what extent does morale, satisfaction, work quality, and present wage level affect overtime policy?

STUDY AND DISCUSSION QUESTIONS

1. What is manpower planning?

2. What are the advantages and disadvantages for a company that has a policy of hiring in skilled occupations during recessions?

3. Do younger employees differ from older workers in the way they view their jobs and the role of work in their lives?

4. What effects do environmental changes have on the manpower planning process in the organization?

5. What is a human resource information system and how does it relate to human resource accounting?

6. Should organizations promote from within? What are the advantages and disadvantages of relying on a promote from within policy to fill job openings?

7. Explain this statement: Manpower planning should be a comprehensive and pervasive function in an organization.

8. Comment on the following statement: "Manpower planning might work in business, but it sure doesn't in government. There's just too much political influence and incompetence in government to allow for planning of *any* kind—let alone manpower planning."

9. Will we ever be able to "account for the value of human resources" in an organization?

10. How heavily should people's aspiration levels influence the manpower planning process in the organization?

11. Should the federal government really attempt to plan manpower utilization in our society?

ENDNOTES

1. Harold Koontz and Cyril O'Donnell, *Principles of Management: An Analysis of Management Functions,* 5th ed. (New York: McGraw-Hill Book Company, Inc., 1972), p. 113.
2. Thomas H. Patten, Jr., *Manpower Planning and the Development of Human Resources* (New York: John Wiley and Sons, Inc., 1971), pp. 1-21.
3. Frank H. Cassell, "Manpower Planning: State of the Art at the Micro Level," *MSU Business Topics,* Vol. 21, No. 4, Autumn 1973, p. 15. Reprinted by permission of the publisher, Division of Research, Graduate School of Business Administration, Michigan State University.
4. *Manpower Report of the President* (Washington, D.C.: U.S. Government Printing Office, 1974), p. 302.
5. See for example: Rensis Likert, *The Human Organization: Its Management and Value* (New York: McGraw-Hill Book Company, Inc., 1967), pp. 146-55.
6. Reed M. Powell and Paul L. Wilkens, "Design and Implementation of a Human Resource Information System," *MSU Business Topics,* Vol. 21, No. 1, Winter 1973, p. 22.
7. R. Lee Brummet, William C. Pyle, and Eric G. Flamholtz, "Human Resource Accounting in Industry," *Personnel Administration,* July-August 1969, pp. 35-36.
8. For a further discussion of management by objectives, see Peter Drucker, *The Practice of Management* (New York: Harper, 1954); George Odiorne, *Management by Objectives* (New York: Pitman, 1965), and *Management Decisions by Objectives* (Englewood Cliffs, N. J.: Prentice-Hall, 1969). Two excellent handbooks for implementing a management by objectives program are George Morrisy, *Management Objectives and Results* (Reading, Mass.: Addison & Wesley, 1970), and Anthony Raia, *Management by Objectives* (Glenville, Ill.: Scott, Foresman and Company, 1974). Also see Stephen J. Carroll, Jr. and Henry L. Tosi, Jr., *Management by Objectives* (New York: MacMillian, 1973) for a discussion of MBO research.
9. Volkswagen in Germany provided workers with a bonus equal to a couple of months pay if they voluntarily quit.

ADDITIONAL READING

Chruden, Herbert J. and Arthur W. Sherman. *Personnel Management.* 4th ed. Cincinnati: South-Western Publishing Co., 1972.
Fisherman, Betty G. and Leo Fishman. *Employment, Unemployment and Economic Growth.* New York: Thomas Y. Crowell Co., 1969.
French, Wendell. *The Personnel Management Process: Human Resources Administration,* 3rd ed. Boston: Houghton Mifflin Co., 1974.
Glueck, William F. *Personnel: A Diagnostic Approach.* Dallas: Business Publications, Inc., 1974.
Hamilton, David. *A Primer on the Economics of Poverty.* New York: Random House 1968.
Mangum, Garth. *The Emergency of Manpower Policy.* New York: Holt, Rinehart and Winston, Inc., 1969.
Megginson, Leon C. *Human Resources: Cases and Concepts.* New York: Harcourt Brace and World, Inc., 1968.

Pym, Denis (ed.). *Industrial Society*. Baltimore: Penguin Books, 1968.

U.S. Department of Labor. *The Manpower Report of the President*. Washington, D.C. U.S. Government Printing Office, published annually.

Weber, Arnold R., Frank H. Cassell, Woodrow L. Ginsburg (eds.). *Public-Private Manpower Policies*. Madison, Wisc.: Industrial Relations Research Assoc. 1969.

Wortman, Max S. (ed.). *Creative Personnel Management: Readings in Industrial Relations*. Boston: Allyn and Bacon, 1967.

6

RECRUITMENT AND SELECTION IN ORGANIZATIONS

In an idealized view of the human resource utilization process, the task structure of jobs and the manpower plan take into consideration the skill mix in the labor force, the vocational aspirations of workers, and the social goals of the nation. To someone seeking employment, the job structure often seems fixed and he must qualify and adjust to the available jobs. Experience and educational job specifications may appear to him to be too restrictive and the opportunity for advancement in the organization very limited. Objective reality is somewhere between the frustrated job seeker's view and the idealized view of the human resource utilization process. In recent years, employee recruitment, selection, placement, and promotion policies have come under more scrutiny than other personnel functions. These aspects of human resource management have begun a process of change that will probably rival the changes brought about by the labor legislation of the 1930s, and the idealized view may soon become a practical reality. In this chapter, we examine these functions of the human resource system in light of there changes. These functions make up two parts of the model as seen in Figure 6-1.

FORCES IN THE MACRO ENVIRONMENT

The forces of change emanate largely from three aspects of the macro-environment: the educational attainment of workers, rising expectations in society, and the changing view of civil rights at the work place. Chapter 3 documented that the level of education in the labor force has increased dramatically during the last fifty years. The effect of this change has doubtlessly been to increase the productivity of labor in the United States and to allow for the increasing use of sophisticated technology in industry. In recent years however, there has been a growing concern that the labor force is becoming too well educated. For example, one study published in 1967 estimated that if the educational attainment required of job holders in 1960 remained the same within occupations, there would be 3.1 million more high school graduates, more than 850,000 persons with less than a college degree, and 3.3 million more college graduates than the economy requires.[1] Of course this has not yet occurred because many jobs have

106

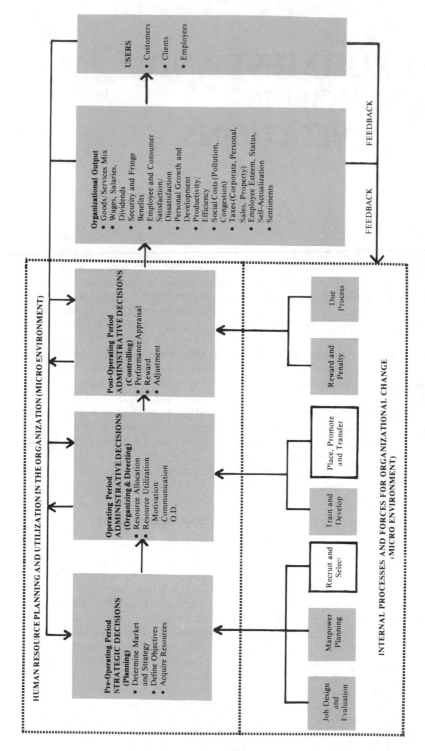

FIGURE 6-1 RECRUITMENT, SELECTION, PLACEMENT, PROMOTION AND TRANSFER IN THE HUMAN RESOURCE SYSTEM

been educationally upgraded in the labor force. The number of years of training required of physicians, attorneys, accountants, nurses, secretaries, etc. has increased over time as each of these jobs have become more complex and far more technologically sophisticated. The problem, though, is that many jobs do not require any more education or training than in the past. The *U.S. Bureau of Labor Statistics* estimates that for 80 percent of the jobs in the economy during the 1970s, a high school education will be sufficient; yet, about one-half of the 18-21 year olds will attend college at some point during the decade.[2] The Carnegie Commission Report summarizes the problem in a somewhat different manner:

> Another way of looking at the problem is to refer, not to the occupations that will be "educationally upgraded," but to the persons who will be occupationally downgraded as compared with past experience. Some of these persons will go into jobs which have been genuinely upgraded, as into managerial levels formerly filled by noncollege graduates but where the assignments are of a truly higher order than in the past. Others will go into jobs which could be and may be redesigned. Some persons, however, will go into jobs that will not and perhaps cannot be raised to the level of their capacity. Some of this happens already. Nearly 30 percent of four-year male college graduates are now in blue-collar, sales, and clerical jobs, many of which do not make full use of their education.
>
> Thus, the realistic problem for the 1970s will be the necessity for the absorption of some college-educated persons into jobs which have not been traditionally filled by persons with a college education, but in a national context where such absorption has been occurring in the past and is less of a traumatic problem than in much of the rest of the world.[3]

In other words jobs that utilize the full educational abilities of workers may not be available to many who seek them.

The second force for change may be largely a function of the first. Popular literature and some serious researchers believe that workers in America are becoming apathetic and alienated because they anticipated personally fulfilling, financially rewarding careers in industry.[4] Instead, many have encountered boring, routine jobs which require little decision-making on their part and few opportunities for advancement. They view their education as irrelevant and wasteful and their present situation almost intolerable. Whether this is an accurate assessment of workers' attitudes or not may make little difference, because many persons in policy-making positions believe this to be true. Lawmakers at state and national levels and chief executive officers of some of the largest firms in the U.S. are increasingly concerned about the quality of work in America.

The third force affecting personnel selection and placement processes is the concern for civil rights that began in the political arena in the 1960s but may have its major social impact in the labor force during the 1970s and 1980s. Legislation affecting the employment of racial minorities, women, and workers over forty years of age has caused widespread effort to create selection procedures and recruitment policies that avoid unfair discrimination and even rectify the effect of unfair practices in the past. (This legislation is discussed in Chapter 10.)

THE RECRUITMENT
AND SELECTION FUNCTION

The recruitment and selection of human resources relates the task or job structure and the manpower plan to the external environment. Career goals, personal abilities and skills, educational preparation, attitudes, values, and social goals are linked to organizational processes through the personnel functions of recruitment and selection.

Job design determines the specific qualifications needed for effective task performance and problem solving on each job, and the manpower plan determines the level of employment in the firm by the number of positions (workers) needed by job type as the organization operates at varying levels of output.

Job design, staffing plans, and recruitment and selection policies of all organizations in the macro-environment determine the *level* and *composition* of employment and unemployment in the economy; therefore, recruitment and selection policies and procedures have been given increasing attention by operating managers in recent years because of social concerns that existing practices discriminate unfairly against certain minority groups and women in society. But equally important is management's concern for matching people and jobs in an effective manner. Effectiveness is defined to include not only the economic goals of the organization, but also the life and career goals of individual employees. Organizations should attempt to attract human resources not only to use them well, but also to help them fulfill life and career goals. This does not assume that work is or should be a central life interest of employees. It does argue for a developmental approach to recruitment and selection that avoids the advertising of hard-to-fill, "dead-end" jobs as glamorous career enhancing positions to meet recruitment quotas. (Have you visited your local Army recruiter recently?) Furthermore, it urges that realistic career ladders be developed and individuals be encouraged (not coerced) to pursue advancement in the organization.

RECRUITING HUMAN RESOURCES

The recruiting activities of organizations have not been subjected to much comprehensive study or systematic evaluation. Many large organizations that undertake extensive recruiting campaigns continuously assess the effectiveness of particular practices, but these studies are seldom made available to the public because of a fear that competitors would benefit from the information in the competition to attract high-quality employees. The following sections review the sources and techniques typically employed in recruiting.

Internal Sources

When job openings occur or are anticipated, an organization should look first to the internal sources of manpower. The advantages of inside sources are: (1) a policy of promotion from within helps keep morale high and acts as a productivity incentive to employees; (2) the cost of recruiting "inside" is typically low compared to an external recruiting effort; and (3) the organization has more reliable information about present employees than about outsiders; therefore, selection from within should result in better placement decisions.

Recruiting techniques may include advertising vacancies in employee newsletters, posting notices on bulletin boards, and notifying supervisors of vacancies and asking for their recommendations. When a union is present, the labor-management agreement frequently establishes job-bidding procedures. These rules typically specify that all jobs covered by the agreement must be filled by qualified applicants from within the bargaining unit. Those interested in the vacancy "bid" the job by applying, if they are qualified; the position is filled by the individual with the highest seniority from among the qualified applicants. In some cases, applicants take competitive examinations and the position is filled by the highest scoring applicant. In either case, only those currently employed are permitted to apply. This has the effect, especially among blue-collar and other unionized jobs, of filling only entry level positions from external sources.

The major disadvantages to a "promotion from within" policy are: (1) it may cause inbreeding in the organization which inhibits the flow of creative ideas; (2) it may foster too much emphasis on seniority as a criterion for promotion; and (3) it may promote nepotism or cronyism in the selection of individuals to fill vacancies. However, neopotism or cronyism can also be practiced by companies that hire "from the outside."

The disadvantages not withstanding, investigators have found that businesses rely on hiring from within to a considerable extent even for managerial, sales, and professional positions.[5] Moreover, the recommendations of friends or acquaintances of current employees constitute an important source of job applicants. Present employees provide employers with information about qualified applicants or contact qualified applicants with little or no cost to the firm. A well-conceived internal recruiting plan may prove to be the most cost-effective source of talent to the employing organization, as well as a help to present employees in their efforts to enhance their own careers and find satisfying and rewarding jobs.

Gate Hiring

Gate hiring or "walk-ins" provide a large number of potential employees, especially during periods of low demand for employees.[6] Malm found that this source is widely used in recruiting manual workers, clerical employees, and sales personnel. The direct hiring of managerial and professional employees is a less frequent source of recruits, but 14 percent of the firms in his study reported the direct hiring of professionals and managers.[7] A study of small businesses in Utah supports the frequent use of gate hiring as an important source of employees especially among manufacturing firms. The prevailing sentiment concerning this source appears to be that it is a low-cost source of potential employees, but the quality of the applicants may be lower than other recruitment sources.[8] Unfortunately, the number of walk-in or write-in applications increases, often significantly, at a time when the firm is least likely to be hiring. This requires a costly effort to process applications and to send notices to many applicants informing them that they are not being considered or that position vacancies do not exist. It is good public relations to treat all such applications courteously and promptly and keep them on file for a limited period of time. Goodwill during a time when labor supplies are plentiful may pay off in a tight labor market situation by building a favorable company image in the area of employee relations.

The Public Employment Service

All states provide employment services to job seekers and employers. A major effort has been undertaken in recent years to improve the image and the services provided by the public employment service. In the past, employers and job seekers alike believed that the public employment system was useful mainly in filling blue-collar, unskilled jobs. In part, this resulted from the association the public employment system has with the payment of unemployment compensation. Another problem with the service has been its preoccupation with filling placement goals or quotas at the expense of effective screening of candidates for jobs. Individuals without proper qualifications are sometimes sent to particular jobs, simply because the service is attempting to meet its referral and placement quotas. However, the service has been used by employers even though this utilization has been mainly to fill unskilled or low skill blue-collar and clerical positions.

Malm found that 29 percent of the employers in his study recruited manual workers from the public employment service, 55 percent recruited clerical employees, but only 22 percent recruited managerial and professional personnel through this source.[9] In recent years the employment service in many states has organized to better serve white-collar professional, technical, and managerial job-seekers. In addition, the service is an excellent source for handicapped persons, minority employees, and veterans.[10]

There are compelling reasons for employers to rely more upon this governmental service to meet their staffing needs. The fact that employer taxes support the system, whether they use it or not, suggests that the service could become the most cost-effective source for the employer and the job-seeker alike. Furthermore, the use of the service could be an important source of qualified minority employees, pre-screened by the service using federal standards, to help fulfill a firm's commitment to a national policy of equal employment opportunities for all persons. Finally, federal and state laws governing private employment practices are likely to gain considerable influence over the recruitment and selection of personnel within the next few years. Many firms may find it too costly to develop their own programs for compliance and are likely to turn to the public employment service to assure compliance with these laws.

Private Employment Agencies

There are about 10,000 employment agencies in the United States helping employers and job seekers meet their employment goals.[11] These agencies vary considerably in size and effectiveness for good sources of employees and must be chosen carefully by employers and job seekers alike. Many firms specialize in certain types of positions such as accountants, engineers, computer specialists, and clerical employees. However, neither agency size nor specialization are sufficient reason to use an agency. Agencies may charge the job seeker a fee if he is hired by an employer through the agency. The employer may agree to pay all or some of the fee, but in either case, the fee is based upon some multiple of the employee's salary. Whatever length of time the employee remains with the employer, the agency is due the full fee. Some agencies seem more bent on placing employees quickly than in effecting a "good match." Agencies must be chosen based on the criterion of how well they match the requirements of the job with the skills and interests of the applicant.

Lopresto points out that these agencies can supplement an organization's recruitment staff and have the advantage that no costs are incurred until the position is filled.[12] Malm's study revealed that only 8 percent of the firms used private agencies in recruiting manual workers, 20 percent of the firms hired sales personnel through private agencies, 22 percent hired managerial and professional personnel through this source, and 62 percent hired clerical personnel through private agencies.

Private agencies have flourished in recent years as the growing economy and an expanding labor force increased employment levels in the United States. Doubtlessly, these agencies survive in the face of competition from the "free" services provided by the public employment service, because they have more effectively met the special needs of organizations and job seekers. A major advantage has been that they were able to carefully cultivate the special needs of organizations without many of the constraints placed upon public agencies (e.g., to find employment for special labor force groups—women, racial minorities, handicapped persons, and other disadvantaged groups). Most likely, these agencies will continue to prosper by specializing in filling certain types of position vacancies within the technical, clerical, and managerial categories. However, the impact of private employment agency practices on social policy will likely bring about more regulation through law and reduce the comparative advantage of using this source of employees.

College Recruiting

In a relatively few years there has been a rapid increase in the number of professional, technical, managerial, and staff specialists needed in industry and government compared to the need for unskilled workers and craftsmen. The vast majority of this need is met through college recruitment.[13] During the 1950–1968 period, the demand for college-educated employees expanded rapidly with the fast growing economy of this period and the increasing sophistication of production processes in industry. The supply of college graduates during this period kept pace with demand, but on balance it was a "sellers" market and the college graduate's starting salary grew rapidly as firms and government agencies bid for the best graduates.[14]

Beginning in 1968, growth in the economy turned down and appeared to be progressing at a much slower pace during the 1970s. The market for college graduates consequently turned into a "buyers" market and many college graduates have experienced difficulties finding jobs in recent years. The *1972 Manpower Report of the President* reflects the social concern that the colleges and universities in this nation are producing too many persons who may be "over-qualified" for available jobs, as we discussed earlier in the chapter.[15] However, the Carnegie Commission Report does not view with alarm the prospects for college graduates over the next thirty years, but points out that in some occupations (e.g. psychologists, college teachers, attorneys) there may be a short-term over-supply of jobseekers.

All during the 1950s and 1960s, college recruiters were engaged in fierce competition on campuses to hire the best of the graduates. In recent years the competition has become less intense, and during the 1970s ten million college trained individuals sought jobs, mainly through college placement offices. For these ten million and the organizations that hired them, the "match" of job vacancy and job seeker that begins on campus is of extreme importance.

There have been numerous articles, books, and reports written on how to improve college recruiting.[16] However, a recent study suggests that prevalent practices of the largest firms are unsystematic and probably inefficient in meeting the needs of employers and job seekers alike.[17] The majority of the large employers in this study sought college students for positions with leadership potential, and those hired could normally expect to participate in policy-making decisions within five years. In view of the importance of securing candidates that "fit" these sensitive positions, one would assume that the recruitment and selection of graduates would be pursued carefully. However, it appears that the majority of these firms allow the college recruiter alone to decide if a candidate should be invited for a second interview, even though the functional head of the department seeking the recruit often made the final hiring decision.[18]

Typically the first interview in the college placement office lasts twenty to thirty minutes. The interviewer attempts to assess a candidate's overall qualifications. Most importantly, the recruiter attempts to judge how ambitious the candidate is, whether he is able to get along with others, and how effectively he communicates.[19] These are complex factors to attempt to judge in such a brief encounter; however, carefully trained interviewers may be quite effective in screening out unqualified applicants. Unfortunately for college recruiting, only about one-half the firms have training programs for their recruiters, and less than half (41 percent) have any method of evaluating the performance of recruiters.[20]

College recruiting is costly for organizations, and mistakes are costly for job-seekers also. George Odiorne estimated in 1964 that the average cost of hiring a college graduate exceeded $1300.[21]

In 1970, the cost per hire was estimated ". . . to be more than $1000 per individual hired, with total expenditures of $100 to $200 million per year for business as a whole."[22] In light of evidence that the turnover rate for college students during the first five years is approximately 50 percent, the process seems inefficient indeed.[23]

There is a second half of college recruiting, the actual hiring of qualified candidates, which is as important as identifying them in the first place.

In other words, the recruiter must sell his company to those applicants with whom he comes in contact. Behling and Rodkin conclude that candidates are attracted to firms primarily based upon the nature of the work done by the company and the company's reputation.[24] While the nature of the work and the firm's image are important determinants of whether the student signs up for an interview, Glueck finds that if students felt that the recruiters performed poorly they stopped considering the company as a potential employer.[25] Furthermore, he found that "... students tended to prefer recruiters who were middle-aged but fairly modern in dress, who had some work experience in the students' specialties and were graduates of their university."[26] What the students did not like were recruiters who treated them indifferently, lacked enthusiasm, practiced pseudo-psychiatric interviewing techniques (such as stress-interviewing), or hurried them through the interview.

Ward and Athos concluded from two studies of recruiting practices in colleges that recruiters typically describe their companies unrealistically. In an effort to attract good students, recruiters often tell students what they want to hear which leads to unrealistic expectations, which, in turn, often results in high turnover among newly hired college graduates.[27] Others have commented on this phenomenon,[28] and we suggest that recruiters who sell students a false image of working conditions not only precipitate high turnover, but foster an unwarranted public image of the business enterprise. Unmet expectations may often result in resentment and rationalizations on the part of the employee. To explain his short tenure with the firm, the departing employee may magnify the adverse conditions he encountered to convince himself and others that the firm is a particularly undesirable place to work. The tarnished image, if communicated back to the campus, will likely inhibit future efforts to recruit desirable students.

Ward and Athos point out that there are many opinions about how to recruit college graduates, but for the most part they "... are hardly worth reading."[29] Obviously what is needed is more systematic research into college recruiting practices. What sound evidence there is suggests that practices are not based upon rigorously evaluated experience and do not appear to be particularly effective in bringing about a good fit between the companies needs and the graduates aspirations.

SELECTION GOALS AND STRATEGIES

The goal of the selection and placement process is to fit individuals into jobs that fully utilize their skills, abilities, and potentialities in a cost-effective manner. Although this is an ultimate and idealized goal from the social perspective, it is important that this perspective be kept in mind when strategies are developed and techniques of selection are used. In the past, many firms operated with an implicit or explicit goal of selecting "the best person for the job" while ignoring the social effects of pursuing such ends. Today, social policy demands that employers operate in such a way that they contribute to the goals of the macro-environment. Equal employment opportunity is no longer merely a socially desirable objective but a legislated requirement for nearly all employers.

Selection and placement strategy must be developed to accomplish these ideal goals. An example of three possible strategies are presented in Table 6-1. If we assume that the aptitude scores are ". . . relative probabilities of success for each applicant on each of five different jobs," the best person strategy corresponds to the pure selection example in the table.[30] Practically, there are several reasons that an organization cannot follow the pure selection strategy. First, in the example, "A" is the most qualified for jobs I and III; likewise, "G" is the most qualified for jobs II and IV. Since they cannot be placed on two jobs, the organization must settle for someone of lesser aptitude or recruit more prospective employees until applicants can be found with as high an aptitude as A, B, and G for the unfilled jobs. Only A, B, and G would be selected; the others would not be given the jobs. The search for more qualified applicants could be costly and the differences in aptitude not sufficiently important to performance on the job to justify further recruitment. Or, a policy of

TABLE 6-1

Hypothetical aptitude scores for ten applicants to each of five jobs, and assignments that would be made under different placement strategies.

APPLICANT	JOBS				
	I	II	III	IV	V
A	.9	.7	.8	.6	.7
B	.7	.6	.4	.4	.9
C	.4	.5	.7	.5	.5
D	.4	.5	.6	.3	.2
E	.3	.5	.1	.4	.4
F	.3	.3	.5	.4	.4
G	.8	.7	.5	.7	.6
H	.5	.4	.6	.4	.3
I	.4	.5	.2	.1	.1
J	.2	.1	.3	.1	.1

PLACEMENT STRATEGY						APTITUDE RATING AVERAGE
Pure selection (most qualified person on each job)	A (.9)	A or G (.7)	A (.8)	G (.7)	B (.9)	.8
Vocational Guidance (person placed on job for which he is most qualifid)	A (.9) G (.8)	E (.5) I (.5)	C (.7) D (.6) F (.5) H (.6) J (.3)		B (.9)	.63
Compromise placement (allocation of available) applicants to job openings	A (.9)	E or I (.5)	C (.7)	G (.7)	B (.9)	.74

Source: *Personnel Selection and Placement,* by M. D. Dunnette. Copyright 1966 by Wadsworth Publishing Company, Inc. Reprinted by permission of the publisher, Brooks/Cole Publishing Company, Monterey, California.

promotion from within or a desire to effect a change in the racial or sex composition of a particular job would lead to selecting others in the group to fill the two remaining positions. Moreover, an individual may not have a personal preference for the job for which he has the highest aptitude. All of these reasons and more make a pure selection policy impracticable for most organizations.

A second strategy is based upon placing individuals in jobs they are best suited for from among the available jobs. In the example, several apparent problems occur if the firm follows this strategy. First, there are more applicants than jobs, and the strategy does not establish a basis for deciding who will be employed if there are fewer jobs than applicants. Furthermore, it appears that no one is best suited to job IV. Finally, if all were hired, the average aptitude of the work force would fall to .63. On the other hand, vocational guidance as a strategy for fitting jobs and applicants is most feasible and desirable from the macro-environmental perspective, and school guidance counselors and manpower economists certainly recognize this as socially desirable.

In practice a compromise strategy is typically followed where ". . . the employment manager makes the best job placement possible with the resources available."[31] This compromise strategy considers the number and type of applicants available relative to the number of openings, the cost of enlarging the pool of available resources through recruiting efforts, the costliness of making wrong selections for jobs, the desires of individual applicants, and other institutional policies and goals. These latter considerations may include policies regarding employment of women, racial minorities, handicapped persons, older Americans or any other group. The selection and placement strategy is simply a means to accomplish organizational goals of all types. Consequently, an affirmative action goal of increasing the distribution of minority groups within various occupations is an organizational goal to be served by personnel selection practices and is not necessarily contrary to good selection theory. Nor is it unacceptable to pursue a goal of high job satisfaction for employees. Regardless, strategies must be designed to accomplish whatever goals are established.

SELECTION THEORY

Good selection practices are based upon three basic principles: the principle of individual differences, the principle of prediction, and the principle of the selection ratio.[32] It is obvious that people differ on many attributes. There are differences among individuals in intelligence, intellectual skills, knowledge, physical skills, personality, ambition, aptitude, motivation, and educational attainment. There are also obvious differences in job performance among individuals. These differences in performance are not fortuitous but relate systematically to individual differences. In other words, it is presumed that differences in individual attributes cause differences in work performance.

The principle of prediction is based, then, on discovering ". . . to what extent and with what significance these differences relate to job performance . . ."[33] The process begins with an examination of the job vacancy and the selection of a performance criterion. The criterion is a measure of how successful a worker is in performing the tasks of the job, e.g., number of parts completed, dollar volume of sales closed, time required to complete a task, etc. The next step is to choose a selection instrument (or a predictor) that assesses or measures some personal attributes. The third step is to obtain measurements using the predictor to determine the extent to which present employees possess varying degrees of the attributes, and then to determine if the criterion measures obtained simultaneously vary systematically with scores on the predictor. When the two sets of scores are highly related, using a statistical term, it is said that the scores are highly correlated. The extent of covariance is an important determinant of good selection. Conceptually, it is roughly analogous to measuring the extent to which variation in the criterion is *caused* by variation in the amount of the attributes possessed by workers or the extent to which variation in both is caused simultaneously by some other unmeasured attribute.

Since many attributes are known to be distributed normally among members of a population, the task of the predictor is to select individuals who are more likely to succeed on the job. By using predictors to select and place individuals who have more of the attributes being measured than one finds in a representative cross-section of the population, the organization is likely to improve group performance over what it would otherwise be. The important point is that the predictor is attempting to predict how likely it is that individuals will perform successfully on the job. The correlation is nearly always less than one, and perfect prediction is unobtainable. But with a given correlation between the criterion and the predictor, good selection then depends greatly on the size of the pool of job-seekers relative to the number of job vacancies. This is referred to as the selection ratio. The selection ratio (SR) may be expressed as:

n/N = SR
where n = the number of job openings
N = the total number of job applicants

The relationship of the selection ratio to the correlation between the predictor and the criterion is easily seen in Figure 6-2. The correlation (r) is .70. If the correlation were 1.0 then the scatterplot would be a straight line. If there was a low correlation the scatterplot would appear to be nearly a circle. In the first example in Figure 6-2, all applicants are hired, so predictors are of no use. In the second example only 80 percent of those who apply are hired. Selection is based upon the highest score on the predictor. In the third example where the selection ratio is .20, the top 20 percent are selected. It should be apparent that as the selection ratio goes down, the predictor score increases and, therefore, the average criterion score should be higher for a group of employees selected on the basis of example three compared to example one.[34]

These three principles of selection—individual differences, prediction, and the selection ratio—are important for implementing a selection strategy successfully, but we need to review a typical selection procedure.

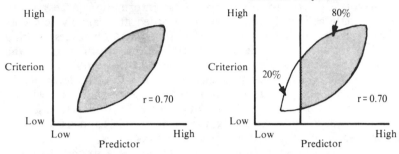

a. Scatterplot showing relationship (r = 0.70) between predictor and criterion. SR = 1.00, i.e., all applicants are being hired.

b. Same scatterplot when SR = 0.80, i.e., there are eight job openings for every ten applicants. Thus the lower 20 percent on the predictor can be rejected.

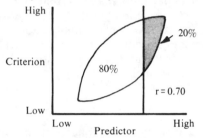

c. Same scatterplot when SR = 0.20, i.e., there are only two job openings for every ten applicants. Thus the lower 80 percent on the predictor can be rejected.

FIGURE 6-2   DIAGRAMS SHOWING THE EFFECT OF SELECTION RATIO ON THE AVERAGE QUALITY OF THOSE BEING HIRED

Source: Reprinted with permission from Milton L. Blum and James C. Naylor, *Industrial Psychology* (New York: Harper and Row Publishers, 1968), p. 47.

SELECTION PROCESS

A typical applicant or job seeker is processed through four separate steps: the application blank, interviews, pencil and paper "tests" (or work sample tests), and a physical examination. Frequently, each step is a hurdle that must be overcome or "passed" to proceed to the next one.

The "successive hurdle approach" is widely used because it is thought to be efficient in eliminating early those who are obviously not qualified, and the organization need not incur the expense of processing all applicants through the remaining steps. In other words, it is assumed that passing all hurdles is both necessary and sufficient to be successful on the job. Each step therefore is a predictor and must be related to job effectiveness to be theoretically correct.

Application Blanks

Each of the steps is intended to measure the qualifications of the applicant to perform successfully. However, it is widely assumed that their purposes differ. The typical application blank requires such information as age, sex, educational attainment, employment history, job experience, and physical characteristics of the job seeker. By having the applicant complete a form similar to Figure 6-3, the information necessary to evaluate his qualifications is conveniently recorded at relatively low cost to the firm and can be made available to functional managers seeking individuals to fill vacancies. The *face validity* of the information on the application blank appears high for employment history, job experience, training, and education, but selection theory requires that the information on the form must be related to a criterion. Most organizations probably do not attempt to determine the correlation between this data and job success in any systematic way, so the use of the application as a hurdle may not be a valid selection procedure in many instances.

Some organizations do attempt to validate this background data and establish statistical weights for the different types of information. Numerous studies have demonstrated that the weighted application blank can result in more effective selection.[35] Another factor which supports the need for a criterion-validated application blank is that if there is evidence of unfair job discrimination, the employer may be legally responsible for demonstrating that the information on the application is related to success on the job. This weighting or validation process is relatively expensive and only justified when a large number of candidates will be hired for a job over a relatively short period of time.

Interviews

The face-to-face interview typically follows if the information on the application blank suggests that the job seeker might be qualified. The interviewer has an opportunity to pursue in more depth the background experience, education, and training to determine "how qualified" the applicant is for the job. Furthermore, such factors as attitudes, personalities, motivations, and job aspirations are explored during the interview. In addition, the interviewer has an opportunity to explain and sell the job to the applicant and respond to any questions the applicant might have concerning the vacancy.

The interviewing process varies considerably among interviewers and from interview to interview, even if one individual meets with all applicants. The subjective nature of the judgements, the dependence on how the interviewer and interviewee relate to each other, and the varied types of procedures used make this step most open to criticism. For example, one study concluded, in the absence of a highly structured interviewing process and well-trained interviewers, that different interviewers evaluated the same experience of the applicants differently.[36] The personal appearance of the applicant affected different interviewers in varying ways. Many could not remember accurately what the applicant had said during the interview. More importantly, there was little agreement among interviewers when they attempted to predict the likely success of job candidates.[37]

In view of the heavy reliance on job interviews, especially in recruiting college graduates, professional, and managerial personnel, considerable effort needs to go into increasing the validity of the process. The previously mentioned study reports improvements in selection by structuring the interview through requiring interviewers to ask certain questions in a particular sequence, allowing managers to learn from their selection decisions by providing them with feedback about individuals selected, and by providing considerable classroom training in interviewing techniques.[38] While there has been little in the way of good validation studies in the

FOR OFFICE USE ONLY	
Possible Work Locations	Possible Positions

APPLICATION
FOR
EMPLOYMENT

(PLEASE PRINT PLAINLY)

FOR OFFICE USE ONLY	
Work Location _____	Rate _____
Position _____	Date _____

To Applicant: We deeply appreciate your interest in our organization and assure you that we are sincerely interested in your qualifications. A clear understanding of your background and work history will aid us in placing you in the position that best meets your qualifications and may assist us in possible future upgrading.

P E R S O N A L   Date: _____

Name _____
          Last   First Initial   Middle Initial

Social Security No. _____

Present address _____
          No.   Street   City   State   Zip

Telephone No. _____

How long have you lived at above address? _____

Previous address _____
          No.   Street   City   State   Zip

How long did you live there? _____

To Applicant: READ THIS INTRODUCTION CAREFULLY BEFORE ANSWERING ANY QUESTIONS IN THIS BLOCKED-OFF AREA. The Civil Rights Act of 1964 prohibits discrimination in employment practice because of race, color, religion, sex or national origin. P.L. 90-202 prohibits discrimination on the basis of age with respect to individuals who are at least 40 but less than 65 years of age. The laws of some States also prohibit some or all of the above types of discrimination.
DO NOT ANSWER ANY QUESTION CONTAINED IN THIS BLOCKED-OFF AREA UNLESS THE EMPLOYER HAS CHECKED THE BOX NEXT TO THE QUESTION, thereby indicating that the requested information is needed for a bona fide occupational qualification, national security laws, or other legally permissible reasons.

☐ Are you over the age of twenty-one? _____ If no, hire is subject to verification that you are of minimum legal age.

☐ Sex: M _____ F _____   ☐ Height: _____ ft. _____ in.   ☐ Weight: _____ lbs.

☐ Marital Status: Single _____ Engaged _____ Married _____ Separated _____ Divorced _____ Widowed _____

☐ Date of Marriage _____ ☐ Number of dependents including yourself _____ ☐ Are you a citizen of the U.S.A.? _____

☐ What is your present Selective Service classification? _____

☐ Indicate dates you attended school:

Elementary _____ High School _____ College _____
          From   To   From   To   From   To
Other (Specify type of school) _____
                                                                          From   To

☐ Have you ever been bonded? _____ If yes, on what jobs? _____

☐ Have you been convicted of a crime in the past ten years, excluding misdemeanors and summary offenses? _____ if yes, describe in full _____

Employer may list other bona fide occupational questions on line below:
☐ _____

What method of transportation will you use to get to work? _____

Position(s) applied for _____ Rate of pay expected $_____ per week

Would you work Full-Time _____ Part-Time _____ Specify days and hours if part-time _____

Were you previously employed by us? _____ If yes, when? _____

List any friends or relatives working for us _____
                                                        Name(s)

If your application is considered favorably, on what date will you be available for work? _____ 19____

Are there any other experiences, skills, or qualifications which you feel would especially fit you for work with the Company? _____

EF 101-2
(FORM 101)

(Turn to Next Page)
Printed in U.S.A.

FIGURE 6-3   EXAMPLE OF A TYPICAL APPLICATION BLANK

past, the concern over unfair discrimination will likely result in either more efforts at validation or in reducing the dependence on the interview as a screening device.

Employment Tests

If the successive hurdle approach to selection is used, then each step in the process of selection is a test in that it is used as a predictor of job success implicitly or explicitly. In a more restrictive sense, pencil and paper examinations or work-sample tests (such as a typing test) have been widely used to select employees for positions. Some tests have high face validity, e.g., giving a typing test to applicants for a clerk-typist position. Others, especially personality tests, may appear far removed from what the job requires. In either case, the relationship of the test to job success is the important concern. In recent years, tests have come under intense scrutiny from government and civil rights groups.

The Equal Employment Opportunity Commission (EEOC) established to enforce the Civil Rights Act of 1964 has published "Guidelines on Employee Selection Procedures." These guidelines define what is included in the category of employment tests:

> For the purpose of the guidelines in this part, the term "test" is defined as any paper-and-pencil or performance measure used as a basis for any employment decision. The guidelines in this part apply, for example, to ability tests which are designed to measure eligibility for hire, transfer, promotion, membership, training, referral or retention. This definition includes, but is not restricted to, measures of general intelligence, mental ability and learning ability; specific intellectual abilities; mechanical, clerical and other aptitudes; dexterity and coordination; knowledge and proficiency; occupational and other interests; and attitudes, personality or temperament. The term "test" includes all formal, scored, quantified or standardized techniques of assessing job suitability including, in addition to the above, specific qualifying or disqualifying personal history or background requirements, specific qualifying or disqualifying personal history requirements, scored interviews, biographical information blanks, interviewers' rating scales, scored application forms, etc.[39]

Furthermore, the guidelines set forth a definition of unfair discrimination as follows:

> The use of any test which adversely affects hiring, promotion, transfer or any other employment or membership opportunity of classes protected by title VII constitutes discrimination unless: (a) the test has been validated and evidences a high degree of utility as hereinafter described, and (b) the person giving or acting upon the results of the particular test can demonstrate that alternative suitable hiring, transfer or promotion procedures are unavailable for his use.[40]

These guidelines have presented a major obstacle to personnel selection. A predictor must be both reliable and valid if it is to be useful as a selection tool. A reliable "test" is one which will show consistency in measurement of the same individual or group of individuals if repeated under the same circumstances. A valid test is one that measures what it is supposed to measure. There are three types of validity that are frequently considered in evaluating a test. The first, *construct validity,* is when a test is measuring the attribute it was designed to measure; e.g., scales should be accurate in measuring body weight. The second concept is *concurrent validity* and is demonstrated by evidence that effective job performers have an amount of the attribute; e.g., all policemen presently on the force for more than 90 days weigh over 150 pounds. *Predictive validity,* the third type, exists where there is evidence that job success can be predicted on the basis of the test measurement; e.g., from among all police officers hired, those who weighed less than 150 pounds did not perform satisfactorily. Of the three, predictive validity is the most difficult and expensive to evidence; however, it appears to be the only acceptable way of assuring that unfair bias does not exist in testing. The EEOC has repeatedly warned that employers using tests may be required to demonstrate predictive validity. From a theoretical point of view this is a desirable requirement. From a practical point of view, however, it may be very time consuming and costly, and small firms may not be able to afford to use employment tests if they must present evidence of predictive validity.

The EEOC is concerned about employment tests because there is considerable evidence that existing tests are culturally biased.[41] Although validity must be demonstrated under the Civil Rights Act only if there is evidence that the use of the test has an adverse effect on a class of employees covered under the law, if racial minorities and women are "underrepresented" in a particular occupation or level in an organization, this appears to be sufficient evidence of an adverse effect and the selection process must be validated.

There are numerous technical questions concerning bias free test construction that are beyond the scope of this chapter. It is sufficient to note, however, that a successful affirmative action plan that integrates underrepresented occupations is only one aspect of overcoming unfair discrimination. The same standard should apply to all hired. To assure that "reverse discrimination" does not occur where a test is valid for two or more groups but one group characteristically scores lower than the others, but without a corresponding difference in productivity (criterion scores), then the scores should be adjusted to predict the same probability of success on the job for all groups. This avoids having to hire low potential employees in order to fill quotas established in an affirmative action plan. However, it may require special recruiting efforts to assure a sufficient number of minority group applicants and/or a lower selection ratio.

Lopez points out that the criterion problem in testing theory is related to the concern of management to select the "best" employees. Most tests are validated using a single index of job performance.[42] He points out:

> To begin with, it is imprecise to speak of *job performance* because this term represents only one aspect of what the employer really seeks, *job effectiveness.* The other and equally important aspect is *job satisfaction.* . . . *job performance* refers to the value of employees' efforts to a company, while *job satisfaction* refers to the extent to which employees' efforts meet their personal needs. . . .

In employment strategy, employers must specify, therefore, the best configuration of *job effectiveness* they need to meet the demands of their business. They may accept a lower *task* performance level to maintain job stability, or they may accept a higher turnover rate in exchange for low training costs and wage rates. They can rarely acquire high task performance, job stability, and low training costs and wages with a uniform set of selection standards simply because the personal attitudes necessary to achieve these three effects do not occur often in the same person.[43]

Whether Lopez is correct concerning the tradeoffs organizations must make is an empirical question that has not been adequately researched. Certainly the object of testing is to measure those aspects which cause a person to be successful on the job. But success is a multi-dimensional concept that requires more than adequate job productivity; it also implies good vocational choice. Effective utilization of human resources requires that more than lip service be given to using the person's skills, and abilities to serve both the organization and the job holder's needs and aspirations.

Another culprit in selection theory Lopez argues is the "successive hurdle" approach.[44] Instead he proposes that each stage of the selection process be focused on what the job requires employees to do (tasks) and what they have to put up with (demands). The testing problem then is to identify the personal traits needed to meet these requirements. These traits should be primary such as strength, creativity, or knowledge of mathematics, rather than secondary traits such as school attainment or years of experience. The selection process is to identify the degree of each trait possessed by the candidates and select from among those who possess acceptable degrees of all *required* traits.[45] From among those determined to possess acceptable degrees of required traits, employers may emphasize job performance criteria which ". . . favor minority groups and women *without* reducing overall job effectiveness."[46] In our view, this is a reasonable strategy to accomplish organization, personal, and social employment goals.

Physical Examinations

The physical examination has become standard procedure for many firms as a final step in the hiring process. One study found that 86 percent of the firms responding to the study required preemployment physical examinations.[47] The primary purpose of the examination is to determine the physical condition of the employee at the time of hiring to prevent expensive liability claims in the future as a result of some pre-condition not known that might make the individual prone to injury or illness on the job. Furthermore, it may reveal whether the individual is physically incapable of performing the job as a result of some existing injury or illness.

The 1970 Occupational Safety and Health Act has made many employers and insurance companies "health conscious," and it is likely that the physical examination will become a more widespread practice as employers attempt to avoid incurring liability for employee-related health problems. This act is discussed in Chapter 10.

CONCLUSION

As a result of changes in the macro-environment, especially the enactment of civil rights laws, the effects of recruitment and selection practices on the utilization of human resources are under close scrutiny. Unfortunately, employers have not undertaken much systematic evaluation of these practices and the result has been an over-emphasis of experience, educational attainment, white, middle-class attitudes, and the personal compatibility of job seekers as criteria for judging employability. This is not to suggest that these factors are unrelated to job performance or to job satisfaction. The published evidence suggests that current practices are not necessarily effective for firms or individual job seekers. This argues, in our view, for a major commitment from firms to sponsor or undertake extensive research into recruitment and selection practices. In a sense, our urging is probably superfluous because legal requirements are likely to require systematic evaluation of these practices or their abandonment among major employers in the next decade.

CASE 1
CARL WATTS' TEMPORARY PROMOTION

Carl Watts was the manager of the planning and budgeting department of a product division of a large manufacturer of electronic equipment. About six months ago, Carl was promoted to the newly created position of division accounting chief with responsibilities for all division accounting functions including his previous department. Ten senior analysts reported directly to him now; the five who reported to him previously and five others were assigned responsibilities in all three departments: planning and budgeting, general accounting, and data processing.

Ted Cobb, the division comptroller, told Carl that he was promoted at this time because there was no other manager experienced in the accounting function who could be promoted and, secondly, it was felt that this experience would enhance Carl's opportunities for promotion to the corporate headquarters in San Francisco.

In addition, Mr. Cobb indicated that he was unhappy with the performance of the three general accounting section analysts. He said that he was unable to get the previous department manager to initiate action to correct the situation. As he saw it, the former manager was too easy going and willing to tolerate a mediocre staff.

Carl eagerly accepted the assignment, indicating to Mr. Cobb that despite losing two of his best subordinates within the past year, he felt that the planning and budgeting department was running smoothly and that he was ready and willing to accept the challenge of managing two additional departments.

At a staff meeting held the first few days after the reorganization, Carl indicated to his staff that because of his expanded role, less of his time would be available to spend with any one individual and that he didn't expect to get as involved in detail as he had done in the past when only one department reported to him. The senior analysts could expect to manage their respective functions with little operational interference, although they were expected to provide him feedback regarding problems they were experiencing and to consult with him on major policy and procedure changes they might be contemplating.

Two months later, Carl noted that the accounts receivable balance of one of the division's major customers had been unusually high for a period of several months and indicated his concern to Bob Gustav, the accounts receivable section manager.

Gustav said that he had had problems with the customer since the division began selling to them over a year ago, but because of a systems and procedures incompatibility in matching seller's invoices and customer's purchase orders, he had never issued credit memos to the customer. He also indicated that the previous department manager had been too busy to get involved in the problem.

Carl asked Gustav to draw up a plan to resolve the paperwork backlog, including cost of working out the backlog and a method of avoiding the problem in the future. He also expressed the hope that automated systems support would be forthcoming but, should systems support not be available, the backlog would have to be worked out manually, even if it required overtime.

Within a week Gustav presented a neatly prepared plan which Carl reviewed, approved, and then asked Gustav to contact the data processing department's financial systems coordinator and present the proposal to him to establish programming priority.

After a few days, Gustav reported back to Carl that he had contacted the systems coordinator and the coordinator said he would see what he could do.

Periodically, over the next four months, Carl asked Gustav how the project was coming. Invariably, Gustav indicated that he had been in communication with the systems coordinator and that the coordinator had other projects of a higher priority, but once he started the programming, it would progress quickly. He also indicated that considerable overtime would be required to work out the backlog manually and that it would be more economical to wait for the systems support.

Two months later, the president of the company wrote a very strong letter to all divisional managers which was extremely critical of the poor corporate accounts receivable collection record and indicated that efforts should be made to bring the accounts down to an acceptable level.

Carl, after seeing the letter, went to Gustav's office to inquire as to the status of the problem customer account.

Gustav informed Carl that the customer had told him that all bills had been paid but that data processing showed a $500,000 unreconciled debit balance in the customer's account.

Carl, expressing deep concern, reiterated that the resolution of the problem was especially important now in view of the letter from the company president.

On his way back to his office, Carl happened to meet the systems coordinator in the hallway and asked him how the project was coming.

The coordinator told Carl that the project had been put on the shelf. He said that in his opinion, it was a low priority project since Gustav had only been down to see him about two times.

Questions
1. How do you explain Gustav's behavior?

2. What criticisms do you have for the promotion process based upon the evidence in the case?

3. Why do you believe the systems coordinator responded as he did at the end of the case?

CASE 2
THE SOLAR ENERGY CORPORATION

Mr. Arnold Becker is the personnel manager for the Solar Energy Corporation (SEC) of Phoenix, Arizona, a small company concerned with solar cell production and research. This company has the good fortune of finding itself in the forefront of a rapidly expanding industry. Despite its small size (presently 150 employees) SEC has many valuable patents and the even more valuable scientists and engineers who developed them.

The demand for solar energy devices is increasing at an exponential rate. Until a few years ago such devices were expensive and sophisticated; the cost of energy produced by them was much higher than that produced by coal, oil, and gas. The National Aeronautics and Space Administration was one of its primary users and developers. It was some of NASA's scientists and managers who realized the potential, practical home and commercial uses of solar energy, and they formed SEC shortly after the Arab oil boycott.

By early 1976 the industry had grown to such an extent—and orders were coming in so fast—that the SEC board of executives decided to increase employment by 50 percent over the next year and by another 30 percent by the spring of 1977.

As a result, Mr. Becker found himself in the position of having to hire a large number of people of various backgrounds and skills within a relatively short period of time. Since SEC did not have regular screening procedures for hiring new employees, Becker was asked to develop a valid procedure. Both Becker and the company were interested in recruiting and selecting those people who would have the greatest long-range success within the company. He decided to split his task into two units, one for blue-collar and clerical work, the other for scientific, managerial, and secretarial work.

To recruit nonprofessional employees, Becker placed advertisements in the Phoenix area newspapers and contacted the state bureau of employment. A surprisingly large number of people responded (112 in all) to the ads, and Becker hoped to hire many of them. He initially had each applicant fill out a form which requested such information as education, work-history, biographical information, vocational interests, and general attitudes and interests. He adopted this form from a manufacturing company he has been associated with previously.

After this initial screening, Becker asked each acceptable blue-collar and clerical applicant to complete a standardized, previously validated test which attempts to measure the candidate's aptitude and specific areas of knowledge and skill. That afternoon the persons who scored highest on this test were given an on-the-job test in their various areas which was designed to discover performance capability at particular skill levels. These combined testing procedures, Becker believed, enabled him and his co-workers to select individuals who would have the highest probability of success on the job. Attention was given not only to the individual's skills but also the person's potential for further advancement at SEC.

Becker decided to recruit his scientific, engineering, and management personnel at professional conferences and through college placement offices, and his secretaries through local employment agencies. At the suggestion of SEC top management, Becker recruited the higher level managers first. These managers were then able to build their own managerial teams and to help Becker form general position descriptions for the other needed professional employees. No tests were used to hire these individuals. Each was interviewed by Becker first, after which he recommended further interviews with management personnel if he believed the applicant was qualified.

After this new management team was chosen, Becker began his recruitment of the other professionals. Again, this process began with the submission of applications containing vitaes, training, and experience. After the application forms were screened, Becker setup interviews for each professional. The interviews were designed to give the applicant contact with the section and division heads, to show them the nature of SEC's work and present and future facilities, and, most importantly, to observe their responses through nondirective interviews. Becker has planned to give these personnel psychological exams to see how they would fit into the organization, but decided not to because of the possible negative reactions that some applicants might have toward the procedure.

SEC decided to hire at least 20 percent racial minorities to avoid problems with government agencies that might be concerned about whether SEC was an "equal employment opportunity" employer. To entice qualified racial minorities to join SEC, Becker was offering a 25 percent salary bonus to members of racial minorities who accepted employment with SEC. This was a one-time cash payment that was called a "dislocation allowance." It appeared to be a successful ploy; the SEC was having no difficulty in attracting qualified nonwhite professionals.

Questions
1. Evaluate SEC's recruitment and selection procedures. What changes would you recommend?

2. Assess the payment of the bonus to nonwhite employees from ethical and legal view points.

STUDY AND DISCUSSION QUESTIONS

1. What changes in the macro environment have led to changes in organization recruitment and selection procedures?

2. What makes a particular selection criterion useful to an organization?

3. Criticize the "succeeding hurdle" approach to selection. Why is it often used? With what can it be replaced?

4. Why are employment experiences and educational performance often used in the selection process? Do these criteria serve as measures for or in place of more basic criteria? What is the danger in using past work experience and educational performance as selection criteria?

5. What are the advantages and disadvantages to using a "promotion from within" policy to fill higher level positions in the organization?

6. What should be the role of public and private employment agencies in the selection process of the organization?

7. Criticize the typical college recruiting and selection process used by companies. How can it be improved?

8. Are all employment tests biased? Should they ever be used in selection?

9. What are some common selection goals and strategies for an organization?

10. How does the recruitment and selection process in the organization interface with the manpower planning function? The training and development function?

11. Criticize this comment recently made by a manager of a small textile mill:
    We have no formal recruitment and selection program and yet we have a good work force. People just know in this town that our company is a good one to work for. We get more qualified applicants than we can use for our job openings and we simply select the most qualified applicant to fill a job.

12. Is there a difference in using the selection criteria of "meeting minimum job qualifications" versus using the criterion of selecting the "person who is most qualified?" What are the implications of your answer as it relates to equal employment opportunity for women and minorities?

ENDNOTES

1. As cited in the Carnegie Commission on Higher Education, *College Graduate and Jobs,* (New York: McGraw-Hill Book Company, Inc., 1973), p. 2.
2. Ibid., p. 2.
3. Ibid., pp. 3-4.
4. For example see: Judson Gooding, "Blue-Collar Blues on the Assembly Line," *Fortune,* Vol. 82, No. 1, July 1970, pp. 69-71.
5. F. T. Malm, "Recruiting Patterns and the Functioning of Labor Markets," *Industrial and Labor Relations Review,* Vol. 7, No. 4, pp. 507-525.
6. Ibid.
7. Ibid.
8. Robert L. Lopresto, "Recruitment Sources and Techniques," *Handbook of Modern Personnel Administration* (New York: McGraw-Hill Book Company, Inc., 1972), pp. 12-22.
9. Malm, op. cit.
10. See U.S. Department of Labor, *Manpower Report of the President* (Washington, D.C.: U.S. Government Printing Office, 1973), pp. 46-50.
11. Lopresto, op. cit., p. 12-19.
12. Ibid.

13. George S. Odiorne and Arthur S. Hahn, *Effective College Recruiting* (Report 13) Bureau of Industrial Relations, University of Michigan, Ann Arbor, 1961.
14. For a detailed analysis of the trends see: The Carnegie Commission on Higher Education, op. cit.
15. For additional discussion see: U.S. Department of Labor, *Manpower Report of the President* (Washington, D.C.: U.S. Government Printing Office, 1972), pp. 103-115.
16. For a review of the literature see: Thomas H. Patten, Jr., *Manpower Planning and the Development of Human Resources* (New York: John Wiley and Sons, Inc., 1971), Chapters 10 and 11.
17. Larry R. Drake, H. Roy Kaplan, and Russell A. Stone, "Organizational Performance as a Function of Recruitment Criteria and Effectiveness," *Personnel Journal,* October 1973, pp. 885-891.
18. Ibid., p. 887.
19. Ibid., p. 888.
20. Ibid., p. 889.
21. George S. Odiorne, "How to Get Men You Want," *Nations Business,* January 1964, p. 70.
22. Lewis B. Ward and Anthony G. Athos, *Student Expectations of Corporate Life: Implications for Management Recruitment* (Boston: Harvard University Graduate School of Business Administration, 1972), p. 6.
23. Ibid., p. 7.
24. Orlando Behling and Henry Rodkin, "How College Students Find Jobs," *Personnel Administration,* 32 September October 1969, pp. 35-42.
25. William F. Glueck, "How Recruiters Influence Job Choices on Campus," *Personnel,* March-April 1971, p. 48.
26. Ibid., p. 48.
27. Ward and Athos, op. cit., p. 51.
28. See Patten, op. cit., Chapter 11.
29. Ward and Athos, op. cit., p. 10.
30. Marvin D. Dunnette, *Personnel Selection and Placement* (Belmont, California: Wadsworth Publishing Company, Inc., 1966), p. 3.
31. Ibid., p. 5.
32. This selection borrows liberally from the clear, non-statistical treatment given the subject by Felix M. Lopez, *Personnel Interviewing: Theory and Practice* (New York: McGraw-Hill Book Company, Inc., 1975), Chapter 5.
33. Ibid., p. 80.
34. For a more complete treatment of this relationship see: Milton L. Blum and James C. Naylor, *Industrial Psychology: Its Theoretical and Social Foundations* (New York: Harper and Row Publishers, 1968), Chapter 2.
35. For example see W. K. Kirchner and M. D. Dunnette, "Applying the Weighted Application Blank in a Variety of Office Jobs," *Journal of Applied Psychology* August 1957, pp. 206-208.
36. Robert E. Carlson, Paul W. Thayer, Eugene C. Mayfield, and David A. Peterson, "Improvements in the Selection Interview," *Personnel Journal* April 1971, p. 269.
37. Ibid., pp. 269-272.
38. For an extensive treatment of interviewing techniques see Lopez, op. cit.
39. Betty R. Anderson and Martha P. Rogers (eds.) *Personnel Testing and Equal Employment Opportunity* (Washington, D.C.: U.S. Government Printing Office, 1970), p. vi.
40. Ibid.
41. Ibid.
42. Lopez, op. cit., p. 96.
43. Ibid., pp. 96-97.
44. Ibid.
45. Ibid., pp. 100-106.
46. Ibid., p. 98.
47. William R. Spriegel and Virgil A. James, "Trends in Recruitment and Selection Practices," *Personnel* (November-December 1958), p. 44.

ADDITIONAL READING

Barnette, W. Leslie, Jr. (ed.) *Readings in Psychological Tests and Measurements,* (rev. ed.) Homewood, Ill.: Dorsey Press, 1968.

Byham, William C., and Morton E. Spitzer. *The Law and Personnel Testing,* New York: American Management Association, 1971.

Calvert, Robert. *Equal Employment Opportunity for Minority Group College Graduates: Locating, Recruiting and Employing.* Garrett Park, Maryland: Garrett Park Press, 1972.

Drake, John D. *Interviewing for Managers: Sizing Up People.* New York: American Management Association, 1972.

Dunnette, Martin D. *Personnel Selection and Placement.* Belmont, Calif.: Wadsworth Publishing Co., 1966.

England, George W. *Development and Use of Application Blanks.* Dubuque, Iowa: William C. Brown Co., 1961.

Fear, Richard A. *The Evaluation Interview,* 2nd ed., New York: McGraw-Hill Book Co., 1973.

Ghiselli, Edwin. *The Validity of Occupational Aptitude Tests.* New York: John Wiley and Sons, Inc., 1966.

Guion, Robert M. *Personnel Testing.* New York: McGraw-Hill Book Co., 1965.

Hasenfeld, Yeheskel. *Manpower Placement: Service Delivery for the Hard-to-Employ.* Ann Arbor: Institute of Labor and Industrial Relations, 1973.

Jackson, Matthew J. *Recruiting, Interviewing and Selecting: A Manual for Line Managers.* New York: McGraw-Hill, 1972.

Kirkpatrick, J. et al. *Testing and Fair Employment.* New York: New York University Press, 1968.

Lawshe, C. H. and Michael J. Balma. *Principles of Personnel Testing.* New York: McGraw-Hill Book Co., 1966.

Levinson, Harry. *The Exceptional Executive: A Psychological Conception.* Cambridge: Harvard University Press, 1968.

Marvin, Philip Roger. *The Right Man for the Right Job at the Right Time: The Executive's Guide to Tapping Top Talent.* Homewood Ill.: Dow Jones-Irwin, 1973.

Stevens, David Walter. *Assisted Job Search for the Insured Unemployed.* Kalamazoo, Michigan: W. E. Upjohn Institute for Employment Research, 1974.

Stewart, Charles J. & William B. Cash, *Interviewing: Principles and Practices.* Dubuque, Iowa: William Brown Co., 1974.

Ward, Lewis B. *Student Expectation of Corporate Life: Implications for Management Recruiting.* Boston: Harvard University Graduate School of Business Administration, Division of Research, 1972.

7

ORGANIZATION DEVELOPMENT

Organization development is a concept that has grown rapidly in popularity over the last decade. It can be rightly called a personnel function, but frequently the organization development staff member reports to a top line executive. There are many definitions of the concept and no widely accepted view of what is to be considered organization development (OD).

DEFINITION OF ORGANIZATION DEVELOPMENT

For our purposes we adopt Professors French and Bell's definition:

> Organization development is a long-range effort to improve an organization's problem-solving and renewal processes, particularly through a more effective and collaborative management of organization culture—with special emphasis on the culture of formal work teams—with the assistance of a change agent, or catalyst, and the use of the theory and technology of applied behavioral science, including action research.[1]

OD, then, is the process of systematically intervening in an on-going organization to bring about some planned change that will improve the functioning of that organization. The intervention is systematic in the sense that the techniques used have either a theoretical base or an experience base for bringing about the desired change. Furthermore, the goal of any OD effort is improving the organization's ability to accomplish its goals.

OD is mistakenly thought of by some as a new label for management training and development. While management training may be used as an intervention technique in an OD effort, to confuse training techniques with this approach to increasing the effectiveness of organizations ignores the more important aspects of the concept. We treat OD in this book, though, as a prelude to the discussion of training and development in the human resources model. Chapter 8 focuses on training and development.

Historically, OD grew out of research and intervention into small groups. Kurt Back points out that OD is a concept with origins that can be traced to the group dynamics and human relations movements in the 1930s and 1940s.[2] However, one of the major influences is the National Training

Laboratory (NTL) at Bethel, Maine. The NTL was created in the 1950s to sponsor research into organizational processes and small group intervention techniques. The pioneers in the movement were all social scientists attempting to use unstructured small-group situations to teach individuals about the effect of their actions on others and the functioning of groups. These training groups (or T-Groups) proved effective in the laboratory, but transferring interpersonal behavior learned in T-Groups into improved organizational processes in permanent and complex systems often proved difficult. Out of this early effort to transfer what seemed effective in the laboratory to on-going organizations, researchers began to look at inter-organizational relationships among sub-systems as well as interpersonal relationships among organizational participants, i.e., organization development.

The concept of OD focuses on planned change in individual, inter-personal, and inter-group behavior. It views the organization as a whole system and concentrates very often on changing the "connections" between the parts of the system to bring about organizational improvement. OD practitioners view the organization as a series of interconnected, inter-dependent parts where a change in one part causes a change in many other subsystems. Therefore, strategies for improving organizational processes often include planned interventions in more than one sub-system in the organization. French and Bell depict the organization as having four major sub-systems connected together by a "goal sub-system" (see Figure 7-1).

This is a particularly useful view of an organization for OD practitioners because they tend to focus on the goal-setting/goal-attainment process. Interventions in the major sub-systems are intended to improve the ability of the organization and its members to reach desired goals. Moreover, Figure 7-1 illustrates that each of the major sub-systems plays an interdependent role in goal accomplishment. Therefore, in an effort to improve the organization's effectiveness, the OD practitioner may intervene in one sub-system to cause a change in another or may intervene in two or more sub-systems simultaneously, or enter each sub-system sequentially to bring about the desired change.[3]

ORGANIZATION DEVELOPMENT GOALS

The objectives of OD programs will vary from organization to organization and differ depending upon the type of intervention techniques used. However, a typical program would include some or even all of the following:

1. To build trust among individuals and groups throughout the organization, and up-and-down the hierarchy.
2. To create an open, problem-solving climate throughout the organization—where problems are confronted and differences are clarified, both within groups and between groups, in contrast to "sweeping problems under the rug" or "smoothing things over."
3. To locate decision-making and problem-solving responsibilities as close to the information sources and the relevant resources as possible, rather than in a particular role or level of the hierarchy.
4. To increase the sense of "ownership" of organizational goals and objectives throughout the membership of the organization.

5. To move toward more collaboration between interdependent persons and interdependent groups within the organization. Where relationships are clearly competitive, e.g., limited resources, then it is important that competition be open and be managed so the organization might benefit from the advantages of open competition and avoid suffering from the destructive consequences of subversive rivalry.

6. To increase awareness of group "processes" and its consequences for performance—that is, to help persons become aware of what is happening between and to group members while the group is working on the task, e.g., communication, influence, feelings, leadership styles and struggles, relationships between groups, how conflict is managed, etc.[4]

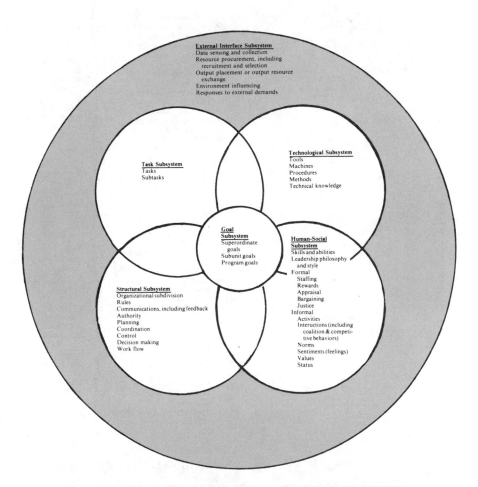

FIGURE 7-1 MAJOR ORGANIZATIONAL SUBSYSTEMS

Source: Reprinted with permission from Wendell L. French and Cecil H. Bell, Jr. *Organization Development: Behavioral Science Interventions for Organization Improvement* (Englewood Cliffs, N.J.: Prentice-Hall, Inc., 1973), p. 78.

ORGANIZATION DEVELOPMENT STRATEGIES

Another way of depicting the organization is as though it were an iceberg (see Figure 7-2) that is composed of both overt, readily seen parts and covert or hidden aspects. This view of organizations suggests that there are depths of organization relationships that are difficult to observe, measure, or change but still very important for the effective functioning of the organization. Some organizational specialists argue that certain techniques intervene "deeper" into organizational processes than others and caution practitioners to avoid techniques intended to change only the overt aspects of the organization.[5] While this caution is well taken because

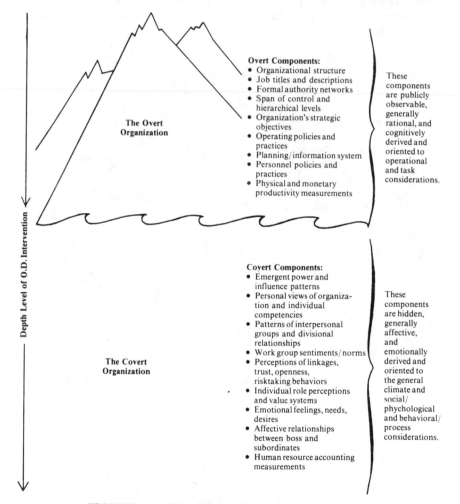

The Overt Organization

Overt Components:
- Organizational structure
- Job titles and descriptions
- Formal authority networks
- Span of control and hierarchical levels
- Organization's strategic objectives
- Operating policies and practices
- Planning/information system
- Personnel policies and practices
- Physical and monetary productivity measurements

These components are publicly observable, generally rational, and cognitively derived and oriented to operational and task considerations.

The Covert Organization

Covert Components:
- Emergent power and influence patterns
- Personal views of organization and individual competencies
- Patterns of interpersonal groups and divisional relationships
- Work group sentiments/norms
- Perceptions of linkages, trust, openness, risktaking behaviors
- Individual role perceptions and value systems
- Emotional feelings, needs, desires
- Affective relationships between boss and subordinates
- Human resource accounting measurements

These components are hidden, generally affective, and emotionally derived and oriented to the general climate and social/ phychological and behavioral/ process considerations.

Depth Level of O.D. Intervention

FIGURE 7-2   THE ORGANIZATIONAL ICEBERG

Source: Richard J. Selfridge and Stanley L. Sokolik, "A Comprehensive View of Organization Development," pp. 47, *MSU Business Topics,* Winter 1975. Reprinted by permission of the publisher, Division of Research, Graduate School of Business Administration, Michigan State University.

easily made, easily observed changes in the overt components may not bring about some desired behavioral change, our experience leads us to believe that permanent change is brought about by modifying relationships and sub-systems in both overt and covert regions of the organization. The strategy of intervention may begin in any sub-system employing techniques designed for or proven effective in bringing about the desired change in that system or determining the nature of hidden relationships in a particular domain. But, this beginning intervention typically suggests or even requires that several other techniques be employed to bring about change in other aspects of the organization's environment.

One of the major strengths of the OD concept is that it is an eclectic, results-oriented view of organizational change. Consequently, little good comes from making disparaging comments about the power of one technique to bring about effective change in complex organizations. Rather, the OD practitioner should be skilled in many techniques and be aware that a change in one part of a system may require a formal intervention into many other parts. A frequently valid criticism of OD efforts is that the practitioner is skilled in bringing about changes in individual attitudes and interpersonal relationships, but is unable to bring about the needed changes in task structure, power relationships, or personnel policies and procedures.

Friedlander and Brown make this same point when they state:

> ... our concept of organization development calls for change in technology and structure (technostructural) or change in individuals and their interaction processes (human-processual), rather than efforts to change only the people, only the structure/process, or only the technology of the organization.[6]

This broad view differs from some of the earlier notions of OD that focused on mainly social, psychological, and behavioral process considerations.

In keeping with this broad definition, Friedlander and Brown classify OD techniques into two categories: technostructural and human processual approaches. Within their definition of technostructural approaches are such concepts as job enrichment, job enlargement, and work technologies (e.g., continuous process technology). These techniques are reviewed elsewhere in the book and therefore only the latter category will be elaborated in this chapter. But you should keep in mind that successful organization development requires attention to and often intervention into the overt or sociotechnical aspects of organizations along with human process change.

HUMAN PROCESS TECHNIQUES

The assumption that seems to pervade these techniques is that *by focusing on improving the fulfillment of human needs in the organization the organization as a whole will become more effective.* While this may not be true if you define organizational effectiveness solely in terms of task accomplishment, it is *necessarily* true if you broaden your concept of organizational success to include job satisfaction as being coequal in importance to the economic or task goals of the organization. We make this assumption and therefore believe that the pursuit of humanistic values through the organizational context is valid for both profit-seeking and not-for-profit organizations.

INTERVENTIONS DIRECTED TOWARD INDIVIDUALS

Some of the earliest efforts in OD focused on individual attitudes, behavior, and beliefs. The humanistic views of McGregor, Maslow, Argyris, and others formed underlying values for laboratory training which has been called T-Group, sensitivity training, and encounter group. Bennis points out that:

> Sensitivity training is a novel and controversial form of education which goes under a variety of names: laboratory training or education (which I prefer and will employ for convenience here), Encounter Groups, "T" Groups, "L" (for learning) Groups, Self-analytic Groups, and many more. Essentially, laboratory training is a small group effort designed to make its participants more aware of themselves and of the group process. The group works under the guidance of a professionally competent behavioral scientist and explores group processes and development through focusing attention on the experienced behavior of its members. The group itself is relatively unstructured and finds its own way, so to speak, by coming together to understand itself.[7]

There are numerous variations using a laboratory approach, but most have common purposes.

Basic T-Groups consider mostly the "public," "here-and-now" data available to all members. The range of these target data is very wide:

1. The specific structures members develop in their interaction, such as the leadership rank-order.
2. The processes of their group life, with special attention to getting a group started, keeping it going, and then experiencing its inevitable "death".
3. Their specific emotional reactions to one another's behavior and to their experiences.
4. The varying and diverse styles or modes of individual and group behavior, as in "fighting" the trainer or in "fleeing" some issue that has overwhelmed group members.[8]

This approach to increasing organizational effectiveness has received the most attention of any OD techniques. Proponents and critics frequently exchange views on the value of the technique to bring about permanent organizational change. Critics argue that there is little "hard" evidence that what is learned in the laboratory is useful in the organization. Furthermore, there is a risk that the technique itself threatens the mental health of some who participate in the experiments. But most importantly, the critics point out, sensitive, open, and trusting behavior may be unproductive in some organizations and even result in people becoming suspicious, uncomfortable, or hostile towards the newly learned attitudes and behavior of recent graduates of "sensitivity" training classes.

Proponents readily admit the need for more systematic evaluation of laboratory methods in bringing about organizational effectiveness. They deny that the technique, in the hands of skilled trainers, presents a significant threat to mental health; and they increasingly recognize that the values of the technique must be consistent with those of the organization.

Golembiewski's taxonomy of values, goals, and means in lab training is presented in Figure 7-3. He summarizes the benefits that can be gained through this technique as follows:

1. The individual can be freed by his experiences in a Basic T-Group so as to remove obstacles to his interpersonal functioning and, perhaps, to his performance in organizations.

2. The Basic T-Group can provide an arena to develop and to test new skills and insights applicable to interpersonal situations that may be modified for use in "action groups" or at work.

3. The experience in the Basic T-Group can reveal the nature and importance of differences between "public" and "private" attitudes in organizations, differences which may be owned up to, analyzed, and perhaps reduced in ways that enhance performance in organizations.

4. The group experience can point up the limitations of existing organization norms.

5. The experience in the Basic T-Group can illustrate in life that alternatives to common organizational norms are available.

6. The Basic T-Group can help generate new norms for work and help enforce them as well, as by inducing a desire in individuals to work actively in a "core group" to try to achieve at their work some of the gratification of needs they experienced by a Basic T-Group.[9]

A Meta-Values of Lab Training	B Proximate Goals of Lab Training	C Desirable Means for Lab Training	D Organization Values Consistent with Lab Training
1. An attitude of inquiry reflecting (among others): a. a "hypothetical spirit" b. experimentalism	1. Increased insight, self-knowledge	1. Emphasis on "here-and-now" occurrences	1. Full and free communication
2. "Expanded consciousness and sense of choice"	2. Sharpened diagnostic skills at (ideally) all levels, that is, on the levels of the a. individual b. group c. organization d. society	2. Emphasis on the individual act rather than on the "total person" acting	2. Reliance on open consensus in managing conflict, as opposed to using coercion or compromise

A Meta-Values of Lab Training	B Proximate Goals of Lab Training	C Desirable Means for Lab Training	D Organization Values Consistent with Lab Training
3. The value system of democracy, having as two core elements: a. a spirit of collaboration b. open resolution of conflict via a problem-solving orientation	3. Awareness of, and skill-practice in creating, conditions of effective functioning at (ideally) all levels	3. Emphasis on feed-back that is non-evaluative in that it reports the impact on the self of other's behavior, rather than feed-back that is judgmental or interpretive	3. Influence based on competence rather than on personal whim or formal power
4. An emphasis on mutual "helping relationships" as the best way to express man's interdependency with man	4. Testing self-concepts and skills in interpersonal situations	4. Emphasis on "unfreezing" behaviors the trainee feels are undesirable, on practice of replacement behaviors, and on "refreezing" new behaviors	4. Expression of emotional as well as task-oriented behavior
	5. Increased capacity to be open, to accept feelings of self and others, to risk interpersonally in rewarding ways	5. Emphasis on "trust in leveling," on psychological safety of the trainee	5. Acceptance of conflict between the individual and his organization, to be coped with willingly, openly, and rationally
		6. Emphasis on creating and maintaining an "organic community"	

FIGURE 7-3   FOUR VALUE-LOADED DIMENSIONS RELEVANT IN LABORATORY APPROACHES TO ORGANIZATION CHANGE AND DEVELOPMENT

Source: Reprinted with permission from Robert T. Golembiewski, "The Laboratory Approach to Organization Change: Schema of a Method," *Public Administration Review,* Vol. XXVII, No. 3, September 1967.

TEAM BUILDING TECHNIQUES

Partly in response to the criticism and short-comings of sensitivity training, some behavioral scientists have tried to increase organizational effectiveness by training work teams in laboratory settings. A typical "family group" might include a middle-manager, several first-level supervisors who report to the middle-manager, and perhaps even a few rank-

and-file employees who work for one or more of the supervisors. As a group they constitute the training class, and the subject matter focused on in the training sessions is their day-to-day interaction. This includes how the group communicates formally and informally, what roles each member sees himself playing in the group, how the group makes decisions about goals and problem-solving, and how effective are the leadership processes.

While there are probably as many team development strategies as there are team trainers, most efforts aimed at increasing team effectiveness rely on an approach whereby the trainer first engages in exercises designed to diagnose problems in one or more of the subject areas. Based upon some agreed upon problem areas, the trainer attempts to create a situation in the group that provides members with quick and accurate feedback about how their interpersonal behavior may be the source of the identified problems and/or how they might change their behavior to avoid the problem in the future. Frequently, the trainer will provide laboratory situations where group members can practice new behaviors with his aid and some encouragement from the group. The trainer may even continue in a consulting role back on the job to assist the team and individual members in learning to interact differently with each other.

The advantages of this approach over early T-Group experiments should be readily apparent. The subject matter of the class is directly relevant to on-the-job relationships. The focus of the training is on group interaction and less on individual attitudes and values. Moreover, if the group supports the behavior in the training sessions there is a greater likelihood of group reinforcement of the newly learned behavior back at the work place. The chief disadvantage to the family group is that because of the continuing nature of their association with group members at the work place, members of this type of T-Group would be reluctant to be honest about their feelings about each other.

There is a growing body of research that suggests, on balance, team building techniques can improve organizational effectiveness, but the evidence is not conclusive. One of the major unanswered questions is what constitutes effective behavior. Secondly, what kind of organizational climate is most conducive to successful team development is debated among several schools of thought. Finally, more evidence is needed to judge what effect team development training has on actual task performance.[10]

SURVEY FEEDBACK TECHNIQUES

The survey feedback method for bringing about organizational change has been developed extensively at the Institute for Social Research at the University of Michigan.[11] Attitude surveys, based upon the work of Rensis Likert, are distributed to members of the organization. The data in summary form are fed to top management who in turn distribute the data to lower levels. As the data moves down the organization, supervisors and subordinates in each work group discuss and interpret the data, plan for constructive changes in the organization based upon the data, and move the data down to the next level. The consultant's or trainer's role is to assist in interpreting the data and helping bring about the desired change.

There are many others who advocate a variation on this approach, and the use of organizational surveys are typically combined with other types of intervention techniques. A recent review of OD research concludes that

> . . . there is evidence that survey feedback can be an effective 'bridge' between diagnostic activities . . . and active intervention, since its primary effects seem to be on attitudes and perceptions of the situation. But there is little evidence that survey feedback alone leads to changes in individual or organizational performance.[12]

INTERGROUP TECHNIQUES

The focus of these techniques is the improvement of interaction among organizational sub-systems. One such technique developed by Blake, Shepard, and Mouton[13] brings together the leaders of two or more related groups and attempts to get a commitment from them to try to improve their relationships. If the commitment is gained, each goes off to complete a list of "like and dislikes" about the other and a list that attempts to anticipate what the other group(s) will say about them. These lists are shared among the leaders of the groups, and they combine them into a single list of issues and problems to be resolved. Next a plan is developed to resolve the issues and assign responsibility for action. Follow-up meetings are scheduled to check on progress toward resolution of the conflict areas and to insure that responsibilities are carried out. The trainer's role varies with the degree of involvement needed to bring about commitment to resolving differences and agreeing on a plan.

Another approach concentrates on the conflict that results in organizations from the extent to which organizational sub-systems are differentiated.[14] This approach attempts to measure the extent to which related sub-systems differ in terms of the formality of their structure, interpersonal orientations toward task accomplishment, time orientations (whether members had long or short time perspectives as they viewed task performance), and goal orientation (whether members of a unit focused tightly on goals or not). Differences among sub-systems are not necessarily undesirable, but where differences exist, the problem is to find an effective way to integrate the activities of the related units. Lawrence and Lorsch conclude that elaborate integrating mechanisms are often used by effective organizations, when dictated by the environment, to facilitate the resolution of conflict, and managers who serve integrating roles had "balanced orientations" and relied heavily on open confrontation.[15]

The role of the OD consultant could range from becoming involved in changing the orientation of sub-units to proposing structural changes in the organization to bring about better integration. This technique is frequently accompanied by a series of interpersonal and team development efforts if a significant organizational change is sought.

There has been little systematic evaluation of these techniques, and as Friedlander and Brown point out, "we simply do not know much about whether OD interventions lead to better management of intergroup relations or not."[16]

OTHER TECHNIQUES

There are numerous other techniques or strategies used in organization development; new approaches frequently emerge, become faddish, and are then integrated with some of the others discussed in previous sections. Two such approaches (management-by-objectives and organizational behavior modification) deserve special attention. In recent years management-by-objectives (MBO) has experienced a growing popularity among organizations, consultants, and academic researchers alike. Less well known, but of increasing importance, are the efforts to increase the effectiveness of organizations through the use of "learning theory," or what are often called *behavior modification principles.*

Peter Drucker's, *The Practice of Management* published in 1954 helped popularize the MBO approach.[17] Drucker argued that every manager should set down explicitly his objectives and help participate in the establishment of higher-level objectives. An MBO approach emphasizes that goals should be quantified, if possible, and the evaluation of performance should be conducted jointly between the supervisor and the subordinate. This enables each manager to know, influence, and understand the goals of subordinate and superior departments in the organization. The established and agreed upon objectives serve as both a guide to behavior and the focus of subsequent performance appraisal for subordinate units.

The current view of MBO emphasizes the mutual goal setting and performance appraisal process. Goals are set by mutual consensus among a superior and his subordinate. Performance reviews are held by superior and subordinate based upon mutually agreed-upon, specific, quantitative performance standards.

One of the early efforts to implement an MBO system took place at the General Electric Company. The efforts there were directed toward the practice of appraising performance rather than implementing a company-wide MBO system. However, the conclusions drawn from this study of goal-directed performance appraisals have had an important impact on the development of MBO. The GE investigators concluded that:

1. Criticism has a negative effect on achievement of goals.
2. Praise has little effect one way or the other.
3. Performance improves most when specific goals are established.
4. Defensiveness resulting from critical appraisal produces inferior performance.
5. Coaching should be a day-to-day, not a once-a-year, activity.
6. Mutual goal setting, not criticism, improves performance.
7. Interviews designed primarily to improve a man's performance should not at the same time weigh his salary or promotion in the balance.
8. Participation by the employee in the goal-setting procedure helps produce favorable results.[18]

A decade after the GE study, Raia concludes that within the past few years MBO has emerged as a system designed to integrate key management processes and activities in a topical and consistent manner.[19] Figure 7-4 describes the elements of a typical MBO process, and Figure 7-5 demonstrates how it fits into the larger human resource system. MBO is a system which integrates strategic decision-making and accomplishment in an effort to improve the use of human resources.

Some authors believe that OD is more basic than MBO.[20] The argument is that MBO concerns itself with only the visible parts of the organizational iceberg (see Figure 7-2). While this is a valid distinction in some cases, it is apparent in others that an MBO program is as concerned with the attitudes, interpersonal processes, and inter-group relationships as any other OD technique.

As with many OD techniques, management-by-objectives has not been subjected to rigorous study. There is little evidence that MBO is related to productivity in either a positive or a negative way, because few experiments using acceptable methodological controls have been undertaken in organizations. Carroll and Tosi, after reviewing the literature concluded that "MBO has a much clearer relationship to managerial attitudes and to the manner in which managers carry out their job assignments."[21]

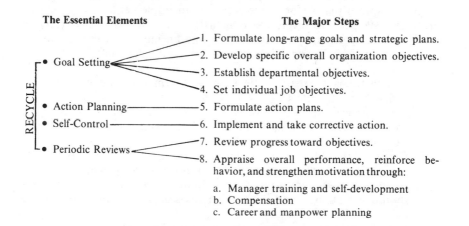

FIGURE 7-4   THE MBO PROCESS

Source: Reprinted with permission from Anthony P. Raia, *Managing by Objectives* (Glenview, Ill., Scott, Foresman, and Company, 1974), p. 16.

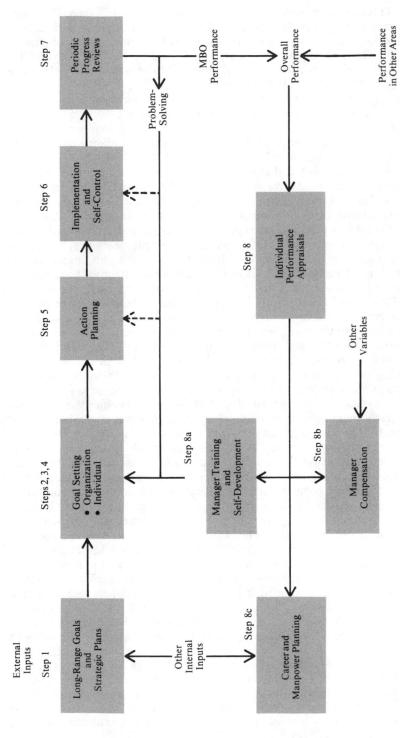

FIGURE 7-5   THE MBO PROCESS

Source: Reprinted with permission from Anthony P. Raia, *Managing by Objectives* (Glenview, Ill., Scott, Foresman, and Company, 1974), p. 21.

MBO tends to improve superior-subordinate relations, engender more confidence in the performance appraisal process, and improve trust among peers and between work groups. However, MBO suffers from problems of over-quantification, much paper work, and a failure to reach beyond the first 2 or 3 levels of management. In short, MBO tends to have the same "track record" as many other OD techniques.

The principles of behavior modification are well-known to students of psychology and have recently become the center of a controversy lead by well known psychologist B. F. Skinner.[22] The work of Skinner and other behaviorists is directly descendent from the classical conditioning experiments of psychologists like I. P. Pavlov and J. B. Watson. The basic premise of this approach is that *behavior is a function of its consequences.*[23] In contrast, psychologists like Abraham Maslow, Douglas McGregor, and Frederick Herzberg, all having had very important influences on OD practices, assume that behavior is the result of some internal state, i.e., needs. Typical OD practices attempt to create organizational environments which better utilize the creative energies of employees by releasing or directing their motivational drives. It is assumed that an inappropriate organizational climate is the *cause* of errant or ineffective behavior. In contrast, behaviorists assert that observed behavior is caused, not by some internal state (such as the need for esteem), but because we have learned that our present behavior will probably lead to desirable consequences.

This last point is a subtle one for the reader unless he is well read in behaviorist literature, but, from an OD practitioners viewpoint it is a crucial nuance. In the practice of OD, it means a shift of emphasis from diagnosing how to create a climate more consistent with the participants' needs, to attempting to determine how to eliminate some behavior and/or substitute desirable behavior patterns. For example, assume that an automobile parts manufacturer is plagued by high turnover and absenteeism; traditional OD consultants may suggest sensitivity training for the supervisors, team building exercises, and a program of job enrichment. An OD practitioner employing behavior modification principles might, after analysis of the consequences of turnover and absenteeism to employees, establish a variable compensation plan that awards bonuses to employees who are seldom absent from the job and defers the payment of the bonuses for two years contingent upon the employees continued employment. The behaviorists avoids speculating about what internal need causes employees to quit their jobs and/or be absent from work; rather he focuses upon establishing contingencies that will reduce the objectionable behavior.

Figure 7-6 is a basic model for an OD strategy that employs behavioral modification principles. Briefly, it requires an analysis of the behavior that needs to be changed to improve performance and the present consequences of that behavior to individuals. Secondly, a baseline needs to be established to see how frequently the behavior is engaged in during a specified period of time. This baseline serves as the "control" to determine whether the organizational intervention is working. Changes can be introduced in one or all of the environmental elements by rearranging or changing the reinforcements (reward-penalty system) to bring about desired behavior and/or eliminate undesired behavior. The focus of the analysis is then upon the effectiveness of the new reinforcements (i.e., behavioral consequences) in bringing about and maintaining desired behavior.

The advocates of this approach point out that it is a more scientific approach to the complex questions surrounding the control of behavior in

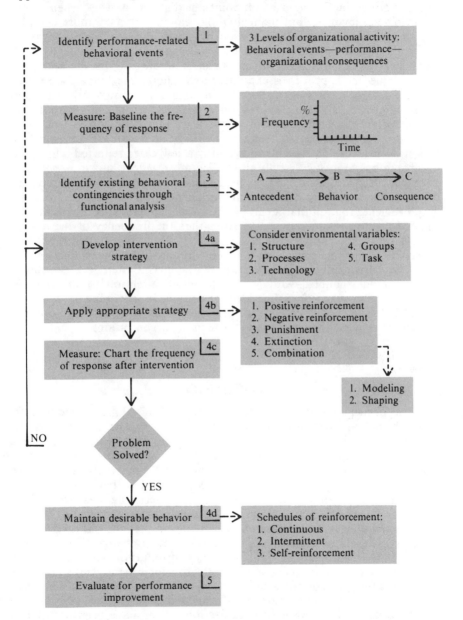

FIGURE 7-6   BEHAVIORAL CONTINGENCY MANAGEMENT
Source: Reprinted with permission from F. Luthans and R. Kreitner "The Management of Behavioral Contingencies" *Personnel* July-August 1974 Vol. 51, No. 4, pp. 13.

organizations and is not dependent upon the validity of assumptions about the nature of man. It makes no assumptions that men work to satisfy a set of needs that are arranged in some hierarchy or that workers inherently seek or avoid challenging work.

The critics, on the other hand, point out that it may work when simple behaviors are involved, but the technology cannot solve the more complex and more important problems associated with organizational behavior. How, the traditional OD consultant asks, can you build highly creative organizations, using behavioral modification strategies? Furthermore, the critics argue, the approach is exploitive and ignores the humanistic values that need to be expressed in the way in which we design organizations. Personal growth, authentic expression of feelings, trust, and collaboration are important dimensions of work experience that behaviorists ignore.

Using the principles of behavior modification as an OD strategy is a recent occurrence. To date there are only a few cases reported where this technique has been successfully used. The most widely known experiment took place at the Emery Air Freight Company where there was a reported $2 million savings over a three-year period resulting from a performance improvement program that identified performance-related behavior and increased positive reinforcements to strengthen the frequency of the desired behavior.[24] This example and a few others are sufficiently intriguing to researchers that the technology of behavior modification is likely to be used more frequently in the near future. Thomas Patten sees traditional OD techniques coupled with MBO and more attention to the reward/penalty system as a "long-heralded new day" in personnel administration.[25] Behavior modification principles may be the long-awaited approach toward improving reward/penalty systems in organizations.

CONCLUSION

The principles and techniques of OD have developed directly from research into small group and individual behavior. The group dynamics movement has been most instrumental in developing techniques to bring about planned change. Of more recent vintage is the emphasis on MBO and behavior modification principles. Although OD has found wide spread acceptance in many organizations, there is evidence that line managers often see it as "another training technique"—interesting, desirable if you can afford it, but dispensable during hard economic times.

These feelings on the part of line managers may be valid. OD consultants have sold value systems along with behavior change. The humanistic values of trust, openness, interpersonal confrontation as a "good," and participative decision-making as most effective for organizations are value judgments that pervade the attitudes of most applied behavioral scientists.

The value question aside, OD consultants have had considerable trouble dealing with power in organizations. They have been accused of trying to sell OD programs on the basis that they would lead to truth and love as the basis for interpersonal relations. W. Warner Burke of the NTL Institute points out that:

. . . OD practitioners . . . do not have sufficient understanding of and experience with power dynamics in organizations. It is obvious that some concentration and exercise of power are required for organizations to function effectively.[26]

Along with learning to deal with power, OD practitioners need to learn how to do more systematic research in ongoing organizations using acceptable methods of scientific control to separate fad from fact and what works from what is only enjoyable as an organization attempts to increase its effectiveness.

Finally, OD as an applied behavioral field of practice and research must establish a procedure that assures that OD practitioners are trained and qualified to intervene (interfere) in organizational processes. Glibness and arcane jargon are the trademarks of many who consider themselves OD professionals. Organizations have a right to demand that they be protected from the sale of behavioral snake oil.

OD holds promise for personnel administration, but its value is suspect among many operation managers who must concern themselves with practical, measurable results. The function of OD is a new personnel function and needs careful nurturing and constant attention if it is to serve a useful role in improving the management of human resources.

CASE 1
THE REORGANIZATION

In April 1974, Mr. Howard, head of the Computation Branch of a large research and development organization, held a meeting to inform the twenty branch members of major organizational changes within the branch. He had already presented these plans to the Computer Center Commander, who had approved them.

Mr. Howard explained to these engineers and mathematicians that the new structure would more closely reflect the nature of the workload—especially since there would be additional computers; it would eliminate the "group-leader" concept and thereby enable the other group members to be promoted, and would possibly allow for a takeover of another small organization. He said he would like to discuss with each person where he or she would like to be in the new organization.

When Mr. Howard asked for comments he was quite surprised at the amount of ill feelings against the change. Many felt that the present organizational structure was quite conducive to good working relationships and to successfully meeting the anticipated workload. They were all willing to share the tasks of the proposed section—which they knew consisted of much drudgery—but as their exclusive responsibility. They felt that the personnel office would not look favorably at the proposed raising of the (civil service) grade structure and that the absorption of an organization that was successfully performing its duties and was very much against the takeover, would lead to no real gain—except for the expansion minded Colonel. Furthermore, many members felt (but would not then express) that Mr. Howard and the section leaders had already basically decided "who was to go where"—an assumption that was verified a short time later.

A few of the reactions six months later:

The new organizational structure reflects the workload poorly—half of the members of the new section, formed to work on task D, were assigned to task S.

Mrs. Mathes, feeling that the talk of promotions was continuing to be mere talk, left the organization. (Her group leader had left the organization a year earlier for similar reasons, his "promised" promotion never materialized.)

Mr. Douglas, who worked effectively when assigned meaningful work he felt he could handle, and enjoyed being with his officemates, was assigned against his expressed wishes to the section which performs task C. This latter task was highly complex and had little relation to Dr. Douglas' interests, background, or education. Further, Mr. Douglas had little in common with his new officemates.

Mr. Opfes, who had repeatedly requested to learn task C but was told that his services were needed for task B, now fulfills his "achievement" needs through his after-hours endeavors.

Unrelated to the reorganization, Mr. Howard's secretary—an ideal secretary when she started to work for Mr. Howard—requested a transfer citing Mr. Howard's lack of understanding.

Questions

1. Why have these problems occurred?

2. Is there a need for an O.D. intervention?

3. What technique(s) would you recommend? Why?

CASE 2
THE BARTLETT CORPORATION

Joe Morgan began working for Bartlett Corporation about one year ago. He came to Bartlett with two years experience as an insurance salesman after attending college for two years. Joe was first employed as a product service specialist, reporting to Bob Hall, supervisor of the product service section. Bob has been with Barlett for thirty years and has functioned as a supervisor for the last two years.

Under Bob's supervision, Joe developed habits that were not considered desirable by the other supervisors, and they began to complain to the manager of the department. They claimed that the other employees were disturbed because they are required to meet certain standards and Joe doesn't seem to be held accountable for them. After eight months, the manager of the department decided to transfer Joe to the administrative section as an administrative specialist. Joe now reports to Jim Moore who was recently promoted to his supervisory position.

Jim has been given the responsibility of improving Joe's production in three months or he will have to terminate him. Jim continually loses his temper and reprimands Joe in front of the entire department whenever he feels it is necessary. Jim is experiencing problems with many of his other subordinates too. He feels that he is not accorded the proper respect due his position by nonsupervisory employees. As a consequence Jim remains on a "businesslike basis" with all nonsupervisory employees.

At the end of the three months, Joe has increased his output; however, his tardiness and absenteeism have increased. Now Jim is faced with the decision of recommending continued employment for Joe or letting him go.

Questions

1. Explain some of the causes for the apparent interpersonal problems at Bartlett.

2. Would an O.D. effort alleviate these problems?

3. What O.D. strategy would you recommend? Explain your answer carefully.

STUDY AND DISCUSSION QUESTIONS

1. What is organization development? How is it related to training?

2. With what organizational systems and subsystems is organization development concerned?

3. What are some "overt" and "covert" components of an organization? What do they have to do with organization development?

4. What is sensitivity or T-group training? What does it try to accomplish? What are its advantages and disadvantages?

5. What are team building techniques? What do they attempt to accomplish? What are their advantages over sensitivity training? How do they differ from intergroup techniques?

6. What are survey feedback techniques and how are they used?

7. What is MBO and how is this concept related to organization development?

8. What is the "behaviorist" approach in organization development and how does it differ from a traditional training approach to organizational development?

9. Can human behavior in organizations really be changed? How? Isn't it necessary to just fire managers in organizations who are unwilling to change and who have outlived their usefulness?

10. Develop a model to implement a program for organization development in a large corporation. Would this model be different for a small corporation? For a University? For a church? For a civic association? For a state governmental agency?

ENDNOTES

1. Wendell L. French and Cecil H. Bell, Jr., *Organization Development: Behavioral Science Interventions for Organization Improvement* (Englewood Cliffs, N.J.: Prentice-Hall, Inc., 1973), p. 15.
2. Kurt W. Back, "Intervention Techniques in Small Groups" in *Annual Review of Psychology* (Palo Alto, Calif.: Annual Reviews, Inc., 1974), pp. 367-388.
3. The reader should be aware that any model of a complex social or behavioral phenomenon is an abstraction that has value only inasmuch as it is a useful tool for understanding and effecting the phenomenon it depicts. No model is complete, but some models are more useful than others.
4. John J. Sherwood, "An Introduction to Organizational Development," *Experimental Publication System* (Washington, D.C.: American Psychological Association, 1971), No. 11, MS No. 396-1.
5. Richard J. Selfridge and Stanley Sokolik, "A Comprehensive View of Organization Development," *MSU Business Topics,* Winter 1975, Vol. 23, No. 1, pp. 46-61.
6. Frank Friedlander and L. Dave Brown, "Organization Development" in *Annual Review of Psychology* (Palo Alto, Calif.: Annual Reviews, Inc., 1974), pp. 313-342.
7. Warren G. Bennis, *Organization Development: Its Nature, Origins, and Prospects* (Reading, Mass.: Addision-Wesley Publishing Co., 1969), p. 61.
8. Robert T. Golembiewski, "The Laboratory Approach to Organization Change: Schema of a Method," *Public Administration Review,* Vol. XXVII, No. 3, September 1967.
9. Ibid.
10. For a review of these points, see Friedlander and Brown, op. cit., pp. 328-329.
11. David G. Bowers, "OD Techniques and Their Results in 23 Organizations: The Michigan ICL Study," *Journal of Applied Behavioral Science,* Vol. 9, No. 1, 1973, pp. 21-43.
12. Friedlander and Brown, op. cit., p. 327.
13. R. R. Blake, H. A. Shepard, and T. S. Mouton, *Managing Intergroup Conflicts in Industry* (Houston, Texas: Gulf Publishing Co., 1965).
14. Paul R. Lawrence and Jay W. Lorsch, *Organization and Environment* (Homewood, Ill.: Richard D. Irwin, Inc., 1969).
15. Ibid., p. 152.
16. Friedlander and Brown, op. cit., p. 331.
17. Peter Drucker, *The Practice of Management* (New York: Harper Bros., 1954).
18. H. H. Meyer, E. Kay, and John R. P. French, Jr., "Split Roles in Performance Appraisal," *Havard Business Review,* Vol. 43, No. 1, 1965, pp. 123.
19. Anthony P. Raia, *Managing by Objectives* (Glenview, Ill.: Scott, Foresman, and Company, 1974), p. 15.
20. Selfridge and Sokolik, op. cit.
21. Stephen Carroll, Jr., and Henry Tosi, Jr., *Management by Objectives: Applications and Research* (New York: The MacMillian Company, 1973), p. 16.
22. At the center of the controversy is the book by B. F. Skinner, *Beyond Freedom and Dignity* (New York: Alfred A. Knopf, Inc., 1971).
23. This section is based in the main, on Fred Luthans and Robert Kreitner, *Organizational Behavior Modification* (Glenview, Ill.: Scott, Foresman, and Company, 1975).
24. _____. "At Emery Air Freight: Positive Reinforcement Boosts Performance," *Organizational Dynamics,* Winter 1973, pp. 41-50.
25. Thomas A. Patten, Jr., "OD, MBO, and the R/P System: A New Dimension in Personnel Administration," *Personnel Administration,* March-April 1972, pp. 23-23.
26. W. Warner Burke, "The Demise of Organization Development," Reprinted with permission of the *Journal of Contemporary Business,* Copyright 1972, p. 61.

ADDITIONAL READING

Albrich, Robert A. *A Theoretical Model of Human Behavior in Organizations: An Eclectic Approach.* Morristown, N.J.: General Learning Press, 1972.
Argyris, Chris. *Management and Organizational Development.* New York: McGraw Hill Book Co., 1971.

Bennis, Warren G. *Organizational Development: Its Nature, Origins, and Prospects.* Reading, Mass.: Addison Wesley, 1969.

Beckhard, Richard. *Organization Development: Strategies and Models.* Reading, Mass.: Addison Wesley Publishing Co., 1969.

Blake, Robert R. and Jane Srygley Mouton. *Building A Dynamic Organization Through GRID Organization Development.* Reading, Mass.: Addison Wesley Publ. Co., 1969.

Boolding, Kenneth E. *The Organizational Revolution: A Study in the Ethics of Economic Organization.* Chicago: Quadrangle Books, 1968.

Dalton, Gene W., Paul R. Lawrence and Larry E. Griener (eds.). *Organizational Change and Development.* Homewood, Ill.: Irwin Dorsey, 1970.

Delbecq, Andre L., Andrew H. Von de Ven, and David H. Gustafson. *Group Techniques for Program Planning: A Guide to Nominal Group and Delphi Processes.* Glenview, Ill.: Scott, Foresman and Company, 1975.

Hage, Jerald and Michael Alken. *Social Change in Complex Organizations.* New York: Random House, 1970.

Lawrence, Paul R. and Jay W. Lorsch. *Developing Organizations: Diagnosis and Action.* Reading, Mass.: Addison Wesley Publ. Co., 1969.

Lorsch, Jay W. and Paul R. Lawrence. *Managing Group and Intergroup Relations.* Homewood, Ill.: Irwin Dorsey, 1972.

Luthans, Fred and Robert Kreitner, *Organizational Behavior Modification.* Glenview, Ill.: Scott, Foresman and Company, 1975.

Margulies and John Wallace. *Organizational Change: Techniques and Applications.* Glenview, Ill.: Scott, Foresman and Co., 1973.

Newmar, William H. *Constructive Control: Design and Use of Control Systems.* Englewood Cliffs, N.J.: Prentice Hall Inc., 1975.

Schein, Edgar H. *Process Consultation: Its Role in Organization Development.* Reading, Mass.: Addison Wesley, 1969.

8

TRAINING AND CAREER DEVELOPMENT SYSTEMS

Work organizations are great socializers of people. They take new members in, nurture them, shape them, move them about, and eventually discard them. They attempt to instill loyalty, obedience, conformity, and proficiency. To accomplish these things, organizations spend much time and effort on the orientation, training, and development of its human resources. This chapter examines the training and career development system found in most work organizations. In some organizations, this system is very sophisticated and quite formalized. In others, it is very informal and unstructured. Whether the system is highly structured, a major responsibility of any organization is to invest in the education and development of its human resources by setting up objectives and procedures for career development programs, on-the-job training, formal classroom experience, and other learning experiences.

In this chapter, we outline the training and career development process, identify the responsibilities of organizations in this area, discuss alternative training and development strategies and techniques, and integrate this system with other human resource systems in the organization.

THE NATURE OF TRAINING
AND CAREER DEVELOPMENT

The term "training and career development" refers to the total structure of on-the-job and off-the-job training and development programs utilized by organizations in developing employee skills and knowledge necessary for proficient job performance and career advancement.[1] Some people use the term "management development" to mean the same.[1] However, management development refers to the training and development programs for managers and often excludes programs for professionals (e.g., engineers, salesmen, accountants), skilled operative employees (e.g., draftsmen, tool and die makers, and bookkeepers), and semi-skilled and unskilled operatives (e.g., assembly line workers, packagers and material handlers).

A comprehensive organizational training and development system is closely tied to subsidiary human resource systems. Crane has identified ten closely related components of a training and development system:

1. Organizational Projection—forecasting future managerial needs
2. Position descriptions for all jobs
3. Management inventory of all managerial talent available now and in the future
4. Replacement charts which indicate successors for each position in the management hierarchy
5. Management recruiting to fill forecasted vacancies
6. Selection and placement systems
7. Specific training and development for:
   a. Pre-supervisory personnel
   b. Supervisors
   c. Middle-management
   d. Executives
8. Performance appraisal
9. Compensation
10. Overall personnel evaluation[2]

While some would certainly argue with Crane's long listing, his analysis does emphasize the point that any meaningful training and development system must be closely integrated with other human resource systems in the organization if it is to operate most effectively. Organizations which have effectively integrated training and development with other human resource systems recognize the importance of the training function, and some have appropriately designated the chief training and development officer as a corporate vice president.[3] This gives the function visibility, prestige, and status in the organization and enables the system to be better integrated with other human resource functions. Figure 8-1 indicates where the training and development system fits into our model of the human resource system.

TRAINING AND DEVELOPMENT
AND ORGANIZATION DEVELOPMENT

As we discussed in the previous chapter, organization development (OD) is a term that has received wide attention over the past two decades. We pointed out that OD differs from training and development by focusing on the overall improvement of an organization—its structure, policies, procedures, objectives, etc., *not* just its managers or other personnel. Thus, training and development is but part of a total organization development system. Even though those who broadly define training and development would probably equate OD with it, we believe training and development to be but one component of organization development and make a distinction between the two concepts.

There is some conflict among writers and practitioners on the relative value of training and development and organization development and the emphasis each should receive in an organization. For example, Miner states:

Organizational development that results in a total restructuring of the organization handles the training need by eliminating it; the organization is changed to fit the members. In contrast, the management development approach takes the existing structures, policies, and procedures as given and attempts to change people to make them more effective in meeting the requirements of the organization as currently constituted.[4]

Probably the greatest criticism which has been leveled at training and development, particularly management development, is the inability of participants in training programs to practice on the job what was learned in the classroom seminar. For example, many management development programs stress participative leadership styles, humanistic management, and Theory Y assumptions about people. Yet when training participants try to practice these beliefs back on the job, they often find that they are thwarted by an autocratic Theory X organizational atmosphere.

This blockage of the "transfer of training" is a very serious impediment to making training effective, and is one reason for criticisms such as that quoted from Miner. After all, if the organization itself needs to be changed rather than the behavior of individuals in the organization, training activities in and of themselves may have little effect. The organization's objectives, policies, structure, procedures, methods, and philosophy should be examined so that the organizational context in which the training will be practiced is consistent with the concepts taught the managers in training and development programs.[5]

Of course, changing the organization is a much more complex and significant undertaking than simply sending a couple of managers off to a three-day management development program sponsored by the American Management Association. Yet it is precisely the organizational context in which the new training will be practiced that must be made congruent with the training and development concepts taught. Otherwise, managers and professionals will find that all the best-intentioned, high-quality training will be of little use back on the job.

MAKING TRAINING EFFECTIVE

How can training be made more effective? This is indeed a difficult task. However, a systematic, comprehensive development program can be remarkably effective if a few guidelines are followed. Probably the first requirement for the program that will influence the organization is that all managers in an organization from top to supervisory should be training and development oriented. Training and development is essentially a line function. Staff should assist and advise, but the major responsibility rests with line managers. Brown concludes:

1. All development is self-development.
2. Specific development activities should be designated for each individual in the organization—managers, professionals, unskilled operatives.
3. Determination of development requires that the manager perceive and understand the needs of the individual.
4. Feedback of training and development results is essential for effective training.

156

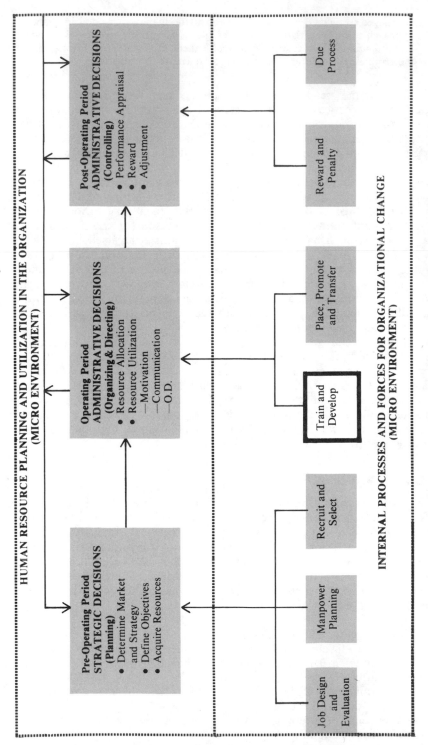

HUMAN RESOURCE PLANNING AND UTILIZATION IN THE ORGANIZATION
(MICRO ENVIRONMENT)

**Pre-Operating Period
STRATEGIC DECISIONS
(Planning)**
● Determine Market
  and Strategy
● Define Objectives
● Acquire Resources

**Operating Period
ADMINISTRATIVE DECISIONS
(Organizing & Directing)**
● Resource Allocation
● Resource Utilization
  —Motivation
  —Communication
  —O.D.

**Post-Operating Period
ADMINISTRATIVE DECISIONS
(Controlling)**
● Performance Appraisal
● Reward
● Adjustment

Job Design
and
Evaluation

Manpower
Planning

Recruit and
Select

Train and
Develop

Place, Promote
and Transfer

Reward and
Penalty

Due
Process

INTERNAL PROCESSES AND FORCES FOR ORGANIZATIONAL CHANGE
(MICRO ENVIRONMENT)

FIGURE 8-1 TRAINING AND DEVELOPMENT IN THE HUMAN RESOURCE SYSTEM

5. Development is a long, continuous process.
6. Improved managerial competence occurs mostly on the job.
7. Internal group instruction and external training supplement and motivate growth on the job.
8. A manager cannot effectively develop others without developing himself.[6]

Following this theme, the role of the chief executive officer and top management is critical for effective training transfer to take place. Managers tend to manage as they are managed. Any developmental program that doesn't have the attention, understanding, and commitment from top management will be severely limited in terms of the basic changes it can bring about in managerial style or attitude.[7]

Another critical ingredient for effective training and development is the liberal use of on-the-job training which directly supplements and is congruent with classroom training. This on-the-job management development should be carefully planned to meet the specific developmental needs of managers and should be fully integrated with and reinforce concepts taught in the classroom training.[8] On-the-job development techniques could include coaching, job rotation, junior boards, "assistant to" positions, and membership in *ad hoc* and permanent organizational committees. (These techniques are defined later in this chapter.)

Competent first line supervisors who realize the necessity for continued training and development both for themselves and their subordinates are also required.[9] First line supervisors are usually not involved enough in organizational decisions, have communication problems, and are usually not smoothly linked up in the chain of command. Any overall training effort must be concerned with improving the supervisor's skills and position in the organization.

Finally, Recknagle suggests several additional points to consider in overcoming training and development program failures:

1. Personalize the training program.
2. Keep the program relatively simple.
3. Focus on the transactional process between boss and subordinates and peers.
4. Use line supervisors as monitors and coordinators.
5. Install at top level first.
6. Integrate the system into the authority structure of the organization.
7. Orient all managerial levels.
8. Humanize the company objectives of the program.
9. Provide training tools.
10. Keep the reporting process simple and brief.
11. Employ a qualified outside consultant, responsible to top management, as an auditor of the system.
12. Establish firm controls to measure and track the system's results.
13. Give people a range of training alternatives.
14. Build an ethical system.[10]

Thus the key to making training and development pay off on the job is through a comprehensive program which fully integrates training and development activities with the structure, objectives, policies, and procedures of the organization.

CAREER PLANNING AND DEVELOPMENT

Just as training and development are part of organization development for the organization, so are they a part of the total career planning and development system for an individual. Figure 8-2 depicts the career planning process. We can summarize the process as having seven steps: self-assessment, determination of life-space goals, determination of occupational requirements, determination of career goals, acquisition of necessary training and education, determination of specific industry and job desired, and job selection. This is a simplification of a very complex process. The seven steps are not discrete but rather interact in a dynamic fashion. (This interaction is indicated by the feedback and evaluation line at each step in the diagram.)

One reason why it is important that we focus on this process is because of its importance as an allocator of resources in the economy. People with ill-defined career plans contribute to a substantial misallocation of resources in the economy. They often accept jobs for which they are either under- or over-qualified and jobs for which they may have little career interest. Once in these jobs, they perform inefficiently because they don't have the necessary skills or lack motivation and interest. From an economic standpoint, this leads to low productivity and a general misallocation of human resources in a society. From an individual's standpoint, this can lead to frustration, job alienation, and anomie (normlessness, drifting). If individual schools and employing organizations concentrated more heavily on the career planning process, these economic and social costs could be substantially reduced.

Self-Assessment

The first step in the career planning process is the self-assessment process which each individual must perform. This involves a thorough and candid assessment of an individual's skills, abilities, interests, and aspiration levels. Usually, personality, interest, and skill tests are very helpful in this stage. Also, discussion with one's peers and family is useful.

Determination of Life-Space Goals

Once a thorough self-assessment has been undertaken, an individual needs to determine the specific goals he hopes to accomplish in each of the important areas in his life. Specific goals should be set for family, church, civic groups, politics, friends, and other important areas. A determination of his role and goals in each of these areas will impinge greatly on his career goals.

Many individuals have a difficult time in this stage and often do not attempt to set these types of goals. They may feel they have little if any

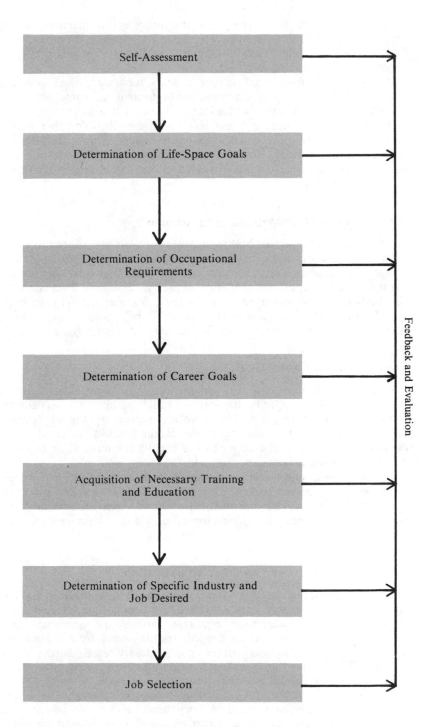

FIGURE 8-2 THE CAREER PLANNING PROCESS

information to use in setting the goals (the future is too uncertain) or that if they set the goals, they feel they are bound to achieve them no matter what. The goals become "cast in concrete" and they then feel committed to achieve them at almost any cost.

A realistic life-space goal setting process recognizes the uncertainty of the future, but also that individuals can control, to some extent, the environmental factors which will affect their lives. It also recognizes that any life-space, goal-setting process has to remain flexible. Just because one specifies his life-space goals does *not* mean he cannot deviate from them because of changing interests or environmental factors. However, it does give him some clear-cut objectives which he is planning to accomplish at a given point in time.

Determination of Occupational Requirements

This phase of the career-planning process involves a thorough examination of the duties, tasks, responsibilities, and training and educational requirements associated with various occupations. It involves a thorough examination of occupational literature as well as extensive discussion with individuals currently employed in the specific occupations. This examination of occupational requirements needs to be made in light of an individual's interests, abilities, aspirations, and life-space goals.

Determination of Career Goals

Once knowledge of various occupations has been ascertained, an individual is able to specify his career goals in light of his abilities, interests, and life-space goals. This involves a process of goal optimization and integration since life-space and career goals often conflict. The balancing of life-space and career goals is usually the most difficult part of the career planning process.

Career goals should be set for the initial time period (one year or less), intermediate time period (one to five years), and long-range time period (five to fifteen years). The specification of short, intermediate, and long-term career goals helps one in developing a system of career or occupational progression.

Acquisition of Necessary Training and Education

Once an individual sets his career goals, he is in a position to begin acquiring the training and education for the occupation selected. Some training will be formal, classroom education paid by the individual. Other training will be seminar and on-the-job training paid by his employing organization. By having his career goals clearly established, he can attempt to ensure that the specific training and education he receives will be of use in furthering his job performance.

It is at this point that an employing organization plays the greatest role in the career planning process. An organization can help its employees with their career development and can ensure that sponsored training is geared to meet the specific career needs of its employees. The role of the employing organization in this phase is discussed in further detail later in the chapter.

Determination of Specific Industry and Job Desired

Here the individual enters the labor market and looks for a job. For many this point occurs after graduation from high school, college, or another formal training program. However, anytime an individual begins looking for a job, even if he is currently employed, he is going through this phase of the career-planning process. It is here that an individual investigates specific job offerings of specific employers. He attempts to weigh these job offers against his interests, abilities, career and life-space goals. If he finds a job that meets these requirements and that provides enough financial and psychological remuneration consistent with his goals, he will accept the job.

Job Selection

This is the final stage in the career-planning process. The individual acts out his career plan and makes a commitment to a set of specific career goals. Life-space and career goals are balanced. The job selected will be the pivotal point in an individual's life around which all else will circle (at least in U.S. society).

THE EMPLOYING ORGANIZATION'S ROLE
IN THE CAREER PLANNING PROCESS

Organizations play a role in each stage of the career-planning process. Perhaps their greatest influence on the formulation of the career plan occurs at the training stage. However, employers should also be concerned with each stage of the process.

ASSESSMENT AND ASSESSMENT CENTERS

Many employers offer a series of personality, aptitude, and skill tests which help individuals in self-assessment.[11] These tests are usually given at the time of recruitment and selection but often are made available to currently employed individuals.

Another method of assessment currently in vogue is the use of an assessment center. Assessment centers involve close examination of an individual in a laboratory situation. The individual is given a series of job-related tasks and is critically evaluated on his performance of these tasks. Tasks often include in-basket games, role-playing situations, case analysis, and small group discussions. He may be evaluated by his peer managers, subordinates, supervisors, or by a group of outside consultants. The session usually lasts two or three days. The results are carefully tabulated and analyzed, and a list of strengths and weaknesses for the individual are developed. This is then used for helping him overcome his weaknesses.

Assessment centers are sometimes used as a selection device to eliminate people for initial job selection or promotion. Here the role of the assessment center changes from one of development to one of screening.

Assessment centers have been criticized on several counts. The observers in the center need to be trained in observation and assessment techniques. It is for this reason that many organizations use outside consultants in their assessment process. Also, the process puts the individual under a considerable amount of stress. Just as in sensitivity training (Chapter 7), he may not be able to cope with the situation unless he has been given some instruction and orientation prior to his assessment as to what he can expect. Finally, the analysis which results from the assessment can hinder a person's promotional opportunities for life. If he happens to have a couple of bad days (as we all do) and is observed by people not versed in assessment techniques, the resultant analysis can be completely invalid. Yet, the analysis becomes a part of the individual's permanent record and can easily be used by superiors to block any further promotion.

It is for these reasons that assessment centers should be used as any management tool—as one of a number of ways to assess a person's present and potential performance, not the only way. It should not be used as a substitute for periodic performance appraisals between superior and subordinates nor for actual observations of a person's job performance and accomplishments over time.

COACHING, COUNSELING, AND LIFE-SPACE GOALS

Most large organizations employ staff psychologists to assist individuals with personal problems, on or off the job. These staff psychologists can be used to help individuals more clearly develop life-space goals. In addition, a sympathetic superior or peer manager may also be of some assistance through informal coaching or advising.

However, most organizations do very little in this stage of the career-planning process of a formal nature. They prefer that individuals develop life-space goals utilizing resources outside of the employing organization such as the church, private psychologists, friends, or family.

DETERMINATION OF POSITION AND OCCUPATIONAL REQUIREMENTS

Organizations should provide individuals with requirements for various occupations and jobs in the organization to which these individuals may aspire. Many organizations have not specified job requirements for middle and higher level positions and, if they have, they are often reluctant to provide these widely throughout the organization to those desiring them. This is because many organizations practice "promotion by surprise." Keeping job requirements vague and ill-defined allows superiors to promote individuals on a very subjective basis and makes it easier to reward one on the basis of personal friendship rather than objectively measured competency.

MBO AND CAREER GOALS

Most organizations on a management-by-objectives program are concerned with developing personal improvement or career goals for individuals in addition to work-output oriented objectives. MBO can be a very effective means of helping individuals to develop specific career goals which they hope to accomplish for a given time period. When MBO is combined with a system of performance appraised by results, an individual is given an excellent opportunity to focus on career strengths and weaknesses.

ACQUISITION OF TRAINING AND EDUCATION

Organizations play a major role in the career-planning process here. The job should be the primary means for training and development. Interesting, challenging, responsible jobs should be a way of providing individuals with a learning experience on almost a daily basis. This refers to more than simple on-the-job training (OJT). OJT is usually concerned with helping the individual master the tasks and duties of a particular job so that he achieves a *minimum* level of performance. Training and development through challenging job experiences allow the individual to continue learning on the job so that he achieves a *maximum* level of performance and also becomes prepared for further promotional opportunities to jobs requiring even greater skill.

Of course, job-learning experiences should be supplemented with both formal and informal off-the-job learning experiences. These include college classes; company, consultant or college sponsored seminars, workshops, or conferences; trade association meetings and conventions; and a host of other off-the-job experiences. These training resources and methods are further discussed later in the chapter.

RECRUITMENT AND SELECTION

The employer's responsibility in the final phase of the career-planning process sometimes does not receive the proper focus. Employers often provide biased information in the recruiting process in an effort to sell the job. This is particularly so in tight labor markets. Of course, employers can't be expected to enumerate all the evils of a given position they have open. However, in the long run, employers are likely to find that being honest and candid with job recruits will pay off with less frustration, higher productivity, and reduced turnover among new job holders in the organization. In other words, employers have a responsibility to provide job applicants with honest and valid job information so that individuals will be in a better position to make an informed, rational job selection choice.

RESPONSIBILITIES FOR TRAINING AND DEVELOPMENT

The preceding section looked at the employing organization's responsibilities in the career-planning and placement process. This section looks at the responsibilities of the parties in the training and development process.[12] Using a framework developed by Morrisey, we can identify specific training and development responsibilities for top management, the personnel department, the immediate superior, and the employee himself. Even though the employee has the prime responsibility for his career development, each of the other areas share a great portion of this responsibility.

TOP MANAGEMENT'S ROLE

Top management needs to be firmly committed to a system of training and development. As we mentioned earlier, lack of commitment by top management is one of the most common reasons why training and development fails. The transfer of training will likely not occur unless the reward system and management example back on the job is consistent with the program. More specifically, top management has the responsibility to:

1. Provide the policies and procedures required to implement the program
2. Provide the administrative controls to ensure compliance with program policies
3. Provide the budget (including allowance for time off from work when necessary) for development opportunities and requirements
4. Demonstrate its interest by action and example
5. Provide the proper organizational climate whereby development can be encouraged
6. Demonstrate to everyone, including other top management personnel, that it is important to continuously work on self-improvement and that such effort is being evaluated[13]

THE PERSONNEL DEPARTMENT

The personnel, staff development, management development, or human resource development department in the organization performs essentially a staff function. It *assists* line management in training and development by providing expertise, resources, and sponsoring training conferences and programs. Line management has the primary responsibility for training and development and the personnel department should not usurp this responsibility. However, the department should:

1. Stimulate interest in the program
2. Train and coach managers in carrying out their appraisal and development responsibilities
3. Administer and interpret related policies and procedures
4. Follow-up and report company activities in employee development
5. Provide the means for satisfying training and educational needs for employees as identified through development plans. This includes sponsoring training programs[14]

THE IMMEDIATE SUPERIOR

He has more direct responsibility in training and development than either top management or the personnel department. It is through his example and attitude that the subordinate learns of the value of training and development in the organization. Furthermore, he is in the best position to monitor and evaluate the developmental efforts of an employee. His specific responsibilities are to:

1. Encourage the employee to develop himself
2. Assist in training the employee to do more effectively the work that he is assigned
3. Demonstrate his active interest in his people's development
4. Determine what he expects of his people or, when possible, assist them in determining realistic expectations of their own
5. Make certain that both he and his people have a common understanding of work and developmental expectations
6. Operate his unit in a way conducive to the growth and development of his people
7. Constructively observe and measure the performance of his employees
8. Assess the strengths and development needs of his employees
9. Effectively plan for employee appraisal and development discussions
10. Hold effective, constructive employee appraisal and development discussions planned to assist and encourage the employee to develop his skills and abilities
11. Assist the employee to make development plans for himself
12. Continually reassess the scope of the employee's job to make certain it provides ample growth opportunities
13. Follow up and carry out his responsibilities in connection with any development plans made
14. Investigate and, when appropriate, encourage the employee to consider transfer or promotional opportunities outside the department (or even the company), if none is available within
15. Identify and make known to higher supervision those employees qualified for greater responsibility[15]

THE EMPLOYEE

The primary responsibility for training and development lies with the employee. However, even though this is so, the immediate superior should not use this as an excuse for not doing anything to facilitate employee development. The immediate superior, indeed the whole organization, must provide the atmosphere, resources, and encouragement for the employee to develop himself. Nevertheless, the employee has the responsibility to:

1. Do the best job he is capable of doing
2. Demonstrate interest in his own development and its relation to the goals of the company and the department

3. Seek out opportunities for development which will benefit him and the organization
4. Follow through in his own development within the prescribed plan
5. Take advantage of development opportunities made available to him
6. Supply the time, effort, and, in some cases, financial resources to increase his education and training
7. Exercise self-discipline in on-the-job application
8. Communicate openly and regularly with superior, peers, and subordinates in development matters which affect them[16]

TRAINING AND DEVELOPMENT METHODS

We have identified a set of responsibilities for top management, the immediate superior, the personnel department, and the employee. How can these responsibilities be carried out? What specific types of training and development methods exist to help individuals meet these responsibilities? Training methods fall into two broad categories: on-the-job training (OJT) and off-the-job training. Any comprehensive training system in an organization will utilize both types of training.

ON-THE-JOB TRAINING (OJT)

Many people associate OJT with simply providing an individual with the skills needed to do a minimum level of performance. However, it can and should be much more than this. A comprehensive OJT program should include the following types of training:[17]

1. *Expanded responsibilities.* This is a frequently used training technique that expands the job duties, assignments, and responsibilities of an individual both horizontally and vertically in the organization. Opportunities are created for the individual in his present job to practice higher level and diverse skills not normally required in the present job.
2. *Job rotation.* This involves moving individuals to various types of jobs within the organization at the same level or next immediately higher level for periods of three to twelve months. Many organizations use this approach during the first two or three years of a manager's career to familiarize him with broad functional operations and processes of the organization.
3. *Staff development meetings.* These are special staff meetings to discuss specific facets of each individual's job and to develop ideas for improving job performance. These meetings may be held away from the job in a "retreat-type" atmosphere.
4. *"Assistant to" positions.* This involves having promising young employees serve as staff assistants to higher level managers for a specified period of time (often three to nine months) to become more familiar with the higher level positions in the organization.
5. *Problem-Solving conferences.* These are conferences called to solve a specific problem being experienced by a group of managers

or the organization as a whole. It involves brainstorming and other creative means to come up with mutually determined solutions to basic problems.

6. *Special assignments.* These are special tasks or responsibilities given to an individual for a specified period of time. It may be writing up a report, investigating the feasibility for a new project, process, service, or product, doing a newsletter, or evaluating a company policy or procedure.

7. *In-Company training done by company trainers.* These programs can cover such topics as safety, new personnel procedures, new products or services, affirmative action, and technical programs.

8. *In-Company training done by outside consultants.* Here recognized experts are brought to the company to conduct training on MBO, assessment techniques, safety, affirmative action, and other current topics of importance. They often supplement training done by company trainers.

9. *Consultant (internal or external) advisory reviews.* Experts in specialized fields meet with various managers or management groups to informally investigate particular problems. The emphasis is on problem solving rather than training.

10. *Distribution of reading matter.* Often one of the most overlooked training methods, this involves a formal program to circulate books, journals, selected articles, new business material, etc. to selected employees. An effective program also includes periodic scheduled meetings to discuss the material.

OFF-THE-JOB TRAINING

An effective training system supplements OJT with various forms of off-the-job training. Most of this type of training is classroom training. Some of the more frequently used types of training include the following:[18]

1. *Outside short courses and seminars.* These are specialized courses conducted by educational institutions, professional associations, or private consulting and training firms which last one day to one week. If managers selectively attend programs that complement their career development plan, these courses can be extremely beneficial.

2. *College or university degree and certificate programs.* More and more universities are offering evening and weekend classes that lead to a degree or certificate. Often these are in professional fields such as management, accounting, finance, or law. Many employers have a tuition refund program which will reimburse employees for all or part of the tuition and book expense.

3. *Advanced management programs at colleges and universities.* UCLA, Harvard, MIT, Ohio State, and other well-known universities offer in-residence programs of two weeks to a full year for top management. Often they cover material typically found in an M.B.A. program but at a very accelerated rate.

4. *Correspondence schools.* If individuals can practice rigorous self-discipline, home correspondence study can be an excellent self-development tool. However, an employee needs to ensure that the correspondence school with which he deals is reputable.
5. *Outside meetings and conferences.* Most managers and professionals have opportunities to attend trade and professional conferences and conventions during the year. If participants actually attend the scheduled meetings and workshops at these conferences, these can be excellent learning experiences.

INSTRUCTIONAL TECHNIQUES FOR TRAINING AND DEVELOPMENT

Within the past few years there has been a virtual explosion in training techniques. These new techniques plus the tried-and-true methods give an organization a wide variety of training techniques from which to choose in building an effective program.

Lecture-Discussion

This is probably the most common teaching technique. Almost all training programs, particularly outside programs, utilize this technique. Most college classes utilize this technique extensively. It has the advantage of being spontaneous and allows the participants to become involved in exploring concepts and in seeking clarification. It requires a professional training leader with broad expertise in the field and related fields under discussion. The major disadvantage is that it's difficult to use with large groups.

Lecture

This method is very useful for large groups. It requires a training leader who is dynamic and who can organize and present his material in an effective fashion. For best use it should be supplemented with additional types of training techniques.

Multi-Media Presentations

Lecture and lecture-discussion work best when a multi-media approach is used. This involves using handouts of materials (such as subject outlines, advanced reading assignments, and cases), films, slides, film strips, videotape, audio cassets, overhead projectors, flip charts, and the old stand-by, the chalk board. The major disadvantage here is that sophisticated equipment can fail at the most inopportune time. Also, the multi-media approach is but one tool for management development. It can't substitute for an effective instructor.

Job Coaching

The best on-the-job technique is coaching. This involves the individual's immediate superior. He acts as a guide, counselor, friend, and interested party in helping his subordinates perform their jobs more effectively and in developing a comprehensive career plan for each subordinate.

Programmed Instruction

Programmed texts and exercises guide students through a step-by-step series of learning experiences. It is a learner-centered method of instruction and seldom, if ever, requires the services of an instructor at the time the training occurs. The technique presents subject matter to the trainee in small steps, which require him to respond and immediately inform him of the appropriateness of his response.

Computer-Assisted Instruction

Actually this is a form of multi-media instruction often combined with other types of instruction such as gaming or programmed learning. Some computer-assisted techniques can be quite sophisticated and expensive. When used as a part of a total educational program, it can be quite effective.

Gaming and Role-Playing

This technique gives participants actual practice in applying concepts in an artificial situation. An opportunity to solve a problem is provided, and the participants actually act out the solution. When gaming is used, there is usually some element of competitiveness with one group trying to out perform other groups. In the hands of a skillful seminar leader, this technique can be an extremely useful training tool since it gives participants actual practice before peers, yet allows them to make mistakes without having the repercussions such mistakes would have on the job.

Case Analysis

Usually combined with role-playing and/or gaming, this technique also gives participants the opportunity to solve an actual or hypothetical problem. If used without gaming or role-playing, it relies very heavily on group discussion without the participants putting themselves in the actual roles of individuals in the case.

Sensitivity and T-Group Training

This method was discussed in detail as an OD technique in Chapter 7. As a training tool it is designed to change attitudes, and, when used with a highly trained, skillful group leader, can be quite successful. It requires individuals in a group situation to give up their psychological defense mechanisms (at least temporarily) and to critically examine their own and each other's basic beliefs, values, and attitudes. It can be quite an emotional experience. Some individuals cannot stand the peer group pressure created in the process and suffer real psychological harm. Yet, it is one of the most effective ways to bring about attitude change in individuals.

Transactional Analysis

This is a relatively new technique which borrows quite heavily from sensitivity and t-group training. It, too, attempts to change basic attitudes and ways of behaving in individuals. It developed from the field of psychiatry and was initially used as a clinical tool by psychiatrists.[19] It has since been developed and applied as a training tool for managers and other individuals in an organization.

Human interaction is viewed as a series of transactions among individuals: "I do something to you and you do something back." This interaction occurs within the context of one of three parts of an individual: Parent, Adult, and Child. A person acts as a Parent when he comes forth with lists of "do's" and "don't's" when dealing with others. He acts as a Child when spontaneous emotion characterizes transactions. The Adult mode of interaction occurs when a person acts as a rational being making decisions based on data derived from experience. The goal of transactional analysis is to strengthen and free the Adult from the archaic constraints in Parent and Child so as to encourage more freedom of choice and new behavioral options.

Harris has developed four life positions that underlie people's behavior.[20] These are:

1. I'm not OK—You're OK (the anxious dependency of the immature).
2. I'm not OK—You're not OK (the give-up or despair position).
3. I'm OK—You're not OK (the criminal position).
4. I'm OK—You're OK (the response of the mature adult at peace with himself and others).

The goal of TA is to move people from one of the first three positions to the fourth, "I'm OK—You're OK" position. Most people operate from an "I'm not OK—You're OK position. If people adopt position four, they will treat superiors, subordinates, and peer managers in a much different manner than if they operated under one of the first three positions.

This technique, like sensitivity and t-group training, rests on the belief that the basic attitude and behavior mode of an individual needs to be changed before he can be taught to be a better leader or decision maker. No leadership, decision making, planning, and other skills of a manager taught in management development programs will be internalized nor used unless this basic change takes place.

As with several other training methods, TA requires a highly skilled group leader. Many "fly-by-night" training and consulting organizations have attempted TA seminars, and they have been failures. It is important that organizations interested in TA use highly reputable training firms and individuals to conduct the training.

INSTRUCTIONAL RESOURCES

Training and development are performed with a wide variety of resources. The most important training resource is the immediate superior of an individual in an organization. His on-the-job advice, counsel, and coaching are the keys to an effective program.

Many organizations also have a department of training and development within the organization. This department normally employs several internal trainers and consultants who can be used in a wide variety of programs.

Private consulting and training organizations such as the American Management Associations (AMA) and the American Management Research (AMR) organization offer a wide variety of management and professional programs on an annual basis. These organizations use private consultants, personnel directors, and university professors to conduct much of their training.

Most universities with programs in business conduct a wide variety of programs in management and related areas. Some outstanding universities with comprehensive programs include Michigan, Michigan State, Ohio State, Harvard, Stanford, MIT, and Northwestern. However, a university in a particular organization's immediate geographic area can usually conduct many programs at a cost substantially below that of the large major universities mentioned above.

The federal government through several agencies conducts various programs and provides other training resources for organizations. For example, the U.S. Civil Service Commission conducts programs in personnel, compensation, management by objectives, and other topic areas. The Small Business Administration provides training and advice to smaller business organizations. Various units in the U.S. Department of Labor conduct programs on safety and health, wage and hour legislation, affirmative action, labor law, and collective bargaining. The Office of Civil Rights in the Department of Health, Education, and Welfare has conducted programs on affirmative action and equal employment opportunity. Most federal programs are offered either free or at very low cost to participants.

States have become increasingly involved in presenting programs in specialized topic areas such as environmental pollution, workmen's compensation, unemployment insurance, electronic data processing, agricultural methods, and consumer issues.

EVALUATION OF TRAINING AND DEVELOPMENT

Assessing the effectiveness of an organization's overall training and development effort is extremely difficult. The ultimate measure of training effectiveness is the health of the organization. Is the organization meeting its objectives? Are its employees competent? Is the work done efficiently and effectively? These are broad questions and good training is but one factor that contributes to a positive response for each question.

IMMEDIATE EVALUATION

Even though it is difficult to assess the training effectiveness of the overall training effort, it is a bit easier to assess the effectiveness of a particular training program. Most programs allow participants to complete a short evaluation of the program at its conclusion. Questions are asked which attempt to assess the effectiveness of the instructors and media used as well as the usefulness of the topics covered. While responses to these questions provide useful information to the planners and instructors in a program, they usually are biased by the high "affect-level" that participants usually experience at the end of the program. The evaluation usually measures feelings and opinions of the program at the very end of the program before participants have had a chance to reflect on and practice the concepts learned.

LONGITUDINAL COST-BENEFIT ANALYSIS WITH CONTROL GROUPS

A methodologically superior assessment technique of training effectiveness would attempt to determine all of the measurable benefits from a training program over given time periods measured at periodic intervals (such as three months, six months, and one year).[21] These benefits would be compared to the costs of the program. Ideally, this information would then be compared with a similar group of employees who did not go through the training program. Any differences in the benefits (as measured by improved job performance) of the group who experienced the training program could be at least partially attributable to the training effort.

The procedure for making this type of evaluation is:

1. Randomly assign employees of a similar occupation or level in the organization to two groups. One group of employees will receive the training, the other will not.
2. Conduct a pre-test measure of performance and/or knowledge of both groups to determine their present level of performance and/or knowledge.
3. Conduct the training for one group.
4. Accurately assess all costs of the training effort including instructor costs, media costs, facilities, and employee time away from the job.
5. Conduct a post-test measure of performance and/or knowledge of both groups at periodic intervals after the completion of training.
6. Compare the benefits of the program as measured by higher performance and more complete job knowledge with the costs of the program for the trained group.
7. Compare the post-test performance and job knowledge of the trained group with the nontrained or control group.

This procedure can be diagrammed as shown in Figure 8-3.

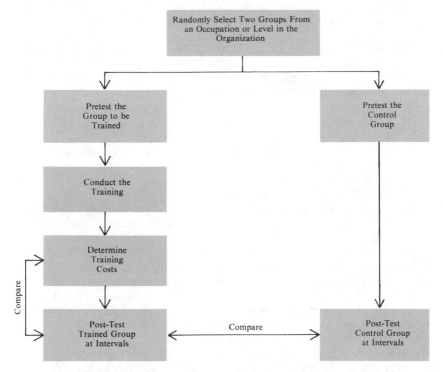

FIGURE 8-3 A MODEL OF LONGITUDINAL COST-BENEFIT ANALYSIS FOR TRAINING EFFECTIVENESS USING A CONTROL GROUP

APPLYING THE TRAINING EFFECTIVENESS MODEL: AN EXAMPLE

Assume you are training director for a large business organization that has a large number of field salesmen. You have noticed, after reviewing a selected number of periodic performance appraisals of these salesmen, that many seem to be having a problem in selling a major new product line which your company has recently developed.

You decide that this problem is significant and that product notices and staff meetings have not helped significantly in reducing the problem. A comprehensive training program is called for. You realize that even though not all salesmen are in need of the program, many are. The procedure you would follow in setting up, conducting, and evaluating the program is:

1. Determine the specific training and development needs of the group. (Use performance appraisals, assessment center results, conferences with superiors, and other methods.)
2. Design specific performance objectives which the training is to accomplish.
3. Identify all the salesmen who need the training.

4. Assign one-half of those identified to a group to receive the training and the other half to a control group who will not receive the training.
5. Conduct a pre-test for both groups on the performance objectives the training is to cover.
6. Design the training program including topics, instructors, media, cases, exercises, handouts, etc.
7. Conduct the training program for the group to be trained.
8. Assess the total cost of the training program including all instructional and travel costs, loss of time away from job, etc.
9. Conduct a post-test at periodic intervals for both sales groups on specific performance measures the training covered.
10. Compare the performance measures of the salesmen who went through the program with those who did not.
11. Compare the benefit (as measured as improvement in performance measures) for the trained group with the costs of the program.

Admittedly, most training directors do not go through such an elaborate procedure. It is costly and often is difficult to withhold training from those who supposedly need it. But this procedure will give an organization a much more documented basis on which to assess training effectiveness and plan future programs. Additionally, this information is very useful for presenting a case to top management on the value of training and development for the organization. When the organization goes through a period of economic downturn, a strong case can be made not to drastically cut or eliminate the training budget as often happens.

CONCLUSION

The training and career development process is a highly complex one. Yet, too often, it is given inadequate attention by many organizations. In this chapter we have attempted to address both major concepts involved: training and development and career planning and development.

Training and development refers to the total structure of on-the-job and off-the-job training systems used by the organization. It is part of the total organization development system of the organization. In fact, an effective training and development program needs to be integrated with a comprehensive OD program to maximize the application of concepts and practices stressed in training. Effective training also requires a commitment to self-development from all employees, top management support, a comprehensive on-the-job training program supplemented with off-the-job training, and support from first line supervisors.

The career planning and development process is also part of a comprehensive organization development process. It consists of seven steps: self-assessment, determination of life-space goals, acquisition of occupational requirements, determination of career goals, acquisition of necessary training and education, determination of specific industry and job desired, and job selection. At each stage the employing organization has an obligation to each employee in helping him formulate his career plan; however, its greatest obligation perhaps lies in the training and development stage.

The responsibilities for effective training and development are shared by the organization's top management, the personnel department, the immediate superior, and the employee himself. The greatest responsibility lies with the employee. The immediate superior has the next greatest responsibility in his role as coach and advisor. The personnel department assists line management in training by acting as supportive staff to line management. Top management must give whole-hearted support to the process.

Methods for training and development involve various on-the-job techniques such as expanded responsibilities, job rotation, assistant to positions and other techniques. Programs include outside short courses and seminars, college degree programs, and correspondence courses. An effective training and development program achieves a unique blend of on-the-job and off-the-job methods suitable for the individuals in the particular organization.

Instructional techniques have mushroomed over the past few years and include lecture, lecture-discussion, multi-media, job coaching, programmed instruction, case analysis, role playing and gaming. Newer techniques include sensitivity training and transactional analysis. Once again, an effective training technique is no better than the instructor who uses it. A good program utilizes all techniques as appropriate rather than relying on any one technique at the exclusion of others.

Instructional resources can be found in universities, the employing organization, private training and consulting groups, the federal government, and some state governmental agencies. It is important that an organization choose resources that best meet its needs for training and development.

Finally, the real success of a training and development program can be assessed ultimately on the basis of the success and health of the organization. However, assessments should be made of specific programs through some longitudinal analysis. The ideal assessment framework would involve a cost-benefit analysis of a training program compared to a control group not receiving the training.

CASE 1
JOHN AND MARY

John: I've called you in today, Mary, to talk with you about your progress in this department. You've been here just over two years. I've noticed lately that your work output has begun declining. Now, I've always thought you were a good employee, but lately you haven't acted that way. You're coming in late, leaving early, and your absence rate has gone way up. What seems to be the trouble, Mary?

Mary: Well, first it shouldn't matter what time I come in or leave as long as I get my work done on time. You know I'm twice as productive as anyone else here. I am entitled to a little time off now and then. What's worse, John, is this whole stinking place. No one cares around here about what happens to the staff. First, we got no raise this year. Second, our work loads increased because we lost some positions last year during austerity, and we can't get any new positions. Finally, no one ever talks to me about my career. They could care less what my career aspirations are.

John: I know, Mary, things have been tough around here lately, but everyone is going through this. It's just not you or our unit. Everyone at this agency is suffering. We just have to learn to live with it.

Mary: You're right it is tough here. It never was like this in business. When I was an executive secretary three years ago, not only did I make more money than I do now, I was also treated better. Our company sat down with each new employee soon after they were hired and developed a career plan with them. An employee knew the promotional opportunities and what she would have to do to get promoted. Hell, around here it's promotion by surprise. No one cares about your career development or about future promotion. We're expendable. We're just hired hands.

John: Well, you have a point, Mary. There isn't a whole lot of career development activity around here. We should try to change it, I guess.

Mary: You're darn right you should. Otherwise, you're going to lose a lot of fine people. Why should they stay around? Your good people will quit and go elsewhere for jobs. They can get them. All that will be left are the low level or marginal people who can't get a job someplace else because no one will have them. Just try to run this operation then!

Questions

1. What seems to be the problem in this case? Which is the most important problem?

2. Is Mary right about good people leaving and marginal ones remaining?

3. What does a career plan do for an employee? For the organization?

4. What should John do at this point with regard to Mary's situation? What should he do within the organization?

5. Do you feel that this situation is fairly typical today among employees in government? Among employees in business?

CASE 2
HECHT SEMI-CONDUCTOR, INC.

Joe Reddig has always prided himself on his progressive attitudes. Joe is a 1968 graduate of the College of Business at Ohio State University.

As a student of the late sixties who had a concern for human rights, Joe thought he knew what was required for more job equality. But he'd never faced this dilemma before.

Mary Collins is 23, attractive, bright, highly motivated, and an extremely competent management trainee. She graduated with a degree in industrial management from Georgia Tech University in 1975. Hecht Semi-Conductor, Inc. has always tried to select the cream of the crop in recruiting college graduates and pays above the market salary to attract bright young college grads.

Mary completed the first 18 months of the rigorous two-and-a-half-year management training program that Hecht Semi-Conductor required of all college graduates. She has performed well up to now. However, during the last two months Joe has questioned Mary's suitability as a manager.

Mary was in a first-line foreman training position in the Blakely, Georgia plant of Hecht. This was the next to the last position she would have to go through in the training program. She was to remain in this position for a total of six months and then spend the final six months as a special assistant to the production department superintendent, Joe Reddig. The first three training positions she had lasted six months each and were in sales, accounting, and personnel. (Hecht Semi-Conductor Corp. believes all management trainees should receive a well rounded training program that gives the trainee a broad prospective of company operations.)

Mary did well in these first three training assignments, but since she was placed in the foreman's job, Joe has begun questioning Mary's competence. He knows she had it tough. She was foreman over twelve middle-aged, semi-skilled to skilled people on assembly line A of the plant. Nine of these persons were men and three were women. None had college degrees, and only four had finished high school. Since Mary took this job almost everything that could go wrong on the line had gone wrong. Output was down 15 percent. Worker absenteeism was up 12 percent. Grievances doubled from an average of two per month to four per month. Production quality was deteriorating. Quality control was rejecting 10 percent of units produced instead of the usual 1.5 percent. Even worse, customers to whom the company shipped had increased their returns of defective products a whopping 125 percent.

Joe was stuck. He thought Mary was competent and still believes she has potential. He thought she knew the relatively simple assembly process. He knew that most of the employees on the line resented her. He's heard men make such comments as: "What does this young girl know about factory work?" "I've been here for fifteen years and never had to work for a woman." "She sure is cute, but boy is she dumb." Worse yet, Mary got little support from the women on the line. Joe had heard them make such comments as: "What's she trying to prove. A woman's place is in the home." "How come she's not married?" "I'll bet she's just looking for a husband," "Who's she trying to impress with her clothes? This is a factory."

Joe had talked to Mary about her dilemma. Mary wants to stick it out. But the company cannot afford such low quality and poor output. Increasing production costs and lower production output cannot be tolerated on assembly line A for four more months. The company, already in a marginal profit position, will have it's back up against the financial wall. Worse yet, Rutherford Hecht, the founder and chairman of the board of the company will use Mary's poor performance as an example of the inability of women to manage, and all that Joe has been working for will be lost.

Joe had just about decided to take Mary out of the foreman's position and approached her one day after work as Mary was sitting in the foreman's office finishing up the daily production reports. The following conversation took place:

Joe: Well, Mary, how did it go today?

Mary: Not bad, Joe. I think I'm finally getting the hang of things. Here, look at these figures. No rejects today, production up 10 percent, and not one person absent.

Joe: That's great, Mary. Has it been going this well the past three or four days?

Mary: Well, no, not as well. You've seen the past days' figures but you know I'm improving.

Joe: But not fast enough, Mary. Our costs have just been too high and output too low since you've taken over assembly line A. You're aware of this, and you know we can't continue under these conditions. Now, Mary, you've done a fine job up to now in the training program. Bob Burwell in Personnel tells me you're one of the best trainees they've ever had in the program. But as you know, Mary, you're the first woman who has ever attempted the full training program, including the foreman's position. We can take you off this position and move you to the final position in the training program. As my assistant for six months, you'll be under a lot less pressure and have an opportunity to learn just as much, if not more, about the production process. Well, Mary, what do you say?

Mary: No way! I'm not giving in now. I've put in two months on this job and am finally beginning to see some improvement. I appreciate your offer, Joe, but I'm not a quitter. If I quit now I could never face those men and women on that line again. In fact, I could never face anyone in the plant again. They would know I lost. I can just hear them now: "Pretty Mary finally cracked. She couldn't take the pressure." "She ought to go back to the kitchen." No way! I'm not going to put up with that. Let me stay on four more months. I'll get production back up. I promise.

Facts On Hecht Semi-Conductor, Inc.

Founded in 1921 by C. A. Hecht, father of present chairman of the board in Marietta, Georgia. Now has eight plants located in Georgia, South Carolina and Alabama. Total 1976 sales $35,382,274. 1976 profit (after taxes) $368,721. Sales are international. Total employment in 1976 is 2566 of which 500 are managerial. Home office is in Marietta, Georgia.

Questions

1. What are the basic issues in this case?

2. What alternatives does Joe have?

3. Is Mary being unreasonable?

4. How would you characterize the style of human resource management in this company? Why? Do you have enough information? If not, what information would you like?

5. What are the implications of the various alternative solutions on future women managers at Hecht? Future male management trainees at Hecht?

6. Is Joe being unreasonable in asking Mary to leave the foreman's job?

7. Is the training program unreasonable?

8. Select an alternative solution that will resolve the issues in this case. How should this alternative be implemented? Be realistic.

9. What might be some hurdles to successful resolution of this case? How can they be overcome?

10. Will your solution prevent similar problems in the future or is it simply a curative solution? That is, does it simply put out the present fire or will it prevent future fires?

CASE 3
HOW AM I DOING?

After graduation in 1975 with an engineering degree, Jeff Lass started working for a large, multi-city, multi-plant corporation. Since that time he has worked in the product assurance department in various capacities. His first assignment was in the staff section of quality control as a Q. C. analyst. Next he was promoted to inspection foreman and from there to quality control engineer. Jeff has consistently improved his job performance ratings and salary scale.

Jeff has survived three product assurance personnel reductions. He attributes this to his achievements in the areas of new or restructured methods and thinking which have made significant contributions to the function of product assurance. Except for the position of foreman, Jeff's assignments have been staff centered, basically unstructured, unclear as to time restraints, dependent upon successful interfacing with other departments, vendors, or customers, and void of authority for implementing the outcome.

Jeff has worked for five different supervisors. He has made a special effort to make known his job preference and promotional aspirations, but has been unable to secure upper management's thoughts in relation to these. Other than his yearly job performance rating, Jeff receives minimal information on "how he's doing," even though he has tried to elicit continuous and specific conversation from his supervisors.

Jeff's immediate supervisor is Jim Toms. One morning Jeff and Jim were talking shop when Bill Nols, Jim's supervisor and department head, walked in. Jeff took this opportunity to come directly to the point and said, "Look, I don't want to stay in my current job for the rest of my life. I want to advance, but honestly, I don't know how you two feel about my strengths and weaknesses nor do I know what positions will be opening in the future." At that instant the phone rang. Something had come up on the production floor requiring Bill's attention and the meeting dissolved.

The next day Jim stopped Jeff in the hall and said, "Bill and I both think you're doing fine, don't be impatient, relax. Bill says he has plans for you but we just can't be specific right now." Four months have passed and no additional light has been shed on the subject. Jeff is currently searching for a new job.

Questions

1. How does performance appraisal relate to training and development? To promotion?

2. Is Jeff being treated fairly?

3. What should Jeff do now? What should Jim and Bill do?

4. To what extent can a manager institute a sound performance appraisal system if his boss doesn't support it?

STUDY AND DISCUSSION QUESTIONS

1. What is training? How is it related to career development?

2. Are organizations "great socializers of people" as the chapter suggests?

3. How is training and development related to other human resource management functions such as manpower planning, selection and placement, and performance appraisal?

4. Why is there a blockage in the transfer of training from the "classroom" to the job? What can be done to reduce or eliminate it?

5. What factors should an individual consider in balancing his "life-space" goals with his career goals?

6. What are assessment centers? How are they used? What are their advantages and disadvantages?

7. What groups have the responsibility for training and career development? What are these responsibilities? How do the responsibilities of the individual interface with these responsibilities?

8. What are some common training and development methods and techniques?

9. How should the value of training and development programs be determined by an organization? Could the value for the organization differ from the value for the individual? Explain.

10. In what way does a college education in business prepare a person for a career in organizations?

ENDNOTES

1. James D. Somerville, "A Systems Approach to Management Development," *Personnel Journal,* Vol. 53, No. 5, Reprinted with permission, Copyright May 1974, pp. 367-371.

2. Donald P. Crane, "A Dynamic System for Management Development," *Personnel Journal,* Vol. 51, No. 9, Reprinted with permission, Copyright September 1972, pp. 667-674.

3. George J. Berkuitt, "Big Shake-up in Management Development," *Dun's Review,* Vol. 101, No. 3, March 1973, pp. 79-81.

4. John B. Miner, "The OD-Management Development Conflict," *Business Horizons,* Vol. 16, No. 6, December 1973, p. 35.

5. Thomas J. Reid, "The Context of Management Development," *Personnel Journal,* Vol. 53, No. 4, April 1974, pp. 280-87.

6. Ralph J. Brown, "A Systems Approach to Management Development," *Financial Executive,* Vol. 38, No. 4, April 1970, p. 25.

7. A. W. Charles, "A Systems Approach to Human Resource Management," *SAM Advanced Management Journal,* Vol. 37, No. 2, April 1972, p. 32.

8. Yoram Zeira, "Introduction of On-the-Job Management Training Development," *Personnel Journal,* Vol. 52, No. 12, December 1973, pp. 1049-1055.

9. Guvenc G. Alpander, "Planning Management Training Programs for Organizational Development," *Personnel Journal,* Vol. 53, No. 1, January 1974, pp. 15-25.

10. Kenneth H. Recknagel, "Why Management Training and How to Make it Succeed," *Personnel Journal,* Vol. 53, No. 8 Reprinted with permission, Copyright August 1974, pp. 589-97.

11. Although more recently these tests have not been used as frequently in selection, placement, and promotion processes because of the lack of validation of the tests to ensure that they do not unfairly discriminate against women and minority groups.

12. Ideas for portions of this section are used with permission from George L. Morrisey, *Appraisal and Development Through Objectives and Results* (Reading, Mass.: Addison-Wessely Publishing Co., 1972), pp. 16-20.

13. Ibid., p. 17.

14. Ibid., p. 18.

15. Ibid., pp. 18-19.

16. Ibid., pp. 19-20.

17. Much of the material in this section is adapted from Morrisey, op. cit., pp. 21-24.

18. Ibid., pp. 23-24.

19. Eric Berne has generally been credited with developing Transactional Analysis as a treatment technique in psychiatry. His ideas were initially presented in "Transactional Analysis: A New and Effective Method of Group Therapy," paper presented at the Western Regional Meeting of the American Group Psychotherapy Association, Los Angeles, November 1, 1957. His book, which popularized his approach, is *Games People Play* (New York: Grove Press, 1964).

20. Thomas A. Harris, *I'm OK—You're OK: A Practical Guide to Transactional Analysis* (New York: Harper and Row, 1967).

21. Most of the significant research employing this evaluation method has been done with technical classroom and Manpower Development and Training Act (MDTA) types of

OJT training. See for example: Max Eninger, et al., *The Process and Product of T & I High School Vocational Education: The Product* (Pittsburgh: The American Institute for Research, 1965); Robert W. Conley, "A Benefit-Cost Analysis of Vocational Rehabilitation Programs." *Journal of Human Resources,* Vol. 4, No. 2, Spring 1969, pp. 226-52; Jacob Kaufman, et al., *The Role of Secondary Schools in Preparing Youth for Employment* (University Park, Pa.: Institute for Research on Human Resources, 1967); and Earl D. Main, "A Nationwide Evaluation of MDTA Institutional Job Training," *The Journal of Human Resources,* Vol. 3, No. 2, (1968), pp. 159-70.

ADDITIONAL READING

Andrews, Kenneth R. *The Effectiveness of University Management Development Programs.* Cambridge: Graduate School of Bus. Adm., Harvard University, 1966.

Argyris, Chris and Donald A. Schon, *Theory in Practice: Increasing Professional Effectiveness.* San Francisco: Jossey-Bass, 1974.

Atherton, J. C. and Anthony Mymphrey. *Essential Aspects of Career Planning and Development.* Danville: Interstate, 1969.

Bailey, Larry Joe. *Career Education: New Approaches to Human Development.* Bloomington, Ill.: McKnight Pub. Co., 1973.

Berg, Ivar. *Education and Jobs: The Great Training Robbery.* New York: Praeger Press, 1970.

Bennett, Willard E. *Manager Selection, Education, and Training.* New York: McGraw-Hill, Inc., 1969.

Biennenvenu, Bernard J. *New Priorities in Training.* New York: American Management Associations, 1969.

Blass, Bernard M. and James A. Vaughn. *Training in Industry: The Management of Learning.* Belmont, Calif.: Wadsworth, 1966.

Craig, Robert L. and Lester R. Bittel, eds. *Training and Development Handbook.* New York: McGraw-Hill, Inc., 1967.

Davis, Russell G. *Planning Human Resource Development: Educational Models and Schemata.* Chicago: Rand McNally, 1966.

Granovetter, Mark S. *Getting a Job: A Study of Contracts and Careers.* Cambridge, Mass., Harvard University Press, 1974.

Holland, John L. *Making Vocational Choices: A Theory of Careers.* Englewood Cliffs, N. J.: Prentice-Hall, 1973.

Hopke, William E. *The Encyclopedia of Careers and Vocational Guidance.* Chicago: J. G. Ferguson Pub. Co., 1972.

Jennings, Eugene E. *Routes to the Executive Suite.* New York: McGraw-Hill, 1971.

Kaufman, H. G. *Obsolescence and Professional Career Development.* New York: AMACOM, 1974.

Lorsch, Jay W. and Louis B. Barnes, eds. *Managers and Their Careers.* Homewood, Ill.,: Irwin-Dorsey, 1976.

McLarney, William J. and William M. Berliner. *Management Training. (5th ed).* Homewood, Ill.: Richard D. Irwin, 1970.

Osipow, Samuel H. *Theories of Career Development.* New York: Appleton-Century-Crofts, 1973.

Powell, C. Randall. *Career Planning and Placement for the College Graduate of the '70's.* Dubuque, Iowa: Kendall/Hunt Pub., Co., 1974.

Ressler, Ralph. *Career Education: The New Frontier.* Worthington, Ohio: C. A. Jones Pub. Co., 1973.

Shertzer, Brice. *Career Exploration and Planning.* Boston: Houghton Miflin, 1973.

Timperly, Stuart R. *Personnel Planning and Occupational Choice.* London: Allen & Urwin, 1974.

9

COMPENSATION, MOTIVATION, AND INCENTIVE SYSTEMS

This chapter examines the reward and penalty system in the organization. Figure 9-1 indicates where this system fits into our model. The reward and penalty system is made up of several factors. An important factor is the compensation system adopted by the organization. The purpose of the reward and penalty system is to provide incentives and hence motivation, to encourage employees to work efficiently toward accomplishing organizational objectives. We begin this chapter by looking at some overall, macro environmental influences in the organization's compensation system.

WAGES IN THE MACRO ENVIRONMENT

In the macro-economic environment, the level and structure of wages and incentives are important because prevailing economic doctrine views wages and other compensation as a price mechanism that determines the amount and type of human resources demanded by the economic system *and* the amount and type of human resources offered for use in the production of goods and services. Furthermore, from the social point of view, wages are one cost of production and, therefore, are important determinants of the price of goods and services in the market place. The level of prices affects consumption patterns for goods and services, determines the attractiveness of national goods on international exchange markets, and is a measure of national affluence.

Without engaging in a lengthy essay on economics, the reader can recognize readily that a major national concern is to maintain a high level of wages and low consumer prices. Since wages are production costs and are, therefore, reflected in consumer prices, the goal of high wages and low prices depends upon how efficiently resources are utilized. In other words, high man-hour productivity can result in both high wages and low prices. It is this commonplace notion that is at the heart of a national concern over wage and incentive systems in the micro environment. A simple example illustrates the principle: if ten employees are employed forty hours per week producing the ever-popular widget and they produce 20,000 per week which sell at $2.00 per widget, then man-hour productivity is equal to [($2 x 20,000) ÷ 400] or, $100 per hour. Assume that the cost of

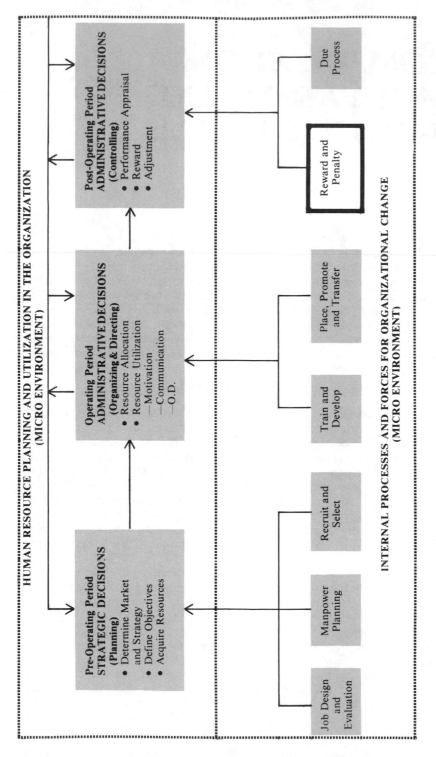

FIGURE 9-1 THE REWARD AND PENALTY SYSTEM IN THE HUMAN RESOURCE SYSTEM

raw materials for widgets is equal to $1.20 per widget, wage costs are $10 per hour, and other costs equal $.60 per widget; unit labor costs are therefore $.20 per widget. If wages increase by 10 percent as in example B of Figure 9-2 the price of widgets must rise to cover all costs. However, in example C if 22,000 widgets can be produced in 400 hours wages can be increased by 10 percent without a necessary increase in the selling price.

Furthermore, wages are thought to be efficient allocators of labor resources. The higher the wage in an occupation, an industry, or a geographical area the easier it is to attract more competent employees. Since it is presumed that more competent employees are more productive, they "earn" the higher wage. Or, in other words, high wages may result in relatively low unit labor costs if competent workers are attracted to the jobs or the high wages act as an incentive to higher productivity.

Finally, wage levels are a macro concern from the viewpoint of social justice. It is thought that workers should be paid a "just wage" that compensates them not only for their productivity, but also for the onerous demands of the job or a "living wage" that allows them to live with a minimum of personal dignity in society. Both of these concepts argue that compensation levels and wage structure must be equitable not only personally but collectively. Some workers or jobs may not be "worth" the minimum wage established by law. Yet, the more productive members of the economy must support, in part, other less productive members not only through the establishment of minimum wages, but through other income supplements such as food stamps, free medical care, unemployment compensation, and other social welfare programs. Society has an interest in protecting individuals from the hazards associated with ill

A. Wages at $10 per hour

Labor cost per widget [($10 × 400 hrs) ÷ 20,000]	$ .20
Materials cost per widget	1.20
Other costs (including capital)	.60
Total unit cost	$2.00
Total unit price	$2.00

B. Ten percent salary increase to $11 per hour

Labor cost per unit [($11 × 400 hrs) ÷ 20,000]	$ .22
Materials cost per unit	1.20
Other Costs	.60
Total unit cost	$2.02
Required unit price	$2.02

C. Ten percent salary increase and a ten percent productivity increase

Labor cost per unit [($11 × 400 hrs) ÷ 22,000]	$ .20
Materials cost per unit	1.20
Other costs	.60
Total unit cost	$2.00
Required unit price	$2.00

FIGURE 9-2 EFFECTS OF WAGE AND PRODUCTIVITY INCREASE ON PRICE

health, physical disabilities, old age, job loss, and early death of family wage earners. In the United States and in other industrialized nations the costs of these programs are assessed to employers mainly through the compensation system.

WAGES IN THE ECONOMY

Wage rates and labor costs never cease to be important and popular concerns in the social arena. When asked what organized labor really wanted, Samuel Gompers is reported as summing it up in one word, "More!" and *more* is an appropriate description of the trend in compensation paid to all employees, not only union members. From 1966 to 1972 average compensation in the nonfarm sector of the economy rose 52 percent.[1] In recent years hourly compensation in the nonfarm sector has risen at higher rates on the order of 8 to 10 percent annually.[2] However, these gains have been accompanied by high rates of inflation and real income actually has declined. (Real income is money wage adjusted for inflation). For example, during the 1966-72 period the price level rose by 29 percent, and in terms of purchasing power the average worker's real income gained 18 percent. At the same time, productivity increased only 13 percent.[3] In comparison, wage gains in the nonfarm sector increased 9.8 percent in 1974, but the increase in prices led to a decline of 2 percent in real income during the year.[4]

There have been a number of other secular trends in employee compensation over the last decade that reflect a continuing emphasis on relatively larger increases in benefit programs (health insurance, pensions, paid holidays, etc.) than in wages for time worked. Pay for working time rose 48 percent during the period 1966-72 but as a percentage of total compensation, wages decreased from 83 percent to 80.5 percent.[5] Benefit programs, on the average, now constitute more than 20 percent of wage costs incurred by employers.

These statistics reflect some of the major trends and problems in the macro-environment. In recent years, average wages have been increasing more rapidly than increases in productivity. As a consequence, the United States has been experiencing a rapid rate of price inflation even in the face of growing unemployment. This situation—rising unemployment coupled with large price increases—is unprecedented for a modern industrial economy and has become a major policy issue for the federal government as well as for employers. In addition, the federal government has continued its emphasis on providing financial security for workers and their dependents through payroll taxes. For example, during the 1966-72 period social security payments increased 73 percent as a result of an increase in the tax rate from 4.2 percent to 5.2 percent of taxable wages. In addition, the tax base rose from $6,000 to $9,000 during this period and in 1976 social security payments were set at 5.85 percent of the first $15,300 of earned wages to be paid by both the employee and employer. Both the percentage rate and the taxable wages are scheduled to increase further through 1980.

In addition to government-imposed increases in benefit costs, there have been larger increases in the relative percentage of total compensation going to such benefit plans as private pensions, insurance, and health benefit plans. Life, accident, and health insurance costs rose by 129 percent from 1966 to 1972, and the evidence warrants a forecast of even more rapid increases in these benefits.[6] The federal government's apparent response to the need for health and retirement insurance has been to encourage employers to provide private coverage to more employees, upgrade existing plans, and encourage individuals to voluntarily purchase insurance from private companies.

The effects of these trends have been to increase the cost of compensation plans and complicate the design and administration of the compensation system in the firm. Coping with compensation problems has become an important and complex part of the human resource system. Increases in social security taxes, new regulations affecting pensions, encouragement of private health insurance plans—all put upward pressure on wage costs and prices of consumer goods at a time when labor productivity has been declining.[7] The challenge for managers and government policy makers alike is to provide high levels of real income through increased man-hour productivity.

LAWS AFFECTING COMPENSATION

There are numerous state, local, and federal laws that have an impact on compensation practices, but the major ones are federal laws that were enacted during the 1930s. These laws reflect the political philosophy that wage levels should not be determined solely by economic forces. This philosophy continues in the macro-environment with surprisingly broad political support from liberals and conservatives alike, and recent legislation regulating wages and prices leads to the conclusion that federal controls over compensation practices are likely to increase in the future.[8]

The Davis-Bacon Act

The Davis-Bacon Act was enacted in 1931 and covers employees working for private contractors engaged in construction projects financed entirely or in part with federal funds. The act establishes minimum wage rates equal to *prevailing* wage rates in the area. Most likely the rate established by the Secretary of Labor is the top rate paid under a current collective bargaining in the area or in a nearby city. Rates are established for each trade and vary considerably from area to area. The effect of this act has been to eliminate the practice of "importing" workers from low paying areas to work on federally funded projects under construction in high wage rate areas. The law is an important support for locally bargained wage rates, and the craft unions consider the act a very important piece of legislation. In 1971 President Richard Nixon suspended the act temporarily to bring pressure to bear on spiraling construction wages. The suspension had little effort on rising wages but did bring considerable criticism of the Nixon administration from organized labor and management spokesmen for the construction industry.

The Walsh-Healey Act

This act formally known as the Public Contract Act of 1936 covers employees other than administrative, professional, office, or custodial employees engaged in work connected with a federal government contract for material or supplies amounting to $10,000 or more. The act establishes minimum wage rates that vary by industry and requires the payment of time and one-half for all hours worked over eight per day or forty per week, whichever yields the highest pay. The act has been a controversial one especially since the Wage and Hour Law provides similar coverage.

The Fair Labor Standards Act

This act passed in 1936 has become known as the Wage and Hour Law because it establishes minimum wages, maximum hours for the calculation of overtime pay, overtime pay rates, and wage rate discrimination prohibition. This act covers nearly all establishments

> . . . except nonchain corner drug stores, undertaking parlors, and so-called "Mom and Pop" stores—stores operated by members of the same family that have no other employees beside the husband, wife, or children of the proprietor.[9]

In 1974 coverage was extended to include domestic workers and all government employees. The act exempts certain white-collar employees paid on a salary basis. These include executives, administrators, professionals, and outside sales persons. There are elaborate criteria that must be met to classify an employee exempt from the act, and as the coverage has been extended to new employers over the years, a considerable amount of litigation has taken place as employers attempted to exempt their establishment or particular occupations from the act. The courts have ruled differently in different jurisdictions, and the effect has been to make interpretation of the act a difficult matter. Added in 1963 to an already complicated act were amendments forbidding wage differentials based upon sex. This has complicated the administering of the provisions of the act and increased the litigation considerably.

The minimum wage as of January 1, 1976, was set at $2.30 per hour except for newly covered workers that were included under the act in 1966 and 1974. These workers were not brought up to $2.30 until 1977 except agricultural workers who are not required to be paid $2.30 until 1978. In addition, the act requires overtime rates of at least time and one-half the regular rate for all hours worked over forty per week. There are some exceptions for certain occupations and seasonal industries but, in each case what constitutes overtime is established by the act. (The act is discussed further in Chapter 10.)

Anti-Discrimination Laws

During the 1960s three civil rights acts were passed which have had a direct impact on compensation systems. The Equal Pay Act of 1963 amends the wage and hour law and prohibits wage discrimination against

women. The Civil Rights Act of 1964 has become a potent force in eliminating wage discrimination against racial minorities and women. And the
Age Discrimination in Employment Act of 1967 prohibits discrimination
in hiring, occupational placement, or wage payment against workers
between the ages of forty and sixty-five. In recent years, numerous charges
have been filed in federal courts alleging wage discrimination on the basis
of age or sex. A dramatic example was the American Telephone and Telegraph Company, which was ordered to pay 15 million dollars to women
and minority workers to compensate them for company policies that discriminated against them unfairly. AT&T also agreed to spend an additional 23 million dollars to improve wages and benefits for this group in
the future.

Many employers are undertaking a careful review of their compensation policies and practices to eliminate or change those which illegally
discriminate against members of these protected groups. Chapter 10 provides additional discussion of these laws.

The Economic Stabilization Act

In 1970 the Congress of the United States passed the Economic Stabi-
lization Act which, among other provisions, gave the president the power
to control wage and price increases in the national interest. This act
represents a sharp break with previous policy in the area of wage or price
controls during peace time. National policy, except during war time, has
been to attempt to control wages and prices through indirect measures.
Fiscal and monetary policy was used to try to stimulate or dampen product
demand. During periods of high demand, labor productivity typically increases and as long as average wage increases do not exceed productivity
increases, price levels, remain relatively constant. If prices rose too fast,
fiscal and monetary policies are used to decrease demand in the economy
which, theoretically, should result in downward pressures on consumer
prices and wages as the level of unemployment rose and consumers
purchased less.

In retrospect this conventional economic wisdom has proven less than
effective in controlling prices and wages during the 1970s. Prices and
wages rose sharply at the same time that unemployment was increasing
rapidly and product demand was falling. To cope with this problem on
August 14, 1971, the president mandated a ninety-day wage and price
freeze. In November of 1971 the president established other economic
controls and established the Cost of Living Council and the Price Commission and Pay Board to oversee and control wages and prices in the
economy. Although most mandatory controls were ended in January of
1973, many employers must continue to file wage and price information
with the Cost of Living Council.[10]

During the control phases, wages were at first frozen and then subject
to maximum increases established by the Pay Board. The basic standard
was that increases must be held to 5.5 percent for direct wages and 0.7
percent for qualified fringe benefits. Exceptions were made on a case-
by-case basis. There is no widespread agreement on how successfully
these controls were in reducing inflation, but the aftermath is a continuing

monitoring of compensation increases by the federal government. A concerned Congress continues to threaten new controls and some congressmen have proposed upper limits on executive compensation.[11]

This episode is, in our view, a major new force in the field of compensation administration and indicates that employers and organized labor are being called upon to act more responsibly in making compensation decisions. The decision makers at the micro level must consider the impact of their decisions at the macro level. A concern for national policies and goals must be a part of the employer's decision process voluntarily or it is likely to be manditorily imposed in the not too distant future. This concern extends not only to the wage level and its impact on prices but must consider such other national priorities as equal employment opportunity, minimum wage levels, and protection against the hazards of ill-health, unemployment, and old age.

COMPENSATION AND MOTIVATION AT THE MICRO LEVEL

The frequently mentioned functions of the wage and incentive systems at the micro level are to attract, retain, and motivate "superior" human resources. Theoretically, high compensation will attract employees of superior ability, reduce employee turnover, and motivate high productivity. Practically speaking, it is difficult to demonstrate that in general one type of incentive plan is better than another in performing these functions. Part of the problem is that there is no adequate theoretical model of motivation that allows researchers to determine how wage incentive plans affect behavior, under what conditions varying results might be expected from different incentive plans, and how individual employee differences relate to the effectiveness of plans.

In recent years there have been four theories of motivation that have been most influential in guiding research and to some extent practices in the area of compensation. Two theories have disparaged the use of financial compensation as general motivators, the third is concerned with the question of what is an equitable wage, and the fourth has only recently appeared on the scene but seems to be a more useful model for examining and understanding the relationship between behavior and incentive systems in industry.

Abraham Maslow's *Hierarchy of Needs* thesis and Frederick Herzberg's *Motivation-Hygiene* theory, briefly reviewed in Chapter 4, have attracted a large audience. A review of compensation books, articles, and research reports published during the past ten years demonstrates that these theories have received considerable attention by academic and compensation practitioners in developing a rationale for the design of compensation systems. Strangely, even a cursory reading of these two theories reveals that their proponents feel that financial compensation is not an important determinant of job behavior. Maslow's thesis implies that money could be a useful incentive for individuals who are trying to satisfy lower order needs such as creature comforts (basic physiological needs), the need for security, or perhaps to some extent money might afford one a measure of esteem. However, Maslow feels that most work behavior is intrinsically motivated by higher order needs, and compensation incentives are not very effective in bringing about desirable behavior. Herzberg's research tends to support Maslow's theory inasmuch as he concludes that although the absence of adequate pay policies may affect productivity adversely, good compensation practices alone will not motivate high performance.

In recent years there has been mounting criticism of these theories both from the point of view of their validity and whether they are practical guides to decision making.[12] Neither of these theories contribute much to the development of effective financial incentive systems.

A third theoretical consideration is more limited in the behavior it purports to explain than the Maslow and Herzberg theses. However, it is more directly related to financial incentives. *Equity theory* is frequently associated with the work of George Homans, Eliot Jacques, and J. Stacy Adams. Essentially, equity theory argues that both performance and personal satisfaction at work are determined by the equity or inequity that workers perceive in the work situation. Equity is defined as the ratio of an individual's inputs (such as effort, educational attainment, etc.) to the outcomes (pay, prestige, security, etc.) compared to a similar ratio he perceives for others. An individual who perceives inequity in a situation experiences stress and attempts to eliminate the perceived inequities. A basic hypothesis of the theory is that most typical workers would try to reduce inequity by increasing outcomes and decreasing inputs on the job.[13] Goodman and Friedman accept this hypothesis and believe that the weight of the research evidence seems to support the following conclusions:

1. Hourly workers who believe that they are overpaid produce more than hourly workers who believe that they are equitably paid.
2. Workers who are paid "by the piece" produce less in quantity but higher quality if they believe that they are overpaid compared to piece-rate workers who believe that they are being equitably paid.
3. Hourly workers who believe they are being paid less than they deserve invest lower inputs than hourly workers who feel equitably paid.[14]

The research is not conclusive, and the theory must be used cautiously in the design of compensation systems. However, it appears reasonable to assume that management should at least try to avoid producing the feeling among workers that they are underpaid for what they are expected to accomplish compared to others doing similar work in the organization or in the community.

The final theory is of recent origin in organizational behavior research but shows promise in providing a more comprehensive model for explaining motivational phenomena than the others. There are a number of variations of the model, but nearly all conclude that a person is highly motivated to act in some manner if he expects that his effort will lead to the intended behavior, and if the behavior is successfully performed, it will likely result in the attainment of some highly desired outcome.[15] The theory is often called *expectancy theory* and hypothesizes that the force or strength of the motivational drive is determined by how strong an individual's preference is for certain outcomes, (i.e., valence), times (x) the extent to which he expects (i.e., expectancy) that certain behavior will lead to the preferred outcomes. Or:

$$\text{Force} = \text{Valance} \times \text{Expectancy}$$

For example, an individual will put forth great effort if he *expects* that this effort will lead to high performance, and he believes that high performance will be instrumental in achieving a raise in salary only if the salary increase is highly valued by him (i.e., has *high valence*).

The importance of this theory is more easily seen in the context of leadership. House and Mitchell have formulated a "path-goal" theory of leadership that incorporates the essentials of expectancy theory. They state:

> The first proposition of path-goal theory is that leader behavior is acceptable and satisfying to subordinates to the extent that the subordinates see such behavior as either an immediate source of satisfaction or as instrumental to future satisfaction.

> The second proposition of this theory is that the leader's behavior will be motivational; i.e., increase effort, to the extent that (1) such behavior makes satisfaction of subordinates' needs contingent on effective performance and (2) such behavior complements the environment of subordinates by providing the coaching, guidance, support, and rewards necessary for effective performance.[16]

The relationship between financial compensation and work motivation is a complicated one that only recently has been subjected to much careful research. The proposition that rewards should be closely tied to performance is commonly accepted as a sound principle advocated by academics, consultants, and managers alike. However, there is evidence that pay is more closely tied to nonperformance factors such as job level and seniority.[17] There are numerous reasons why pay may not be closely tied to performance but no doubt an important reason is that it is difficult to assess performance. Even if differences in performance are apparent, managers may be reluctant to reflect these differences in compensation increases. Hamner concludes that compensation increases among employees are likely to be based on such factors as length of service, employee potential, or need to bring the employees' salary up to others in the group.[18]

In other words, the evidence suggests that good pay is not contingent upon good performance in many cases or the relationship between performance and pay is not perceived as an instrumental one. If pay was contingent on performance what would be the effect on productivity and job satisfaction? Hamner cited two studies that support the expectancy theory of motivation and concludes that both satisfaction and performance are dependent upon whether pay is contingent upon performance.[19]

In summary, because of the popularity of the theories of Maslow and Herzberg there is a widespread notion that pay is not an effective motivator of job performance. However, equity theory and especially expectancy theory argue that pay as a reward can and does motivate performance and has an effect on job satisfaction. Present research supports both of these latter views but finds that compensation systems tend to be poorly administered, supervisors are unable or unwilling to use pay to discriminate among employees who perform well and those who do not, and the secrecy that surrounds compensation decisions may lead to unrealistic expectations about the relationship between pay and performance.[20]

Lawler, after an extensive review of the research on compensation, concludes that if pay is tied to performance it can motivate performance, reduce absenteeism and turnover, lead to high satisfaction with pay, and increase the perceived importance of pay among employees. If pay is not tied to performance Lawler concludes pay becomes less important to employees, it does not motivate high performance, results in low satisfaction and high rates of turnover and absenteeism among all employees.[21]

WAGE PAYMENT PLANS

Lawler in his review of pay and organizational effectiveness states that:

> There are virtually as many methods of relating pay to performance as there are organizations, and at times it seems that every organization is in the process of changing its approach.[22]

For our purposes we classify wage payment plans as either time wage or incentive wage plans. Our major interest is however on the latter.

Time Wages

Most employees are paid on the basis of hourly wage rates or annual salaries. It is assumed that the employee paid for the time he spends on the job is doing a "fair day's work" for the pay he receives. Furthermore, since every person doing the same job is typically paid at the same hourly rate established by the job evaluation system, it is assumed that there is little variation in output among employees on the same job. Most of us with even a casual knowledge of the world of work know that reality is often at variation with these assumptions. However, there are often good reasons to pay employees for time worked rather than what is produced. In situations where employees have little control over the pace of work, or the quantity of work flows unevenly and at times there is forced idleness and at other times there is a rush of work, time payment is appropriate. If units of output are not easily identifiable or attributable to certain individuals or identifiable groups, such as the output of a staff of security guards, time payment is probably preferable. If quality considerations are clearly more important than quantity considerations time payment is advisable.[23]

Incentive Plans

The prevalance of plans that pay workers according to their productivity rather than on a time basis only is not known. It was once believed that incentive plans were falling in disfavor with workers and management alike and therefore were being abandoned. What evidence there is suggests that while in certain industries there have been changes from incentive wage systems to time payment, in others the change has been the opposite. Stelluto found that among manufacturers,

> . . . the proportion of production and related workers paid under incentive wage plans have remained almost unchanged over the past several years for most industries studied.[24]

Lawler classifies incentive plans into individual plans, group plans, and organization wide plans (see Table 9-1). The most well known incentive plan is the individual *piece rate* plan whereby employees are paid, in its simplist form, a fixed rate per piece produced. In practice careful work measurements and job evaluations establish productivity standards for each job. These standards, if expressed in hourly production, are measurements of what an average worker should produce during an hour under typical working conditions. Normally, an individual is paid an hourly rate for all that he produces up to the standard. Over standard he is paid an additional increment per piece produced. For example, if the base rate is $2.50 per hour and the standard is ten pieces per hour at $.20 per piece, the incentive might be established for all pieces produced over eighty per day.

There are numerous variations on piece work plans. Some pay low rates per piece up to standard and higher rates per piece above standard to encourage employees to exceed standards. A standard hour plan such as the Halsey premium plan, the Rowan plan, or the Bedaux plan pays bonuses on the basis of time saved.[25] For example if the standard is eighty per day and an employee is paid $20 per day if he produces a hundred per day, that is a rate of 125 percent of the standard, his pay is calculated at (1.25 × $20) or $25 for the day. He has saved one-quarter of a standard day.

There are numerous variations on these plans and as many advocates as critics. Slezak reports on a study of a hundred companies in Sweden where employers who switched from fixed salaries to a premium payment system had an average increase in productivity between 25 and 35 percent. In contrast, those firms that switched from simple piecework systems to fixed salaries experienced a 15 to 25 percent drop in efficiency.[26] Lawler in reviewing the research literature concludes that piece rate payment systems can increase productivity. He also points out that:

> . . . when workers are placed on individual piece rate plans, they often feel that a number of negative social and economic consequences will result if they are highly productive. There is also some evidence that they do not believe that the company will continue to reward them for higher productivity.[27]

Group norms may restrict output. Fear of working oneself or others out of a job, fear of management raising the standard, and the possibility of maximizing individual output at the *expense* of the group and other units in the organization are all frequently cited as reasons why piecework systems fail to meet management expectations.

TABLE 9-1
A CLASSIFICATION OF PAY-INCENTIVE PLANS

| | Performance Measure | Reward Offered | | |
		Salary Increase	Cash Bonus	
Individual plans	Productivity Cost effectiveness Superiors' ratings	} Merit rating plan	} Sales commission Piece rate	
Group plans	Productivity Cost effectiveness Superiors' ratings		Group Incentive	
Organizationwide plans	Productivity Cost effectiveness Profit	} Productivity Bargaining	Kaiser, Scanlon Profit Sharing (e.g., American Motors)	

Source: Reprinted with permission from E. E. Lawler, *Pay and Organizational Effectiveness* (New York: McGraw-Hill Book Co., Inc., 1971).

Group plans do not appear to be as widespread as individual plans, but Dunn and Rachel believe that for a group plan to work well the group should be homogeneous and concerned with a single operation, and each employee should share equally in the bonus.[28] The advantages of a group incentive plan are that they can be used effectively where it is difficult to measure individual performance, where cooperation among group members is especially important, and where the group can exercise a powerful effect on individual output. Lawler concludes that group plans will not motivate employees as effectively as individual plans, but suggests they are preferable to time payment plans if one wishes to increase output.[29] Group plans also violate expectancy theory since workers often do not see the tie between their individual effort, group performance, and rewards.

Organizationwide plans are common, and a number of them have been dramatically successful. The Kaiser Steel Company Plan and the Scanlon Plan are two of the most well-known plans. The Kaiser Plan is tied to cost savings through increased labor productivity and technological change. In return for a "guarantee" of employment, management is given a free hand by the union to introduce method changes. As costs go down relative to a base year, bonus funds accrue to workers. The formula is a complicated one and the plan has not worked without major problems in recent years.[30] Lawler concludes that it is much less successful than the Scanlon Plan.[31] The Scanlon Plan was first developed for use in a steel mill but has subsequently received wide application. The basic plan calculates a base line ratio of total sales to total labor costs. If, during a given period, labor costs fall below the base line percentage the labor cost savings becomes available for bonuses. Seventy-five percent of the labor cost savings is distributed to labor and 25 percent to management. Individual bonuses are based upon individual earnings during the period.[32] Both the Kaiser and the Scanlon Plans are based upon motivating increased effort, employee teamwork, and improved work methods. It appears that these company wide plans probably relate pay to performance more closely than time payment plans; however, there is little reliable evidence to suggest that they work better than individual incentive plans.

EXECUTIVE COMPENSATION PLANS

Executives are typically paid on the basis of an annual salary, plus fringe benefits, and perquisites. As in the case of non executives, time payment appears to be the most frequent method; however, performance related bonuses, both cash and noncash, frequently accompany base salaries.[33] There is considerable controversy over how much an executive is worth, and there is evidently no acceptable answer. Foster found that although job level was the single best predictor of managerial salaries, years of professional experience, number of employees supervised, average salary of employees supervised, and the size of the firm, are highly related to pay differences among managers.[34]

A typical compensation package for an executive includes a base salary, a cash bonus based upon performance criteria, stock option or purchase plans, and deferred compensation that is typically tied to profits.[35] The range of fringe benefits are more extensive and the levels of benefits are higher than for non executives, but there are also perquisites that accrue to executives that are not part of a non manager's compensation package. Financial counseling, executive dining rooms, automobiles, club memberships, company airplanes are but a few of the typical perquisites available.[36]

The primary problem in executive compensation is to determine what measure of performance salary should be related to such as growth in sales, earnings per share, return on investment, or some other measure of success. Once the measure has been chosen, the level of salary, including base, bonuses, and perquisites, can be related to the measure and the total salary then can be distributed among the components in a manner that suits the executive. From the firm's point of view, though, the important question is to determine what results need to be tied to the incentives. The evidence is mostly of the "expert opinion" type and varies considerably. Deardon suggests that companywide profit is the most acceptable standard to use in determining executive incentive compensation.[37] Patton argues that there are too many problems with this approach because even in bad years, some executives should be paid for outstanding performance under adverse conditions.[38] In many cases it is difficult to determine who contributed what to the goals of the firm. Or, the interdependence of effort required to accomplish complex goals at the executive level suggests a group approach to incentive pay might be more appropriate. These are but a few of the unsettled questions in executive compensation. Less systematic research has taken place at this level to determine the relationship of pay plans to productivity than among other groups of employees.

EMPLOYEE BENEFIT PLANS

The early trade societies of the eighteenth and early nineteenth centuries were associations of craftsmen, masters, and journeymen, who came together to form "mutual aid societies." These societies provided sickness and death benefits to members and were formed to accomplish collectively what was difficult to do individually, i.e., find protection from the hazards of life that threatened the interruption of income. Economic security was the motive force then and in large part is the motivation behind today's growth in supplementary compensation programs. The rapid growth in fringe benefits is often attributed to governmental policies during World War II. During the war, wages and prices were rigidly controlled, the demand for labor was at an all-time high, and labor unions were constrained in what they could "win" at the bargaining table by wage control policies administered by the War Labor Board. However, the area of fringe benefits was less tightly controlled and employers were willing to provide nonwage compensation to attract employees and placate organized labor, and the War Labor Board was ready to accept this form of higher compensation.

The policies of the government during the Second World War only accelerated a trend toward providing noncash benefits to workers. The paternalistic attitudes of many employers during the 1920s gave both rationale and impetus to the growth of fringes. Economic theory argues that this form of compensation like other forms should serve the function of attracting, retaining, and motivating employee productivity. On the other hand, the rationale of the early Mutual Aid Societies and the paternalistic feelings of employers are similar in that they recognize that the organization may be better able to meet the common security needs of employees collectively than the employees are able to individually. Both of these approaches underlie benefit programs today.

Previously, it was indicated that nonwage benefits constitute 20 percent of the labor costs. This estimate is based upon a sample of nonagricultural, civilian employees who hold mainly blue-collar jobs. Other estimates of benefits put the costs closer to 33 percent.[39] Regardless of the source, nearly all research indicates that fringe benefits are a rapidly increasing part of employee compensation. This section will review some of the more popular forms of benefits, review past trends, and speculate about future changes in benefit plans.

Life Insurance Plans

Employers have provided group life insurance for employees for many years. This benefit is intended to financially assist the family in the event of the death of the wage earner. Nearly all employers provide some life insurance plan for office and nonoffice employees.[40] Research by The Conference Board found that the median amount provided nonoffice employees was $5,000 with only 18 percent providing $10,000 or more. Among office, clerical, and managerial employees the insured amount is some multiple of an individual's salary, typically twice the annual salary. Some employers require employees to contribute to the cost of the plan if they wish to receive the entire benefit. Employee contributions are usually 50 percent of the cost, but contributory plans are more likely to be found among nonoffice workers. Some firms are beginning to provide insurance coverage for dependents and retired workers but at substantially lower levels than for active employees.

Disability Benefits

A major hazard faced by most workers is the loss of income that accompanies short-term or long-term disabling illness or injury whether it is work-related or not. Work-related disability is covered by workmen's compensation laws in all states, and the federal social security system provides benefits to covered workers in the event of total disability.

In addition, most organizations provide paid sick leave for salaried employees and, increasingly, for hourly employees. The most significant development in this type of benefit has been the rapid growth of long-term disability insurance during the last decade. Seventy-four percent of the companies in the Conference Board study provided long-term disability to managerial employees, 68 percent provided it to office employees, but only 28 percent made it available to nonoffice employees.[41] Benefit amounts are usually 50 to 60 percent of the disabled worker's salary up to a maximum of $1500 or less. Only 30 percent of the firms in the Conference Board study provided higher maxima.[42]

Nonoffice employees are typically covered by short-term disability and sickness insurance which provides benefits for as long as 26 weeks. Most of the plans are paid entirely by employers and are frequently negotiated by the union. Dollar benefits for nonoffice employees typically range from $50 to $124 per week with most paying less than $100 per week.[43]

The major trends in disability insurance have been the growth of long-term disability, increased benefit levels, and a decline in the percent of plans paid, in whole or in part, by employees. Most likely these trends will continue into the future, but expanded coverage is likely to occur mainly in the nonoffice worker group as a trend toward equal benefit coverage for all employees continues to be brought about by management and labor unions alike.

Health Insurance

In the past ten years, along with increases in prices throughout the economy, health care costs have increased even more rapidly. New and expensive diagnostic and treatment techniques and facilities have improved medical care for the typical patient but at much higher costs than previously. There is a medical ethic that emphasizes the best medical care available be provided patients regardless of costs, and, consequently, a major illness of a family member whether he survives or not can be financially devastating. As a consequence of these changes in the macro-environment, there is a recognized need for a collective solution to the individual need for affording "the best medical care." For the elderly, Medicaid provides some benefits during a time in life when incomes may be the lowest but medical expenses the highest. However, there remains a considerable amount of political pressure for a comprehensive national health care program. Although it is speculative, we believe that any national health care plan will be built upon the present growing system of employer-provided privately funded health insurance.

The Conference Board study found that the vast majority of companies provide both a base plan and major medical coverage for the employee and his family.[44] The base plan usually covers specified or "scheduled" medical services, limiting payment to a maximum fee established for each service. Room rates, hospital expenses, surgical fees, and others are limited to the scheduled amount and the maximum length of covered hospital stay is most often specified. Illnesses, procedures, or services not scheduled are not covered. Major medical coverage is broader based and covers a portion of the total medical bill, regardless of the illness or treatment above a specified amount. For example, if a major medical plan has a deductible of $1500 and a coinsurance provision of 80 percent, once medical expenses exceed $1500 the major medical plan will cover 80 percent of all expenses over $1500, typically up to a limit of $15,000 to $50,000. The limits are higher and coverage is broader for office and managerial employees, but comprehensive plans are growing which tend to equalize coverage for all employees, broaden the hospitalization coverage, reduce the amount of coinsurance that must be borne by the employees, and provide higher maximum amounts. In addition, some plans have included family dental care, prescription drug costs, annual physical examinations and doctor's fees for routine visits.[45]

The major trends appear to be in the direction of comprehensive medical expense coverage, paid for by the employer, to cover the employee and his dependents. From the macro view these are desirable trends, but employer related health care plans leave important groups uncovered in society. Typically, employees who are retired, unemployed persons, and individuals working in seasonal employment remain uninsured against catastrophic medical expenses. The next decade is likely to bring government incentives for employers to provide comprehensive medical insurance coverage as well as government plans to cover individuals who are not likely to be protected through the employment relationship.

Retirement Plans

Private pension plans have become a major social concern in recent years. Since the 1940s unions have been bargaining for pension plans, higher pension benefit levels, and earlier retirement for workers. Emerson Beier found that in 1968 over 32 million workers amounting to 58 percent of private nonfarm employees, were employed in establishments that offered private retirement plans.[46] The incidence of retirement plans is greater among larger, unionized firms, especially in manufacturing industries. The Conference Board study found that 87 percent of the companies in their survey provided pension plans for employees for retirement typically after the age of 65 but some offering full benefits after age 60. In comparison to a previous study the Conference Board found the incidence of plans up from 74 percent in 1964. Eighty percent of the companies pay for all of the plan while only 20 percent require an employee contribution.

The major concern with retirement plans in recent years has been over the extent to which employees receive benefits that they anticipate at the end of their working careers. Many employees who change jobs frequently never remain under a plan long enough to be vested, i.e., have a guarantee of a certain level of benefits. Under some plans employees had to be employed for fifteen to twenty years before benefits were guaranteed. Presumably, if an employee was laid off with twenty-one years of service he should be entitled to some benefit at retirement age since the employer paid a sum every year in his behalf. Only if he was vested would he be entitled to a benefit upon retirement. In addition, some pension funds were not set aside or funded by the firm, but benefits were paid to retirees from current revenues. Therefore, future benefits were dependent upon the continued financial success of the company.

To remedy pension fund problems, Congress passed the "Employee Retirement Income Security Act of 1974." This act has several implications for employers. First, there must be 100 percent vesting after ten years of service for every employee or graduated vesting where, after five years of service, the person is vested at the 25 percent level, and this increases in regular intervals up to 100 percent after fifteen years of service. Or, according to an age-plus-sum-of-years-service formula, the employee is provided gradual vesting to 100 percent by the fifteenth year of service. Secondly, eligibility for participation in the plan must be no later than age 25 or three years of service. Finally, the law provides more stringent rules for funding pensions to guarantee sufficient funds to meet the future obligations even if the firm is financially unsuccessful.[47]

One trend in pensions is toward earlier retirement ages. Some unions have negotiated "twenty year and out" provisions regardless of age. Higher retirement benefits continue to be bargained for, and some employers attempt to lure employees to retire early by offering benefits that are higher than they are typically entitled to at their age to accomplish a reduction in the workforce. Other trends are toward earlier vesting and fully funded plans with outside agencies such as insurance companies or banks. Moreover, there is likely to be growing scrutiny by government to assure that workers receive their anticipated benefits.

Rationale for Benefit Plans

There are numerous other supplementary benefits that are popular and seem to be increasing as a part of the incentive package. Time off with pay for vacations, holidays, sick-leave, and other reasons are on the increase. Supplemental unemployment benefits that augment the state unemployment benefits paid to unemployed workers are frequently found in labor contracts. Educational benefits, short work weeks (without a loss of pay), financial and personal counseling are but a few of the many and varied benefits currently offered by some employers. Since these benefits are increasing as a percentage of labor costs, is there good reason for this trend? From the micro viewpoint, firms tend to view these benefits as a help in attracting, retaining, and motivating employees. There is scant evidence to support this notion.[48] Since benefit plans typically are not linked to performance of the employee, they are not motivators. There is even some evidence to support the notion that employees are not very aware of the benefits they are receiving.[49] From the individual employees' point of view there may be better reason to provide more benefits; he may prefer benefits to direct compensation. It matters little in terms of costs to the firm whether a dollar is paid in wages or used to purchase a dollar's worth of benefits. Therefore, employee preferences should be an important part of the decision process in allocating dollars to wages or benefits. Finally, we believe there is a major reason for firms to be concerned about the level and kind of benefits they provide that begins at the macro-environment level. Private employment continues to be the main vehicle for providing economic security to the bulk of the citizens in the United States. This imposes on private decisions an obligation to consider the social ramifications of human resource decisions in the firm.

CONCLUSION

The socio-economic goals of low prices for consumer goods, high wages, economic security, and equitable wage differentials among jobs must be accomplished through private employers. Our national concern over increasing productivity is of primary importance because only through increasing productivity can prices remain low and real wages continue to rise. The employer meets this concern through the compensation and incentive system he creates. Most researchers who survey compensation practices conclude that many firms establish compensation and incentive systems that are not very effective motivators of high productivity. But, more importantly there is evidence that if rewards were made more contingent on performance, productivity would increase. This calls for not only changes in incentive systems but also job redesign; some jobs are not designed in such a manner that performance and rewards can be closely tied together.

Supplementary fringe benefits continue to grow as a proportion of total compensation. The rationale that they attract, retain, and motivate workers of superior ability lacks sufficient evidence. We believe that a social rationale is more appropriate. These forms of compensation should be viewed in terms of whether the firm can better meet the common needs of workers by providing these benefits to all rather than through individual worker choice.

Finally, the federal government is a potent and pervasive force in wage decisions. The legislation of the 1930s remains and added to it is the legislation of the 1960s and 1970s. Two thrusts are likely to have major impacts on employer compensation practices in the future. First, the struggle for equal pay for women and minorities will force firms to further rationalize their practices to avoid civil rights litigation. What is needed is a justification of differences in pay where they exist. Secondly, some form of wages and price monitoring and perhaps controls are likely to continue to be used by the federal government. Executive salaries are likely to become a target for policy makers because there appears to be little in the way of systematic evaluation of what an executive is worth.

CASE 1
THE BONUS SYSTEM

The Allison Janitor Company is a small janitorial contracting business owned by Bill Allison. The business employs approximately thirty people. Over the past twenty years, the business has grown largely because of its good reputation. The economic outlook shows signs of a continued growth for many years to come.

Mr. Allison's 27-year-old son Jim has been working in the business for six years. Two years ago, Mr. Allison opened a division of the parent company. The new division is called Allison Janitorial Supply House. Its function is to act as a wholesaler of materials used by the parent company. The materials are sold to the parent company as well as to other janitor service companies. Jim was placed in charge of the division and manages it as a separate entity from the parent company.

Bob Smith is the general manager of the parent company. His function is to act as the general manager, foreman, and right-hand man to Mr. Allison. Bob's knowledge of the business, his expertise, his friendly relations with the employees, and his long length of service to the company has made him almost irreplaceable. Mr. Allison considers Bob a friend and has said that, without him, he would not wish to continue to operate the business.

Mr. Allison places emphasis on getting the jobs done with the least cost, but without sacrificing quality. Mr. Allison often goes out to the job sites to check on work progress and to inspect the work done. He usually gives Bob instructions about the jobs. Bob, in turn, gives detailed instructions and helps the employees get the jobs done. He usually listens to employee suggestions and takes them seriously. Employees are very loyal to him.

Mr. Allison is happy that his son is running the new division. As an incentive, he is giving him a quarterly bonus of 2 percent of net sales produced by the division, even though the net profit of the division is still low.

Because Bob had been in the business fifteen years longer than Jim, and was in charge of the main income producing unit, it was considered only fair that he should receive the same bonus percentage of net sales from the parent unit. For the first year, the net sales bonus system was working fine, with Bob getting a larger bonus. But recently, the net sales of the division has jumped higher, even though the net profit has been rising slowly when compared to the parent company. This is to be expected since a wholesale supply business' mark-up is usually small compared to the service mark-up of the parent firm. Thus, the net sales of the division were much higher than the parent unit, but the net profit of the parent unit was much higher than the division's net profit.

Bob, like Jim, is a minority stockholder in the company. When Bob saw the difference between his bonus and Jim's, he mentioned this to Mr. Allison. He felt that Jim should not be getting more bonus than he received. He felt justified because it was well known to all concerned that Jim was new to the business and had relied on Bob's knowledge and advice for wholesale price bidding while learning the job. Without Bob's advice, Jim would not have been as successful with the new division.

Mr. Allison did not know what to do. He wanted his son to get the bonus, yet he wanted to keep Bob happy, too. The next quarter showed a bonus to Jim that was three times greater than Bob's. The difference amounted to several thousand dollars. He decided to talk to his accountant, who also acted as an advisor to him, during a business trip coming up next month.

The next day, Mr. Allison stopped in the accountant's office to pick up some papers and briefly mentioned the bonus problem. Immediately, the accountant insisted on a meeting to discuss the problem the next morning.

Questions

1. Is it "fair" to base a bonus on sales volume?

2. What should be the basis of an equitable bonus?

3. How will Bob react when he discovers the difference between his and Jim's bonus?

4. Discuss the ethics of the present bonus system.

CASE 2
HANSON FREIGHT SERVICES

Hanson Freight operates within the continental United States as well as Alaska, engaging in the delivery of parcels from firm to firm, firm to consumer, and consumer to consumer. At its Cleveland, Ohio, terminal managed by Bob Wilson, there has been significant pressure exerted upon the hourly employees who sort and load packages to raise their piece rate from an average of 130 to 180 pieces per hour. Regional management feels that significant labor savings should be realized in Cleveland because of the presence of a new automated parcel sorting system which is unique among its national operations. The new Cleveland facility has been on-line for fifteen months. The employees involved are part-time and work the early morning shift, 3:30 to 8:30 a.m. Almost all of the part-time employees are either full or part-time college students. Their job description indicates that they are responsible for loading Hanson Freight's delivery vehicles. The employees' immediate supervisors are part-time as well and have been promoted from the ranks. Each supervisor is responsible for ten packers.

On the morning of April 15, the terminal manager directly informed the hourly employees that as of the next day all employees would work only three hours and were expected to load all trucks during this period. This was in accord with the collective bargaining agreement provision governing the minimum number of hours that could be paid once the employee reported for work. The employees reacted the following morning by staging a work slowdown. They were ordered off the clock after three hours. In order to eliminate the tremendous backlog of unloaded parcels, all drivers were called in two hours early at a pay rate of time and one-half. Bob Wilson ended up with a significant labor rate variance which more than offset any payroll savings due to the early dismissal of the part-time employees. The regional manager is on his way to the Cleveland terminal.

Bill Towson, one of the loaders who has been with the company for a long period of time, suggested to Bob Wilson that he should eliminate the incentive rates and pay straight hourly rates. He argued that a good dock supervisor can get as much work out as a poor incentive system. Bob a-greed to consider Bill's comments.

Questions

1. Evaluate Bill Towson's suggestions.

2. What caused the present dilemma?

3. What should have been the approach to changing the standards?

STUDY AND DISCUSSION QUESTIONS

1. What role do wages play in the macro-environment? What relationship do wages have to labor costs and productivity? To inflation?

2. What are the major laws affecting compensation and what are their basic purposes and coverage? Why do you think so many laws have been passed?

3. Discuss this statement:
   A concern for national policies and goals must be a part of the employer's decision process voluntarily or it is likely to be manditorily imposed in the not too distant future. This concern extends not only to the wage level and its impact on prices, but must also include such other national priorities as equal employment opportunities, minimum wage levels, and protection against the hazards of ill-health, unemployment and old age.

4. How does Maslow's need hierarchy and Herzberg's motivation theory relate to compensation and motivation? What are their limitations?

5. What is equity theory? What are its implications for compensation practices?

6. What is expectancy theory? What are its implications for compensation practices?

7. Explain this statement:
   Good pay may not be contingent on good performance in many cases and the relationship between performance and pay is often not perceived as an instrumental one.

   What are the implications of this statement?

8. Explain the major wage payment plans in use today.

9. Explain the Kaiser and Scanlon Plans.

10. How and to what criteria should executive payment plans be structured?

11. What are the major types of employee benefit plans? Why have they been developed by employers?

12. Comment on this statement made by a manager of a medium-sized textile manufacturer.
    I don't care what Herzberg says, money will motivate. Pay a guy enough and treat him fairly and he'll produce. In fact, most of my workers just want more money and couldn't care less about good benefits and job conditions. They'll work hard if you pay them well.

13. Do the Scanlon and Kaiser incentive plans negate Herzberg's findings?

ENDNOTES

1. Paul L. Scheible, "Changes in Employee Compensation," *Monthly Labor Review*, March 1975, p. 10.
2. Joseph E. Talbot, Jr., "An Analysis of Wage Gains in 1974," *Monthly Labor Review*, April 1975, p. 4.

3. Scheible, op. cit., p. 10.
4. Talbot, op. cit., p. 4.
5. Scheible, op. cit.
6. Ibid.
7. Talbot, op. cit., p. 4.
8. The review of these laws is based upon the book by Russell L. Greenman and Eric J. Smertz, *Personnel Administration and the Law* (Washington, D.C.: The Bureau of National Affairs, Inc., 1972).
9. Ibid., p. 15.
10. Daniel J. B. Mitchell and Ross Azevedo, "A Pay Board Assessment of Wage Controls," *Monthly Labor Review,* April 1973, p. 21.
11. U. S. Congress, Joint Economic Committee, *Executive Compensation Rules, Hearings,* before the subcommittee on Priorities and Economy in Government (Washington, D.C.: Government Printing Office, 1973).
12. For example, see Edward E. Lawler and J. Lloyd Suttle, "A Causal Correlation Test of the Need Hierarchy Concept," *Organizational Behavior and Human Performance,* Vol. 7, 1972, pp. 265-287 or Robert J. House and Lawrence A. Wigdon, "Herzberg's Dual-Factor Theory of Job Satisfaction and Motivation: A Review of the Evidence and a Criticism," *Personnel Psychology,* Vol. 20, 1967, pp. 369-389.
13. For a review of the theory and research see Paul S. Goodman and Abraham Friedman, "An Examination of Adams' Theory of Inequity," *Administrative Science Quarterly,* Vol. 16, 1971, pp. 271-288.
14. Ibid.
15. Robert J. House and Terence R. Mitchell, "Path-Goal Theory of Leadership," Reprinted with permission of the *Journal of Contemporary Business,* Copyright 1974.
16. Ibid., p. 82.
17. E. E. Lawler and L. W. Porter, "Predicting Managers Pay and Their Satisfaction With Their Pay," *Personnel Psychology,* Vol. 19, 1966, pp. 363-373.
18. W. Clay Hamner, "How to Ruin Motivation with Pay," *1974 National Conference Proceedings, American Compensation Association* (Pittsburgh: American Compensation Assn., 1974), p. 44.
19. Ibid., p. 47.
20. For a comprehensive review see, E. E. Lawler, *Pay and Organizational Effectiveness* (New York: McGraw-Hill Book Company, Inc., 1971).
21. Ibid., pp. 273-74.
22. Ibid., p. 162.
23. For a more complete discussion of these considerations see J. D. Dunn and Frank M. Rachel, *Wage and Salary Administration: Total Compensation Systems* (New York: McGraw-Hill Book Company, Inc., 1971), pp. 243-246.
24. George L. Stelluto, "Report on Incentive Pay in Manufacturing Industries," *Monthly Labor Review,* July 1969, p. 49.
25. See Dunn and Rachel, op. cit., p. 249.
26. Lester Slezak, "Effects of Changes in Payment System on Productivity in Sweden," *Monthly Labor Review,* March 1973, p. 51.
27. Lawler, op. cit., p. 126.
28. Dunn and Rachel, op. cit., p. 250.
29. Lawler, op. cit., p. 129.
30. Dunn and Rachel, op. cit., p. 251.
31. Lawler, op. cit., p. 131.
32. Dunn and Rachel, op. cit., p. 253.
33. Harland Fox, *Top Executive Compensation,* (New York: The Conference Board, Inc., 1974).
34. Kenneth E. Foster, "Accounting for Management Pay Differentials," *Industrial Relations,* Vol. 9, 1969, p. 86.
35. Fox, op. cit.
36. "Executives Perquisites," *1974 National Conference Proceedings* (Pittsburgh: American Compensation Association, 1974), pp. 109-112.
37. John Dearden, "How to Make Incentive Plans Work," *Harvard Business Review,* July-August 1972, pp. 117-124.
38. Arch Patton, "Why Incentive Plans Fail," *Harvard Business Review,* May-June 1972, pp. 58-66.

39. Mitchell Meyer and Harland Fox, *Profile of Employee Benefits* (New York: The Conference Board, 1974), p. 1.
40. Ibid., p. 68.
41. Ibid., p. 43.
42. Ibid., p. 45.
43. Ibid., p. 41.
44. Ibid., pp. 10-13.
45. Ibid., pp. 22-24.
46. Emerson Beier, "Incentive of Private Retirement Plans," *Monthly Labor Review,* July 1971, p. 37.
47. Thomas H. Paine, "Pension Reform: Implications for the Employer," *Compensation Review,* 4th Quarter, 1974, pp. 14-20.
48. See G. L. Palmer, et al. (eds.), *The Reluctant Job Changer: Studies in Work Attachment and Aspirations* (Philadelphia: University of Pennsylvania Press, 1962).
49. Joyce Gildea, "What's Happening in Employee Benefit Communications?" *Pension and Welfare News,* Vol. 8, March 1972, pp. 31-35.

ADDITIONAL READING

Andrews, Robert (ed.). *Managerial Compensation.* Ann Arbor: Foundation for Research in Human Behavior, 1965.

Belcher, David W. *Wage and Salary Administration,* 2nd ed. Englewood Cliffs, N. J.: Prentice-Hall, Inc., 1962.

Bloom, Gordon F. and Herbert R. Northrup. *Economics of Labor Relations.* 7th ed. Homewood, Ill.: Richard D. Irwin, Inc., 1973.

Carter, Allan M. and F. Ray Marshall. *Labor Economics: Wages, Employment and Trade Unionism,* rev. ed. Homewood, Ill.: Richard D. Irwin, Inc., 1972.

Crystal, Graef. *Financial Motivation for Executives.* New York: American Management Associations, 1970.

Dunn, J. D. and Frank M. Rachel. *Wage and Salary: Administration: Total Compensation Systems,* New York: McGraw-Hill Book Co., 1971.

Famularo, Joseph J. (ed.) *Handbook of Modern Personnel Administration.* New York: McGraw-Hill Book Co., 1972.

Gellerman, Saul. *Motivation and Productivity.* New York: American Management Associations, 1963.

Henderson, Richard L. *Compensation Management: Rewarding Performance in the Modern Organization.* Reston, Va.: Reston Publishing Co., Inc., 1976.

Kahn, C. Harry. *Employee Compensation Under the Income Tax.* New York: National Bureau of Economic Research, 1968.

Moore, Russell, F. Ed., *Compensating Executive Worth.* New York: American Management Associations, 1968.

Niebel, Benjamin W. *Motion and Time Study,* 5th ed. Homewood, Ill.: Richard D. Irwin, Inc., 1972.

Rock, Milton L., ed. *Handbook of Wage and Salary Administration.* New York: McGraw-Hill Book Co., 1972.

Sullivan, John. "Indirect Compensation: The Years Ahead." *California Management Review,* 15 (Winter, 1972), pp. 65-76.

Tolles, N. Arnold. *Origins of Modern Wage Theories.* Englewood Cliffs, N. J.: Prentice-Hall, Inc., 1964.

Williams, C. Glyn. *Labor Economics.* New York: John Wiley and Sons, Inc., 1970.

INDUSTRIAL JURISPRUDENCE: RIGHTS TO ECONOMIC AND SOCIAL SECURITY

10

Up to now in this book, we've focused primarily on the various kinds of decisions an organization makes regarding its human resources. We've examined job design, recruitment and selection, training and development, and reward and penalty issues among others. In the course of making these decisions, an organization deals with employees who have certain rights granted to them either explicitly or implicitly by social institutions and by the particular employing organization.

In this Chapter, we attempt to identify some of these rights, indicate how they evolved, and examine how organizations modify and implement them. The specific issue of due process as the way to ensure fair treatment in exercising individual rights is also examined. Figure 10-1 shows how this due process component fits into our human resource system.

These issues are examined from the perspective of industrial jurisprudence. *Industrial jurisprudence* is the system whereby individual members of a society attempt to fully exercise their rights with regard to economic and employment matters. It includes an examination of the process of exercising the rights as well as the vehicles that society has developed to protect and enable employees to exercise their rights. This chapter examines the role of the federal and state government in passing legislation and establishing regulatory agencies to protect these rights. The role of pressure groups is also examined, including the role of unions as a pressure group. Finally, the obligations of the employing organization are examined in insuring its employees adequate due process in the exercise of their rights.

HUMAN RIGHTS AND SOCIAL VALUES

There's bound to be disagreement over any listing of individual rights in U.S. society. However, we can develop a tentative listing based upon cultural values of our society. *Cultural values* are the basic beliefs of a society which are adhered to by the vast majority of people. They tend to be ambiguous, very general, and very slow to change. They are the glue which holds a society together. Most of us think immediately of such concepts

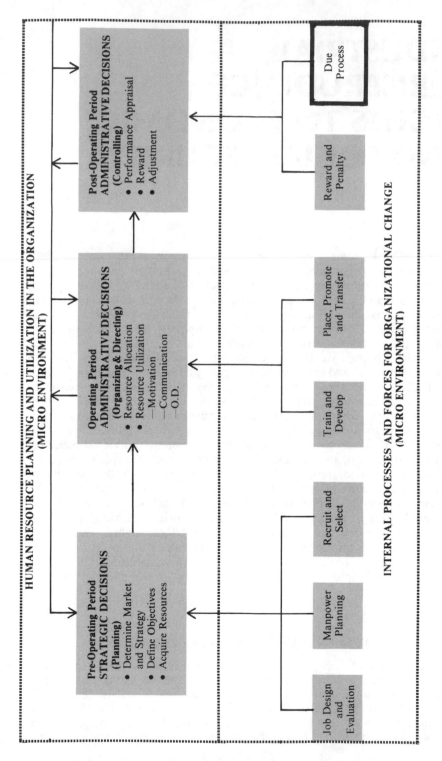

FIGURE 10-1. DUE PROCESS IN THE HUMAN RESOURCE SYSTEM

as "freedom," "brotherhood," "equal opportunity," "love," "peace," "hard work," and "human dignity." These values are quite broad and ambiguous. Our definition of freedom might be somewhat different from our neighbor's definition. These broad concepts serve as one umbrella which encompasses differing definitions. Who is against freedom, peace, and love? No one. Who's against drafting men to fight a war in Viet Nam? Many people, yet it still becomes national policy.

Thus, the way values are interpreted and implemented in particular situations often causes great disagreement. We value both patriotism and peace. Do we fight a war in Viet Nam? The values conflict. In many instances, the actual implementation of values causes conflict in society because the very *operational definitions* of two or more values conflict.

CULTURAL NORMS

Norms are standards of behavior. They are derived from values and manifest the values. They are guidelines of behavior that should be followed to adhere to the value. One value of U.S. society is brotherhood; one norm based on this value is to attempt to "get along" with everyone as well as possible. Another value is the integrity and importance of the family. A norm representing this value is making divorce a rather difficult legal process for a married couple to try to ensure that the family has every chance to stay together.

Figure 10-2 depicts some common values and norms which manifest these values. (Note that for each value there is more than one norm which actually represents this value even though Figure 10-2 does not show this. Also note that a particular norm may represent two or more values.)

Sample Values in U.S. Society	Example Norms Associated with Each Value
Democracy	Everyone should vote on election days.
Peace	The U.S. should not start a war.
Freedom	A person should be free to choose any job for which he is qualified.
Brotherhood	A person should try to help others in need.
Human Dignity	The life of a garbage collector is just as important as that of a corporate president.
Love	A person should treat others as he would wish to be treated.
Equal Opportunity	A person should have the opportunity to become all he is capable of becoming.
Hard Work	A person should work hard for his living and not be on welfare.

Sample Values in U.S. Society	Example Norms Associated with Each Value
Patriotism	A person ought to fight in a war to support his country's position.
Integrity of the Family	A married couple should try to stay together and be divorced only as a last resort.
Belief in a Supreme Being	Everyone ought to go to church as often as he can.
Honesty	Everyone should tell the truth.
Private Property	A person has a right to protect his property.

FIGURE 10-2   SOME COMMON CULTURAL VALUES AND NORMS IN U.S. SOCIETY

CULTURAL VALUES, SOCIAL INSTITUTIONS, AND WORKER RIGHTS

Dominant cultural values are expressed through social institutions such as government, the corporation, the church, labor unions, etc. Each of these institutions play a role in securing human rights that derive from our values. It is difficult to express the varied roles that these institutions play in such a pluralistic society as ours; however, our concern here is with the role of these institutions in securing and protecting rights that accrue to workers.

Any discussion of rights in the United States must begin with the notion of property rights. The birth of our nation and the early struggle to define a body of law unique to this nation focused on property rights. Our constitution and the body of common law that grew out of it in the early nineteenth century is, in great part, an affirmation of the individual's rights to acquire and use property for purposes of private gain and be protected from seizure of that property or restrictions on its use without benefit of legal due process. Out of the rights of private property grew our basic economic philosophy of capitalism, the corporation as a "legal person" with property rights, and the notion of job rights.

The traditional logic of private property is eloquently expressed by Berle and Means:

> From earliest times the owner of property has been entitled to the full use or disposal of his property, and in these rights the owner has been protected by law. Since the use of industrial property consists primarily of an effort to increase its value—to make a profit—the owner of such property, in being entitled to its full use, has been entitled to all accretions to its values—to all the profits which it could be made to earn. Insofar as he had to pay for the services of other men or other property in order to accomplish this increase in value, these payments operated as deductions; the profit remaining to him was the difference between the added value and the cost of securing these services. To this difference, however, the owner has traditionally been entitled. The state and the law have sought to protect him in this right.[1]

In today's modern corporation there remain those who strongly believe that all authority rests in the stockholders. Since many corporate managers are not majority stockholders in most large corporations, the stockholders (according to the traditional logic) delegate authority to them. The stockholders elect a board of directors who, in turn, elect officers (top managers). These officers then select other top managers. Top managers select middle managers, and middle managers select first line supervisors, who in turn select operative workers (often with the aid of a personnel department).

Each level of management derives its authority to manage its subordinate level from its superior level. This authority to manage can be traced to the top, or to the stockholders of the company. Figure 10-3 depicts this traditional view of the flow of authority for a corporation.

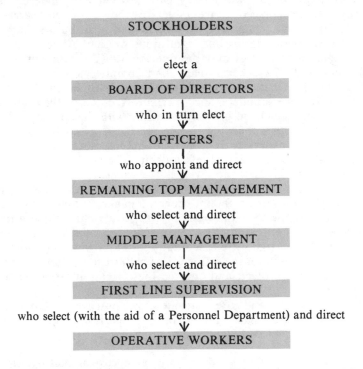

STOCKHOLDERS

elect a

BOARD OF DIRECTORS

who in turn elect

OFFICERS

who appoint and direct

REMAINING TOP MANAGEMENT

who select and direct

MIDDLE MANAGEMENT

who select and direct

FIRST LINE SUPERVISION

who select (with the aid of a Personnel Department) and direct

OPERATIVE WORKERS

FIGURE 10-3   THE TRADITIONAL VIEW OF THE FLOW OF AUTHORITY IN A CORPORATION

Notice that in this traditional view the right to manage individuals in an organization derives from the right of the people who own the property which the business uses to operate. Each layer of management commands the layer of management below them, and ultimately the worker, and each layer obeys. If an individual dislikes the command or the job, he is free to quit and seek employment elsewhere. In fact, the bargaining power of an individual in this view is to threaten to seek employment elsewhere. If he is a valued employee or if his skill is in short supply, the organization might change things to suit him better so that he would remain with the company. However, the employee can do little else within the organization to secure changes since authority flows from the top down.

In view of this traditional approach to private property and the authority of management, what rights accrue to workers? To answer this question the notion of rights to contract should be examined. The development of authority based upon property rights of stockholders has not been as neat as we've explained it. Others who have a stake in a business operation have also exercised authority in the operation of that organization. For example, customers have the authority to buy or not to buy the company's product or service and hence are voting "yea" or "nay" on company offerings each time they make a purchase decision. Financial lenders, such as banks, which extend loans to businesses often attach specifications as to how the money can be used and, indeed, how the company is to be managed. Lease-holders can affect the company's use of building, land, and equipment. Suppliers and distributors bargain for mutually agreed-upon terms and conditions of sale. All of these parties are exercising some control over the operation of the company.

So the owners have never really had complete authority to run the organization. This authority has been shared with customers, financial institutions, leasors, suppliers, and distributors. Each of these groups had rights which they sought to protect in dealing with the company. The concept that parties other than the owners of the firm could have a major say in how the firm was to be run is, therefore, not new; rather it is a result of established contractual relationships.

What is relatively new, however, is the concept that an outside party could have some influence as to how the organization should treat its employees. One can justify the influence of banks, suppliers, distributors, leasors, and customers on the basis of property rights; these groups are providing property or taking title to property associated with the organization. But employee's rights are based upon jobs and work and not property ownership and, therefore, the influence of a third party (union or government) to preserve, protect, and enforce these rights must be justified on other grounds.

Only reluctantly, and after considerable controversy, did the courts recognize that workers had rights, akin to property rights, that should be protected by the law.[2] Wellington points out that:

> The worker's property is his ability to be productive and his right to sell his skills. Freedom of contract is necessary for him, too, because unless he can sell his work freely he loses control of his property and his destiny. These attributes of property, combined with political rights to speak and vote, add up to a good portion of the individualism which we value today, and deeply so.[3]

On the basis of this logic, the courts upheld the legality of organized efforts to protect and foster the rights of workers. Unions, collective negotiations, strikes, and other tactics designed to improve labor's bargain in the contractual process were first recognized as legal by the courts and then protected more specifically by the legislative branch of government by the passage of the Norris-LaGuardia Act and the Wagner Act during the 1930s. Today, we view collective bargaining as a contractual process between labor and management that is as legitimate as that carried on between management and suppliers or management and bankers.

Job rights accrue to employees in another sense in the United States. As a nation we have asserted that individuals are entitled to a *decent job, steady work,* and *good working conditions.* These are rights that emanate from the cultural values of hard work and equal opportunity and embody the concept that anyone who wants to work ought to be able to obtain a job in the labor market. This is expressed as a national policy in the Employment Act of 1946 and has led to many federal programs designed to assist people in obtaining jobs in the economy. These laws and programs designed to foster and protect job rights are reviewed in the remainder of this chapter.

GOVERNMENT PROTECTION OF EMPLOYMENT RIGHTS AND INDUSTRIAL JURISPRUDENCE

What kinds of action did the government take to enforce and protect worker rights? Much has been done. In the remainder of this chapter we do not provide a detailed listing of all legislation and other actions taken. What we do is to simply outline the basic purpose and thrust of most major government activity. The reader is referred to more detailed discussions of each law or case in footnotes. Our concern is to paint a rather "broad brush" of government activity in six major areas as follows: The level of economic activity, minimum standards, protection from economic hardship, training and development, equal employment opportunity, and regulation of unionization activities.

LEVEL OF ECONOMIC ACTIVITY

The depression of the thirties was an extremely difficult period for the U.S.[4] Annual unemployment rates of approximately 25 percent of the labor force in the U.S. were not uncommon. Unlike earlier depressions this one lasted a full decade. It was not self-correcting. The traditional free enterprise system seemed to have broken down. It took a war to pull us out of it.

Following WW II, there was considerable concern that we would once again drift into a depression. Therefore, Congress passed the Employment Act of 1946. For the first time, the federal government decided it had an obligation to take action to ensure that we had a viable economy—one that would provide jobs for all who wanted to work. The Act had four major goals:

1. To ensure full employment
2. To ensure economic growth
3. To keep inflation at an acceptable level
4. To ensure a balance in international trade

The act recognized the fact that in the absence of high level economic activity, an individual's "right to work" is sufficiently curtailed. It also recognized that normal *laissez-faire* market operations would not automatically correct themselves to ensure full employment. Government now had to take some action.

The government uses *fiscal policy* (government taxation and spending) to create budget deficits and surpluses to either increase or decrease the level of economic activity. It also uses *monetary policy* (the operations of the Federal Reserve System) either to increase or decrease the monetary supply, which in turn increases or decreases economic activity. Monetary and fiscal policy actions are taken to increase economic activity and hence employment opportunities in an effort to ensure a high level of employment. They are also used to hold down inflation to ensure that the wages and salaries received do not lose purchasing power.

The act has been fairly successful to date, in stimulating economic activity, although in the mid-1970s unemployment did reach 8 to 9 percent for a brief period. However for most of the period since the act was passed, the rate has stood at between 4 and 5½ percent, a rate now considered to be full employment.[5] The act has not been as successful in controlling inflation. At one time a rate of inflation of 3 percent or more (as measured by the Consumer Price Index) was considered too high. However by the late sixties we experienced inflation rates of 6 percent or more and by the mid-1970s it was around 10 percent. The rate for 1974 in particular was very high standing at about 12 percent.

MINIMUM STANDARDS

The level of economic activity is important to ensure rights to jobs and employment. But once employed, what protection did the worker have against low wages, long hours, unsafe working conditions, and other abuses? As we indicated previously, the operation of the labor market did not correct these abuses automatically. Once again government took action to insure certain rights and to protect the public good by passing and enforcing various types of legislation.

State Laws

Some of the earliest legislation to set minimum standards were passed by states just after the turn of the century. These laws were designed to protect women and children from certain abuses.[6] For example, mandatory school attendance laws and laws prohibiting children from working in certain jobs below a specified age (often 14 or 15 years old) were created to keep employers from hiring children, paying low wages, and otherwise exploiting child labor. Similar laws were passed restricting the hours, and types of work for women. For example, it was not uncommon for such legislation to prohibit women from doing certain foundry jobs, from working after dark, or from lifting objects heavier than a certain weight.

This protective legislation was consistently attacked in the courts as unconstitutional on the grounds that it violated the principle of "freedom to contract." These state laws were never widespread having been passed primarily in some industrial states in the north and midwest. For example, the first stringent regulation limiting child labor to eight hours per day was passed in Illinois in 1903, but few laws were enacted in the south, midsouth and east.[7]

Fair Labor Standards Acts Of 1938

The federal government began to be interested in setting certain standards relating to wages, hours, and other protective measures after the turn of the century. Several bills were introduced into Congress but failed to be passed. However, during the depression the Fair Labor Standards Act of 1938 (FLSA), or the Wage and Hour Law, as it is commonly known, was passed and concerns wages, hours, and child labor. As we discussed in Chapter 9, the law has been amended several times since passage to expand its coverage and to raise certain minimums. The law is concerned with establishing minimum wages, maximum hours, overtime pay, equal pay, and child labor standards for covered employment.[8] The law now applies to retail and service employees, farm workers, domestic homeworkers, factory and office workers, universities and colleges, hospitals and nursing homes, laundries, and hotels and motels unless specifically exempted. (At the time of this writing, the U.S. Supreme Court ruled that the law does not apply to state and city governments even though Congress specified it should.)

The law originally established a minimum wage of $.25 per hour which was raised to $2.30 per hour by 1976 for most workers and to $2.00 for farm workers. It also stipulates that any time worked over forty hours in a week must be paid at 150 percent the normal rate (time and one-half for overtime). (This provision, in the original Act of 1938, was originally included so as to spread out the employment opportunities available during the depression.) The 1963 Equal Pay Act which amended the 1938 act stipulates that employers may not discriminate by paying employees of one sex at rates lower than he pays the opposite sex in the same establishment for doing equal work on jobs requiring equal skills, effort, and responsibility performed under similar working conditions. The purpose of this amendment was to prohibit employers from paying women less for similar work performed by male employees. Finally, the law also established minimum ages for various types of occupations. The basic minimum age is sixteen years of age with a higher minimum age of eighteen for employment in nonagricultural occupations declared hazardous by the U.S. Secretary of Labor and a lower minimum age of fourteen for specified occupations outside of school hours.[9]

While this law has just about replaced state child labor laws, state laws are allowed to exist if their standards are higher than federal standards. Even though this law does not address female employment (except for the equal pay provision), most states have repealed this type of protective legislation because of various equal employment opportunity laws passed since 1964. These laws are discussed later in this chapter.

Occupational Safety And Health Act (OSHA) Of 1970

The third field of legislation concerned with establishing minimum standards in the work place is safety legislation. Here, as in child and female protective legislation, certain states passed laws to set minimum health and safety standards soon after the turn of the century. Also, some states and the federal government established certain standards in particularly hazardous fields of employment such as mining. The federal government also had established several safety standards for facilities of commerce such as aviation, shipping, railroads, and highways. However, it wasn't until 1970 when the Occupational Safety and Health Act was passed that comprehensive safety and health standards were established for the vast majority of employers throughout the U.S.

OSHA established a wide variety of safety and health standards for all firms engaged in interstate commerce.[10] The standards are very stringent and precise and affect almost every conceivable operation, process, or piece of equipment used by American industry. Employers have a general duty to furnish employment free from recognized hazards causing, or likely to cause, death or serious physical harm. Employers and employees alike are expected to comply with the standards. The Occupational Safety and Health Administration has the responsibility of enforcing the law and has been given extensive power including on-site, surprise inspections and the authority to fine, imprison, or close down a firm's operations. An employee can also file complaints with OSHA asking for enforcements of the law if he feels that he is being subjected to a hazardous or unsafe work process, condition, or piece of equipment.

PROTECTION FROM ECONOMIC HARDSHIP

In addition to establishing minimum standards at the workplace, government has also attempted to provide for the economic security of employees. These laws and actions attempt to cushion the impact of being without a job for one reason or another and to assist workers in getting a new job if need be. In this section, we briefly examine four primary types of protection provided as follows: workmen's compensation, unemployment insurance, social security, and job location assistance.

Workmen's Compensation

In the past if an employee was injured on the job, he had little chance of collecting monetary damages from his employer. If the injury was serious enough for him to miss work, he was out of luck unless he had a private income insurance plan, which the vast majority of employees did not have. Therefore a system evolved over the years to provide some protection for occupational injuries. This system is known as workmen's compensation.

Prior to workmen's compensation, employees received little, if any, restitution from employers for occupational injuries because of three common law doctrines based on risk and negligence.[11] Under the *assumption of risk doctrine* an employee assumed all of the ordinary risks and hazards of a job when he assumed employment. It was generally held by the courts that an employee fully understood the risks associated with a given job, assumed these risks when he took the job, and therefore could not hold an employer liable.

Under the *contributory negligence doctrine* where the employee was also negligent in an accident on the job he could not hold the employer liable. This held even where the employee's negligence was far less than the employer's in a given instance. Finally, the *fellow servant doctrine* held that if an injury was caused by the actions of another worker the employee could not hold the employer liable.

Obviously, under these three comon law defenses few employees ever collected damages from employers when the employee was injured on the job. Therefore, in view of the abuses perpetuated under these doctrines several states began passing laws to provide a system whereby employees could collect payments to compensate for job injuries. Maryland is generally credited with the first workmen's compensation act which was passed in 1902 and covered employees in mining, quarrying, steam and street railways, and certain construction and excavation jobs.[12] However, the law was declared unconstitutional in 1904. Other states soon passed similar laws including Massachusetts, Montana, and New York. In 1908, the federal government passed a law for certain federal employees, such as those working in arsenals, navy yards, and river and harbor fortification establishments. Soon after, various groups such as the American Bar Association and the National Civic Federation threw their support for workmen's compensation legislation and a host of states enacted such laws.

Today each of the fifty states, the District of Columbia, and Puerto Rico have workmen's compensation legislation. All of these state laws are based upon the principle of liability without fault, but since they are individual state laws their benefit and coverage provisions vary widely from state to state. However, we can summarize these coverages and benefits as follows: (1) one must be an "employee" working in "covered employment"; (2) one can receive benefits only for disabling injuries and sickness, the nature and origin of which are compensable under the law; and (3) one's disability must have resulted from employment.[13] Basically an employee can collect cash or indemnity payments and payments for medical services. More recently states have also provided physical and vocational rehabilitation services (or payments for such services).

Workmen's compensation laws have done much in protecting employees from economic hardship caused by a job injury. When this coverage is coupled with a private group insurance plan often made available to the employee by the employer, workers can also collect additional benefits. These benefits often include a salary for a period of time during which the employee is unable to work.

Unemployment Insurance

Even though several states had passed legislation which provided payments to employees out of work (most notably Massachusetts in 1916) and Wisconsin in 1921), the major impetus for unemployment insurance came about with the passage of the Social Security Act of 1935. This act established a federal state system for paying unemployment insurance. It was an enabling act designed to encourage states to pass their own laws and, second, it provided a set of minimum standards for state laws.[14]

Employees earn coverage by working for a certain length of time in covered employment. The system is financed by a payroll tax on employers. It is administered by the U.S. Secretary of Labor through the Bureau of Employment Security. The states retain considerable autonomy in administering the law on a day-to-day basis. Most states have established bureaus of employment security to administer the law.

Provisions of the law can be changed as need be by both the states and the Federal government. For example, a state can raise the weekly payment (within limits) if its legislature votes to do so. The federal government can extend the period during which benefits are paid from the normal 26 weeks to 39, 52, 64 weeks, or more. For example several extensions were granted during the 1975 recession when unemployment hovered around 9 percent.

In general, unemployment insurance provides the majority of the workforce with income protection they previously did not have. Even though weekly payments are rather low (averaging roughly one-half the average wage paid while employed), a subsistance level of living is provided to get the worker through a rough period until another job can be found.

Job Placement Services

How can the new job be found? In 1933 the federal government passed the Wagner-Peyser Act which established a network of employment exchanges. The intent of this legislation was to provide a system of publically financed employment offices which would be available at no cost to individuals who were out of work and looking for employment. Like unemployment insurance, this job placement service program is a joint federal-state venture. The offices are managed by the states, but the funding and overall policy direction comes from the federal government. Most states have established divisions or bureaus of employment services to administer the local employment offices.

Since the program started during the depression and serves basically unskilled and semi-skilled workers, and since most states require those seeking unemployment insurance to register with the employment office, the offices suffer from an image of "unemployment" or "welfare" offices rather than true job exchange centers. Even though the federal government is trying to upgrade the image of the office by providing computer-based job information systems and by serving higher skilled applicants, there still is much progress to be made. Yet the offices have been fairly effective in providing job location assistance to the lower skilled occupational categories. And, after all, it is usually these individuals who need job placement services most.

Social Security

As we mentioned earlier, the Social Security Act of 1935 created the system of unemployment insurance in the U.S. However, the act is more commonly known for the social insurance program it created. This program is known as Old-Age, Survivors, Disability and Health Insurance or OASDHI. This program is what most people refer to when they say "social security." The program is divided into four parts: (1) Old Age and Survivors Insurance, (2) Disability Insurance, (3) Hospital Insurance, (4) Supplemental Medical Insurance.

Not everyone has full coverage under social security. To receive benefits from all aspects of the program, one must be "fully insured." To receive partial benefits he may be "currently insured." The definitions of these terms have varied over time. However, one is fully insured if he has paid into social security for forty quarters or has reached a certain age by a certain date. For example, persons who reached age seventy-two before 1968 are eligible for minimum monthly payments even though they have never worked in covered employment.

To be currently insured one must be covered by social security in his present or past job but need not have had forty quarters of coverage or meet the age requirement.

The greatest portion of the payments made under the program fall under old age and survivors benefits (OASI). Old age benefits are payments made to a person when he retires. Survivors benefits are benefits paid to his survivors should he die. It's a form of life insurance plan. Benefits paid under disability insurance, hospital insurance, and supplemental medical insurance, while growing, do not constitute the great bulk of payments.

The theory underlying social security is that workers and employers should share the cost of these benefits by paying premiums as in any other insurance program. The program differs from the common definition of welfare since premiums are paid into a fund, and workers earn their rights to coverage.

The Social Security Act of 1935 and especially its amendments have done much to protect workers and their families from economic hardship. Total reliance on individual resources and the operations of the free labor market had caused many problems in our society. However with the passage of social security legislation, workers in the U.S. now enjoy a far greater amount of income protection than most would have thought possible just forty years ago.

EDUCATION AND TRAINING

Even though our country has provided tax supported, public education to our citizens from kindergarten through college for many years, the concept that specific occupational training should be provided at public expense is relatively new. Public instruction has been available at the college level in various professional fields such as law, medicine, and business for many years, but the cost of this education was shared by the state and the individual and only a very small percentage of the individuals desiring such education were able to receive it because of limited funding and facilities. Thus, these programs tended to draw individuals primarily from middle and upper income groups who had the influence and money to enter the school and then pay their portion of the cost (tuition).

State land grant colleges began changing this as studies were added in agricultural and other fields so individuals could obtain the necessary professional education. Still, most of the funding for the programs came from state governments and individuals had to share in the costs. Education was still pretty much based on the philosophy of individual and state initiative with a relatively minor amount of federal government involvement. Those who were qualified and motivated for advanced training were able to receive it—if space was available and if they had the money for tuition, books, and living expenses.

Of course, many did not receive such education and in the absence of it possessed few, if any, job skills upon graduation from high school. This fact became a matter of national concern in the late fifties for various reasons. Sputnik scared us. Would the Russians beat us in the space race and eventually overpower us both technologically and economically? Furthermore, were our children receiving the proper type of education to prepare them for productive and rewarding jobs?

These questions, plus the nagging problem of a national unemployment rate thought to be too high (about five to seven percent in the late fifties and early sixties), prompted the federal government to look at job and occupational training and education as a national problem requiring action at the federal level. This action was manifested in a series of acts passed in the sixties to enhance the skills—and hence the employability—of people in the labor market. Three types of legislation were passed: (1) manpower training and development, (2) vocational education, and (3) aid to elementary, secondary, and higher education.

MANPOWER TRAINING AND DEVELOPMENT

The impetus for this type of legislation originally came about because of a concern over skill obsolescence brought about by automation. This obsolescence was causing a certain amount of structural unemployment in the labor market. Jobs were available, people were unemployed, but a mismatch was occurring between the skill requirements of the jobs and the skills of the people who were unemployed.

The first act passed to rectify this situation was the Area Redevelopment Act of 1961 which provided job training to individuals in Appalachia (primarily displaced coal miners) who were having difficulty in obtaining jobs. However, the major training and development act is the Manpower Development and Training Act of 1962 (MDTA) which has subsequently been amended and enlarged several times since its initiation. MDTA originally focused on providing job skills to adult workers. However, the focus changed with the "Great Society" programs of the Johnson Administration to provide not only job skills, but also general employment orientation, such as counciling, basic education, and communication skills, to the disadvantaged including teenagers. The Employment and Training Administration (formerly the Manpower Administration) of the U.S. Department of Labor administers the act and offers both institutional (classroom) and on-the-job (OJT) learning experiences.

Many other programs were passed in the sixties and early seventies. Some of these programs were decreased in scope, funding, and authority by the Nixon administration and some of the functions were transferred to the states and local area manpower councils under revenue sharing. However, the major programs include the following:

1. The Neighborhood Youth Corps—Provides work and income for students of high school age from low-income families.
2. The Job Corps—Provides preparation for youth who have left school in either job skills or basic education skills so they may resume school.
3. The Work Incentive Program—Provides training or work for welfare recipients (other than mothers with young children).
4. The Public Employment Program—Encourages state and local governments to hire unemployed workers by providing a federal subsidy covering part or all of their wages for a specified period.

Under the Comprehensive Employment and Training Act of 1973 (CETA), the major responsibility for administering manpower development and training programs rests with state and local government through area manpower councils. These councils receive requests for funding of various programs, including those listed above, in their local areas and then allocate funds on the basis of priority, need, and program effectiveness. CETA has decentralized the operation of manpower training and development to local areas on the theory that they can better spend the funds since they know their local requirements. Overall policy direction and guidance is provided by the Employment and Training Administration in Washington and various reporting procedures to Washington have been instituted as control measures to ensure that the funds are spent effectively.

VOCATIONAL EDUCATION

Manpower programs have dealt primarily with unemployed and disadvantaged members of the community. Vocational education programs attempt to provide job skills primarily to youth who are not disadvantaged. Although adult workers and some disadvantaged individuals enroll in vocational programs, these groups have not been the primary focus of the programs.

High schools and some private schools have traditionally provided vocational education to the youth of this country. However, there was no conscious effort to ensure that job skills being taught would be those required of a technologically complex society. With the passage of the Vocational Education Act of 1963 and its 1968 amendments, this situation has improved considerably. Federal appropriations for vocational education were increased substantially, and strong encouragement was provided to existing and new schools to make their curricula job relevant for the future. New schools, such as post-secondary, two-year area technical schools were funded, and new programs for existing schools were established.

Since the passage of the 1963 act and its amendments, enrollments in vocational education programs have increased substantially, particularly in the two year post-secondary schools. Adult enrollment has also increased. In addition enrollments in growing occupations of the future, such as computer and electronic technicians, have increased while enrollments in the traditional vocational education fields of agriculture and home economics have declined.

Public expenditure in manpower and vocational training has been justified on an investment basis. Several studies have been conducted indicating that returns on educational expenditures are quite high—often higher than other investments that could be made with the same expenditure.[15] The federal government has placed a high priority on skill training and has realized that when left strictly to individual initiative and resources, necessary skill training needed in a technologically complex, dynamic economy often does not take place.

ELEMENTARY, SECONDARY AND POST-SECONDARY EDUCATION

Additional financial support has been provided to educational institutions through the Educational Acts of 1964 and 1965 and subsequent amendments. This support is provided for the construction of new facilities, the purchase of teaching equipment and materials, and for special programs for slow learners and high achievers. The primary thrust of these acts is to provide support for programs in basic, college, and professional education rather than for specific job skill training. The rationale is that people need a strong educational foundation which will assist them in functioning as literate, concerned individuals in a democratic society. As a result of this, their job and occupational opportunities are likely to be expanded even though the purpose of this legislation was not to provide specific job skills.

EQUAL EMPLOYMENT OPPORTUNITY

In the past, certain employees with necessary training, education, and job skills still found themselves unable to obtain satisfying jobs because of other reasons such as their race, sex, or age. These factors, which have nothing to do with their potential job performance, often were used as criteria by employers to ensure that certain privileged jobs went to certain groups and that other groups were relegated less desirable jobs.

Employment discrimination based on factors other than job-related characteristics exact a heavy toll on U.S. society. This toll is economic, psychological, and sociological. Poverty, high crime rates, lost productivity, unemployment and underemployment, welfare, lost tax revenues, dispair, anomie—all are costs of discrimination. When discrimination is practiced consistently against certain groups such as blacks, women, and older workers, it is especially harmful to a society since the resultant discrimination becomes so institutionalized in the society that people practice discrimination without even realizing it. Attitudes become hardened, generally accepted, and are never questioned. Social institutions and processes perpetuate the discrimination. "Women should be secretaries and never doctors because they are better at typing and aren't smart enough." "Blacks can do strong physical work but little that requires mental effort." "A younger worker is more ambitious and aggressive, and thus will do a better job than older workers." These are but some of the once commonly accepted beliefs seldom questioned by people in our society.

Obviously, any governmental action to overcome these attitudes and institutional arrangements which perpetuate discrimination would have little success unless it was comprehensive and strongly enforced. Elimination of job discrimination would be difficult unless discrimination in education, training, housing, voting, and health care were also eliminated.

The first efforts toward eliminating employment discrimination were taken by the federal government through presidential executive orders. Executive orders are quasi-legislative pronouncements that have the force of law and can be issued by the president in certain limited areas. In the thirties, Roosevelt issued an order prohibiting racial discrimination in federally financed public works programs. During WW II this order was extended to employers in war industries. After the war and through the fifties, executive orders were issued which prohibited discrimination in the armed forces, federal employment, and in defense contract work. Additional orders later extended coverage to all federally funded government contract work, such as road construction, and to sub-contractors as well as prime contractors.

However, these executive orders, while having some effect, did not significantly reduce racial discrimination. It was not until the landmark 1964 Civil Rights Act and Order 4 (revised) were passed that the federal government took comprehensive action. Title VII of the Civil Rights Act prohibits discrimination based on race, religious belief, ethnic group, or sex in all aspects of employment—selection, promotion, tenure, discharge, discipline, etc. It covers employers engaged in interstate commerce with twenty-five or more employees. The Equal Employment Opportunity Commission (EEOC) was established to enforce the law and through a series of amendments to the act, the commission was given greater enforcement powers.

An additional regulation known as Order 4 (Revised) issued in 1970 specifies Affirmative Action requirements for contractors (including cities, counties, state and private universities) with fifty or more employees and a government contract of $50,000 or more. Affirmative Action requires employers to develop employment goals and timetables for the employment of minorities in job categories where they have been underutilized. Order 4 is enforced by various offices of civil rights or of contract compliance within each of the major federal departments.[16]

In the meantime, the Age Discrimination in Employment Act of 1967 was passed to prohibit discrimination toward workers over forty years of age. Many states have also passed Fair Employment Practice Acts (FEP) to cover employees employed in firms engaged in intrastate commerce. Also in 1963, the Equal Pay Act amended the FLSA to prohibit the payment of a differential wage to women engaged in the same jobs as men as we discussed in Chapter 9.

In addition to this legislation, the federal government has also passed legislation to attempt to eliminate discrimination in education, training, housing, and health care. While a discussion of this legislation is beyond the scope of this book, it is important to realize that deeply rooted attitudes and behavior in our society usually pervades all of our institutions. In order to correct job discrimination, discrimination in education, housing, and other institutional areas also needs to be corrected, and action has been taken to attempt to achieve this correction.

The current issue in equal employment opportunity is the affirmative action concept. The debate is whether the goals and time tables required for minority group employment in under-represented occupations are indeed quotas. If they are quotas, then the implication is that minorities and women should be hired and promoted to "fill the quota," regardless of their present or potential qualifications. Of course quota hiring of this nature does a disservice to the employing organization and to the individual involved. However, a strong case can be made for goals and time tables if they are viewed simply as are other management goals frequently established in production, finance, and marketing. They are targets to be reached, but not at all costs. They serve as the basis for program development. They guide managerial action.

Using this approach, programs can be developed to recruit and train members of minorities based upon their *qualificability*. That is, they may not be presently qualified for a job but through both on the job and classroom training, they can learn the skills and knowledge required in the job. This type of approach is needed if the vicious cycle of discrimination is to be broken, and if all individuals are to be allowed to exercise their employment rights based upon their present and potential skill and knowledge and not their age, race, ethnic group or sex.

EMPLOYEE ORGANIZATIONS AND UNIONS

The final issue with which we deal in the industrial jurisprudence area is employee organization. Once again, we do not deal with all the specific details of union-management activity nor with all of the details of labor-management law. However, as with previous issues we discuss unionization from the perspective of due process. We attempt to answer the question: how do employee organization and unionization protect the employee's rights at the workplace?

As we pointed out earlier in this chapter, employees had little real individual bargaining power in the labor market when faced with the massive resources of large employers. However, as a group acting in concert, they could exercise some influence over employers simply by their sheer numbers. An employer could refuse or ignore the demands for higher wages from one or two employees, but when all employees acting together demand higher wages, he had better listen or find himself without a workforce. The bargaining power of the individual employee was enhanced by the concept "in unity there is strength."

EARLY UNIONIZATION ATTEMPTS AND
THE LEGAL RESPONSE

Early attempts at unionization met with limited success. The courts ruled in *Commonwealth vs. Hunt* (1842) that unions were not criminal conspiracies *per se* but their legality depended on whether their ends were legal. Unions which organized around a craft and did not attempt to reform the economic and social system of the U.S. made some headway. These unions could collectively withdraw their prized labor market skills if need be by striking, and an employer would have some difficulty in replacing the employees.

Early attempts at organizing industrial workers and unions which espoused radical economic and social reform met with little success. Industrial workers were plentiful and any radical economic or social philosophy was not understood by the average worker and was characterized as communistic or even traitorous by employers and government. These unions would experience some growth during prosperous times but had a very difficult time of it during periodic depressions that hit the country when there were plentiful supplies of unskilled and semiskilled workers.

The Court Injunction

A particularly successful technique used by employers and sanctioned by the courts to break up union activity was the injunction. An injunction is a court order issued to compel a party to take a certain action or to refrain from taking such action. Such court orders were easy to obtain by company lawyers early in the labor movement and were used to break up strikes, picketing, and organizational activities. The theory behind the issuance of such injunctions rested on the legal doctrine of *equity*. This doctrine applies where a given action will cause irreparable harm which no amount of financial compensation in a legal suit will "make whole" or repair. Concerted employee action was viewed as causing irreparable harm to the property rights and the right to do business of the owners.

Sherman And Clayton Acts

The injunction received even greater use under the Sherman and Clayton Acts. The Sherman Act of 1890 was passed to break up business monopolies and trusts. However, it was initially used almost exclusively to break up unions since they were viewed as monopolies "in restraint of trade." The passage of the Clayton Act in 1914 sought to exclude unions from prosecution under the Sherman Act, but the U.S. Supreme Court in the *Duplex Case* (1921) served to simply reaffirm the courts' earlier decisions on prosecution of unions.

Railway Labor Act Of 1926

Since railroads were viewed as facilities of commerce, Congress and the courts viewed this as a legitimate area of federal regulation under the interstate commerce clause of the U.S. Constitution. Thus, when Congress passed legislation authorizing the right of railway workers to organize and bargain collectively, this act was upheld by the courts as a valid regulation of interstate commerce. This law, therefore, became the first federal legislation guaranteeing the right of collective bargaining to a group of workers, even though this was a limited group in society.

Norris-La Guardia Act Of 1932

This act, passed during one of the bleakest periods of the depression, was the first major piece of federal legislation that made it easier for the vast majority of workers to unionize. The act did essentially two things: (1) it made the court injunction much more difficult for an employer to obtain, and (2) it outlawed "yellow dog contracts." Yellow dog contracts, often used by employers, required an employee to sign a contract as a condition of employment agreeing never to advocate or join a union as long as he worked for the employer. Needless to say, the widespread use of these contracts was a severe limitation on employee unionization activity.

LATER UNIONIZATION ATTEMPTS
AND THE LEGAL RESPONSE

As indicated elsewhere in this book, the depression of the thirties was an extremely difficult period for the U.S. During this time the U.S. experienced major social change, often brought about through federal legislation, in an effort to break out of the depression. In particular one type of change attempted was to bring about harmonious labor-management relations. It was reasoned that if this could be obtained, management and labor would be able to devote their energies to the task at hand—that is, work and productivity rather than battling each other in the streets and the courts. Harmonious labor-management relations would help pull us out of the depression.

It was with this in mind that Roosevelt supported, and Congress included, a major labor provision in the National Industrial Recovery Act of 1933. This provision guaranteed employees the right to organize and bargain collectively with employers over wages, hours, and other terms and conditions of employment.

The act, however, was soon declared unconstitutional by the U.S. Supreme Court on the basis that it was an invalid regulation of interstate commerce. Efforts were soon made to extract the labor provisions of the act and to repass them in a separate law. This was soon done.

National Labor Relations Act Of 1935 (Wagner Act)

What resulted was the Wagner Act, which, for all practical purposes, legalized unions and collective bargaining throughout the U.S. The law soon became known as labor's *magna charta* after the *Magna Charta* of England. The act guaranteed the rights of employees to form, join, assist, bargain collectively, and take other mutual aid or protection with regard to wages, hours, and other terms and conditions of employment. It established the use of the petition and the secret ballot election as the means to decide if employees wanted a union. For the first time a legal definition of employer, employee and supervisor was provided. This was important because employers claimed supervisors were employees and thus eligible to join the same union and be in the same collective bargaining unit with employees. Employers thus would infiltrate supervisors into union activity and encourage them to work against organization activity.

The law also made illegal certain activities of employers labeled as *unfair labor practices*. For example employers were prohibited from interfering with employee rights to organize; from discriminating against union members in hiring, firing or tenure; and from refusing to bargain collectively in good faith. The National Labor Relations Board (NLRB) was established to administer the law and to regulate union-management affairs.

In the *Jones and Laughlin Steel Case* of 1937, the U.S. Supreme Court upheld the Wagner Act as a valid regulation of interstate commerce. Employee rights to organize and bargain collectively, if they so choose, had now become legalized, in effect, by the federal government. Employees were finally guaranteed a means to enforce certain rights at the workplace that they previously were unable to enforce.

Labor Management Relations Act Of 1947 (Taft-Hartley)

This law, passed soon after the close of WWII, was actually an amendment to the Wagner Act. The purpose of the law was to correct some perceived abuses on the part of unions and attempted to balance the scale of power between management and labor. The Wagner Act gave much power to labor, and union membership grew tremendously during the 1935–1947 period.

Taft-Hartley, in attempting to balance this power, placed some restrictions on union activity. The unfair labor practices prohibited for unions included refusal to bargain in good faith, discriminating among members of the same bargaining unit, and establishing hot cargo agreements and secondary boycotts against employers with whom the union had no direct bargaining relationship. Also prohibited were the charging of excessive initiation fees, featherbedding (receiving pay for time not worked), and jurisdictional disputes, which were actions attempting to force an employer to assign work to one union or group of employees over another. Unions were also prohibited from bringing pressure on an employer to bargain with a union not certified or to picket for certification within twelve months of a valid election.

The law also reinstituted the use of the injunction under certain circumstances and provided for the use of the eighty-day "cooling-off" period whereby workers could be ordered back to work for eighty days in presidentially declared national emergency strikes. Finally, the law prohibited the closed-shop (where employees had to be a member of a union before being hired), except in certain circumstances in certain industries such as construction. The law also allowed the union shop (where employees had to join a union after being hired), except in those states that specifically prohibited it.

Labor-Management Reporting And Disclosure Act Of 1959 (Landrum-Griffin)

The last major piece of labor legislation discussed here also amended the Wagner Act by attempting to provide greater protection for the individual employee's rights in dealing with his union. Union members were provided with a bill of rights in election procedures including certification elections and election of union officers. Requirements for the public reporting of union officers' salaries and possible conflict of interest situations were also strengthened.

Summary Of Labor Legislation

Thus, the three major pieces of labor legislation—Wagner, Taft-Hartley, and Landrum-Griffin—were passed in an attempt to balance the power of the three parties to the union-management relationship. Employees were guaranteed rights to organize and bargain collectively with their employers, which gave much power to employees and their unions. Some of this power was restored to management under Taft-Hartley through provisions restricting union activity. Individual employees were given protection for their rights in dealing with their union under Landrum-Griffin.

This approach of federal legislation in laying out the rules of the game to attempt to maintain a balance of power among the parties involved follows the approach the government has taken in most other conflict areas. The basic philosophy is to write and enforce the rules of the game and to let the parties work out their difficulties within these rules without government interference. This is why the eighty-day cooling off clause has been used so infrequently since its passage. This is also why compulsory arbitration as a means to settle contract negotiation disputes has never caught on in the private sector and why federal mediation and concilliation in contract disputes is generally provided only at the request of the parties involved.[17]

DUE PROCESS AT WORK

We have been discussing various measures which have been taken primarily by the federal government to enforce and protect employee work and job rights. We next need to examine the way in which our system allows for complaint resolution and justice when these rights are violated by employers. How do employees "make themselves whole" when their rights have been violated? What system exists to adjudicate alleged violations of employee rights?

Basically, depending on the situation, employees have three primary options open to them if they feel their rights have been violated by the employer: (1) they can bring the issue directly to the employer for restitution; (2) they can appeal to a government regulatory agency; or they can (3) file suit in court. The most commonly used methods are the first two, and our discussion will focus on these.

DEALING DIRECTLY WITH EMPLOYER

As indicated several times in this and the last chapter, employees have always had the option of seeking restitution for the violation of an employment right directly from the employer. However, because of the very great difference in bargaining power between the two, most employees are at a considerable disadvantage when dealing with employers. It wasn't until unionization that employees obtained the necessary power to deal effectively with employers.

The most common way employees seek restitution is through the *grievance process,* which is a method of adjudicating a complaint usually spelled out in the agreement or contract which governs the union-management relationship in a particular organization. In most unionized organizations, grievances and the use of the grievance process are limited to alleged violations of specific classes in the contract. However, in some organizations, including nonunion companies, grievances can be filed on any issue, and they are adjudicated through a formal grievance procedure. Yet because of the imbalance in bargaining power, the grievance process is usually effective only in union situations where the union acts as an agent in representing the employee's interests.

Most grievance procedures in unionized firms allow for a three or four step process with outside arbitration being the final step. Generally an employee first brings his grievance to the attention of his immediate supervisor. Most grievances are settled here to the employee's and company's satisfaction. However, some go to the second step, which is usually an appeal to the department head and may include the union shop steward. Even fewer go to a third step, which usually involves the industrial relations director, personnel manager, or plant manager of the operations and the president of the union local. The final step, and very few of the total grievances actually reach this stage, is arbitration. Here an outside neutral third party is brought in to settle the grievance. His award then becomes binding on both parties and, even though it is appealable to the courts, it seldom is. In those cases where an arbitrator's award has been appealed, the courts have almost universally refused to over-rule the arbitrator's decision.[18]

Arbitration

Arbitrators are professional third party neutrals who may be lawyers, professors, or former company or union officials. Most are members of the American Arbitration Association or the Federal Mediation and Concilliation Service Panel of Arbitrators. The parties generally agree to the person who will be the arbitrator in a particular grievance hearing. Arbitrators are like a judge and hold a quasi-jurisdictional hearing where both parties are represented in the hearing. They then rely on the wording in the contract and common employer practices in determining their award. Arbitrators have a good deal of authority and in certain cases can order payment of back pay and reinstatement as part of the settlement. However, arbitrators do not fine, imprison, or otherwise penalize employers or employees for violations.

The most common types of grievances brought to arbitration involve discipline and discharge. Management has the duty in the employment relationship for maintaining law and order either under the collective bargaining agreement or under company policies, rules, and regulations. The worker has the obligation to adhere to the agreement, policies, rules, and regulations. The best way for management to maintain law and order is through worker self-discipline. Employees adhere to the regulations because they feel that they are just, proper, and benefit the work relationship. Discipline thus becomes self-discipline or "positive discipline."[19]

However, there are instances when management takes direct action to penalize an employee because he has violated a regulation. At times this penalty takes the form of discharge—"the capital punishment" of the employment relationship.

The grievance process and arbitration play a particularly important role in discipline and discharge cases since under most contracts, employees lose all seniority rights they've built up in an employment relationship when discharged. As we'll see later, seniority serves as the foundation for many employment rights and benefits.

Since discharge is such a severe penalty in today's industrial society, arbitrators have been particularly careful and thorough in the hearing of discharge cases. Professor J. Fred Holly, after examining 1,055 discharge arbitration cases, formulated eight principles which are widely used by arbitrators for handling these cases.

1. Policies must be known as reasonable.
2. Violation of policies must be proven, and the burden of proof rests with the employer.
3. The application of rules and policies must be consistent:
    a. Certain employees cannot be singled out for discipline.
    b. Past practice may be a controlling consideration.
4. Where employees are held to a standard, that standard must be reasonable.
5. The training provided employees must be adequate.
6. The job rights of employees must be protected from arbitrary, capricious, or discriminating action.
7. Actions must be impersonal and based on facts.
8. When the contract speaks, it speaks with authority.[20]

As you can see, the application of these principles to individual cases is difficult and allows for a rather large amount of discretion and judgment on the arbitrator's part. However, the guidelines do provide a basis whereby the arbitrator can act to provide fair and equitable treatment in the protection of employee rights.

Seniority

Many rights and benefits, which accrue to employees under union contracts, accrue because of a worker's seniority. The criteria for accruing seniority can differ from contract to contract. For example, there can be company, plantwide, departmental, occupational, or position seniority. A person's seniority in the department might be different than his seniority with the company.

Seniority is usually tied to such issues as layoff, recall, pension benefits, vacations, job bidding rights, and promotion. In some cases, departmental seniority might apply, as is often the case in job-bidding rights; in other cases, company seniority applies as in the case of vacation time earned. Workers earn *protective* seniority which establishes the relative job rights of employees in layoff and recall. They also earn *seniority of opportunity* which involves job promotions and transfers. And they earn *seniority of privilege* which establishes worker's relative claim to wage supplements and worker insurance and income continuity benefits, such as pensions.[21]

Seniority serves to limit management discretion in these areas by substituting an objective criterion for management judgment. This criterion—length of service—becomes the critical factor in determining many personnel-related decisions in a unionized situation.

Seniority also does something else for the worker. It lays his claim to job rights. He actually develops a quasi-legal right to his job through seniority. This right approaches the rights one possesses through the ownership of private property. John R. Commons, an economist who assisted in developing the institutional school of economics, argues that the courts have ruled in several cases that a man's calling—his labor, his occupation—is indeed his property. Property is not merely physical objects but expected earning power.[22] Seniority protects this expected earning power in the organization and for this reason plays a very strong role in the protection of worker rights under collective bargaining agreements.

APPEAL TO A GOVERNMENT ENFORCEMENT AGENCY

Often times an individual employee may find it inappropriate to bring certain complaints to his employer through his union. This is particularly so regarding issues not covered by the contract. He also may find little satisfaction in bringing his complaint directly to his employer without having the union represent him on this issue. Therefore, employees have appeal to another set of adjudicating bodies: federal and state agencies which enforce various pieces of legislation dealing with issues at the workplace.

In our previous discussion in this chapter, we identified numerous federal agencies which administer the various employment laws. In this section, we do not reiterate the function and purposes of these agencies but will simply highlight some of their operations.

Most government agencies in the employment area rely on individual complaint for the initiation of government activity. For example, if an individual feels that he has been discriminated against because of his race, he can file a complaint with the Equal Employment Opportunity Commission (EEOC). The commission will first attempt to resolve the complaint through the state human relations or human resources commission, should one exist in the state where the complaint originated. If it cannot be resolved at this level, then the EEOC will take action usually starting with concilliation and perhaps ending with a court injunction.

The National Labor Relations Board (NLRB) also relies on individual complaints for the initiation of action on unfair labor practices. The same is true of the Wage and Hour Division of the U.S. Department of Labor in resolving issues related to wage and hour law.

However, in two areas government enforcement has become more aggressive and does not rely as heavily on individual complaint. The Occupational Health and Safety Administration (OSHA) conducts unannounced inspections of operations to determine safety and health violations. They also will respond to individual employee complaints on an alleged violation. Also the various offices in federal departments, such as the Office of Civil Rights in the U.S. Department of Health, Education, and Welfare, and the Office of Contract Compliance in the General Services Administration, require government contractors and subcontractors to file affirmative action plans. These can be required even though no one in the organization has claimed he has been unjustly discriminated against.

The trend is toward stronger government enforcement and involvement in all of these areas. In particular, recent amendments to the 1964 Civil Rights Act have strengthened the EEOC enforcement powers considerably and have extended the coverage of the act. The commission can now seek court injunctions to enforce its decisions in a wide variety of firms including businesses, universities, and hospitals.

Of course, many businessmen decry this increasing scope of government authority as a violation of our free enterprise system. However, as we've pointed out several times before, government will continue to take such action as long as the problems exist and as long as actions of employers in the labor market do not work to alleviate such problems.

The action that can be required of employers by these agencies is essentially one of making the wronged employee(s) whole again and of preventing such action on the part of the employer in the future. Seldom do the agencies levy heavy fines on or imprison the employer. However, lately some employers, most notably AT&T, have been required to compensate all affected employees in a class who had been discriminated against in the past. This "class action" type of restitution can be quite expensive for an employer and may become a more common form of government action. Generally the employer is required to undertake any of the following types of remedies:

1. Hire or rehire the wronged employee(s) with back pay (if appropriate).
2. Cease and desist from continuing the practice which violated the law.
3. Publicize his efforts to the employees admitting his guilt and inform employees of their rights on the issue.
4. Change company policy which led to the violation.
5. In some cases (such as safety and health), pay a fine or cease operations until the violation is corrected.
6. In some cases, pay all employees in a particular affected class a portion of back pay lost as a result of discrimination.

These penalties, coupled with the large amount of publicity which often surrounds a case, generally serve as a deterrent for many employers. The deterrent value of publicity should not be underestimated for in today's era of social responsibility and corporate accountability, most companies are very much concerned about their reputation in the community.

CONCLUSION

This chapter has dealt with the issue of industrial jurisprudence and has addressed the basic issue of employee rights in the labor market and at the workplace and the ways in which these rights are enforced and protected. We've seen that the definition of employee rights has evolved over time and that these rights are concentrated in five major areas: economic and social security, training and education, equal employment opportunity, unionization, and due process.

A list of procedures and government activities have evolved to protect and enforce these rights. Employees can appeal directly to employers either as individuals or through their unions. Through arbitration, they can rely on the judgments of outside neutrals who provide impartial adjudication on issues much faster and less expensively than that which could be provided by courts or government agencies. However, employees still have recourse to several government and some state agencies on various employment issues and to the courts on others.

Notice that in this area of human resource management, there is action in all three environmental areas: macro, intermediate, and micro. At the macro level government and pressure groups bring about legislation; at the intermediate level, specific government regulatory agencies, arbitrators and unions play a role; and at the micro level, the specific union local, the employee and the employing organizations are involved.

In the final chapter of the book, we examine certain activities and procedures that employers can take to enhance the productivity and efficiency of employees. The goal of any employment situation ought to be the achievement of productivity and the protection of employee rights, not productivity at the expense of employee rights. Protection of employee rights and productivity are not mutually exclusive goals, but rather go hand in hand. Both will continue to be required of organizations in the future.

CASE 1
SYLVANIA CITY

Bob Hanington is Public Works Director of Sylvania City. Sylvania is a city of about 80,000 located in Southeastern Tennessee. Recently, Sylvania signed an agreement with the Atlanta Regional Office of the U.S. Office of Civil Rights of HEW that specified the development of an affirmative action plan to upgrade the employment of women, blacks, and American Indians employed by the city. HEW contended that these groups were systematically discriminated against in hiring, promotion, discipline, and discharge and were over-represented in unskilled job classifications and under-represented in skilled and professional job categories.

Bob had held several meetings with the city manager and the city personnel director in an attempt to develop procedures to meet the agreement which had been signed with the Office of Civil Rights. He thought he now understood what was expected of him but was having trouble communicating this information to the managers that worked for him. He was particularly troubled by a meeting he had held yesterday with his immediate subordinates. Out of nine people who report directly to him, two—Jack Perkins and Marv Smith—were particularly outspoken at the meeting.

Bob, therefore, decided to call Jack and Marv into his office to further discuss the implementation of the affirmative action agreement. Jack and Marv arrive at Bob's office and the following discussion takes place:

Bob: Jack and Marv, it's good to see you. I appreciate your coming in to further discuss some points you all raised yesterday. I . . .

Jack: Well, I hope this doesn't take long. We've got a rush job. You know that paving job on. . . .

Bob: No, it shouldn't take long, but it is important. Now, yesterday you both gave me the impression that you were going to stonewall this whole affirmative action thing and I . . .

Marv: No, no, Bob, you misunderstood us. We're all for hiring more blacks and women if they're qualified. The trouble is there are damn few qualified and we're not about to hand them their jobs on a silver platter. They need to earn their good paying jobs as we did and as does everyone else.

Bob: How do you know there are no qualified blacks? We just started the program and already we have over 100 applications on file of blacks who can fill many higher level jobs above unskilled laborer.

Jack: Well, I'd like to see them. If you're talking about Jack Johnson and Fred Jones, forget it. Their high school degree is not worth a plugged nickel. I talked to them yesterday and they can barely communicate.

Bob: Well, I'm not familiar with Mr. Jones and Mr. Johnson, but they may very well be qualified. Personnel has. . . .

Marv: Yeah. Personnel. What do they know? What right do they have to snoop around in our area? Jack and I have been with the city for over fifteen years, as you know. We've been getting along fine without a personnel group and. . . .

Bob: Hell, Marv. We've had a terrible personnel system. Poor records, arbitrary and capricious treatment by supervisors. We're very lucky we haven't had a big law suit or a union. Very lucky.

Jack: Well, Bob, what I resent are these federal bureaucrats telling us what we have to do. It's none of their business who we hire.

Bob: Ah, but it is, Jack. As long as we receive federal funds we've got to abide by federal regulations. And we receive plenty of federal funds under revenue sharing and grants. So I'm asking you two to go along with me and the city manager on this. It's something we simply have to do. I also expect each of you and the other seven superintendents to meet with your respective supervisors and to explain the situation. I'll help you in any way I can.

Thanks for coming by.

Questions

1. What are the major issues in this case?

2. How well did Bob handle the meeting? What should he have done differently?

3. Were Marv and Jack out of place in making an issue over the affirmative action procedures?

4. What should Marv and Jack do now?

5. What should Bob do in terms of follow up?

CASE 2
IN THE PUBLIC SERVICE?

Jack: I've called you three in today because of a problem we're facing. As you know we have been under affirmative action guidelines now for four years. Also as you know, these guidelines are becoming more rigidly enforced. In particular, you know that we're being cited for discriminating against females in several job classifications—middle and upper management, administrative services, and regional office managers. Well, the secretary and I have met several times with Jeff Donnelly of the Atlanta office of HEW, and we've come to an agreement as to what we need to do. Here's what we agreed to. From now on we cannot ask female applicants to state on the application blank their marital status, future marriage plans, the number of children they have, husband's occupation, and their age. We're going to be a pilot operation on this for the rest of the state agencies.

Now we know that this is important information. We don't want to be hiring women managers who are going to be getting pregnant soon and leaving us. We also know that women with pre-school age children have higher absence rates than men. Also, we know that single women will soon be getting married and leaving the agency, either immediately or as their husbands are transferred. Therefore, I'm asking each of you to note the women's marital status, age, and number of children during the employment interview.

Now we've got to be tactful about this. Don't come right and ask them, but get at it in general conversation with the applicant. Make a note of it but keep it in a separate file from their application file. Mark it confidential. Don't even let the secretarial pool type up the information.

I know this all sounds secretive, but we've just got to have this information if we're going to make good hiring decisions.

Burt: Secretive, hell! It sounds illegal to me, Jack. I don't think we should do it.

Bob: Come on, now Burt. I think it's reasonable. We've just got to do this. It costs us a bundle each year because women leave to get married and have children.

Sally: Not all women do. We have many women who have been with our agency for over twenty years.

Bob: Come on, Sally. We're not talking about secretaries and office clerks. We're talking about high priced managers.

Sally: Well, several of our women are administrative assistants making over $10,000 per year. I make more than that and I've been here for ten years.

Bob: Yeah, but you're fifty years old. You're stable. You won't be having any more kids or leaving to get married.

Sally: Bob, you're stereotyping. All young women aren't out to get married or have half a dozen kids. Let's just judge each individual on work potential not on age, sex, marital status or the number of children. Ours is the largest state agency. We employ about 40,000 people statewide, yet we have less than 1 percent women in managerial or professional jobs paying more than $10,000 per year. We ought to set a better example.

Jack: Hold on, hold on, Sally and Bob. You know we're trying to improve things. There are many things we're implementing like the talent bank and special training programs for women. But we can't invest all these funds in young women and have them quit. We've got to recoup our investment. We've got to start running this operation more like a business and stop wasting the taxpayer's money. Now as head of personnel for this agency, I'm asking each of you to start getting this information on the women you interview.

Sally: More like a business? O.K., then let's stop hiring these retired military types who come to us with their hard-lined military attitudes, stay a few years, do almost nothing, and then retire. Talk about wasting money! Think of all these people who are already semi-retired and who only stay a few years. We'd be better off replacing them with women who appreciate the opportunity and the challenge to manage. There are hundreds of women who would love some of these traditional male jobs and who would do a helluva better job.

Jack: So you're not going to go along with my suggestion, Sally.

Sally: No, I'm not. If the rest of you want to do it, fine. But I think it's clearly unethical and probably illegal.

Jack: O.K., Sally, what do you suggest we do? We just can't ignore the marriage problem. We want good women with management potential but we must have some assurance that they stay with us. What do you suggest?

Questions

1. What are the major issues here?

2. Is Jack's suggestion unethical and/or illegal as Sally maintains?

3. What are the ramifications of implementing Jack's suggestion?

4. What would you suggest if you were Sally?

5. Is there a need to have some assurance of permanency from all people—male and female—before they are hired for a managerial position? How about before they are hired for a clerical position?

6. Is Jack prejudiced? Is he operating on the basis of stereotypes?

7. What would Jack's superior say if he knew of Jack's suggestion?

8. What should the role of a large state agency be in promoting affirmative action and employment opportunities for women?

CASE 3
THE GRIEVANCE

Arbitrator: Now let me get the facts straight in this case. Mr. Grunfeld, you say that the company laid you off when they shouldn't have and violated the contract. In addition you say that the union has not vigorously pursued your grievance. You claim that because you're black you've been treated unfairly by both the company and the union. In addition you claim that the seniority clause in the contract actually discriminates against blacks. Is that right?

Mr. Grunfeld: That's right, your honor. Up until five years ago, few blacks were employed by this company and only in the worst jobs—mostly in the dip room. Well, I've got a lot of seniority in the dip room, yet I was one of the first to be laid off. The company claims my seniority ain't no good.

Mr. Johnson: No, that's not what we claimed. Under the contract you had
(company the option of staying in the dip room or moving to another
representative) department when we opened all of our jobs to blacks. You chose to move to the machine shop. Of course, you knew that all the seniority you had in dip would not transfer to the machine shop. Therefore, when we cut back two months ago, you were laid off because you had the lowest seniority in the machine shop.

Mr. Grunfeld: But it just ain't fair. I've been a good employee for this company. When I finally get a better job in the machine shop, I get penalized. It just ain't fair.

Mr. Johnson: But we're simply following the contract and under the contract your layoff is justified.

Questions

1. Why might the union not have pursued this grievance vigorously?

2. How do common seniority clauses found in contracts penalize minorities?

3. Does Mr. Grunfeld have a good case?

4. If you were the arbitrator, how would you rule?

5. Should the company attempt to negotiate a different seniority clause next year? Should the union? If so, how should it read?

STUDY AND DISCUSSION QUESTIONS

1. How are human rights related to social values?

2. What are property rights? How does this concept compare to the concepts of job rights and work rights?

3. Why does government protect certain job and work rights for workers? What gives them the authority to so protect?

4. Why was the Employment Act of 1946 passed? What does it attempt to do? Why is it significant?

5. Discuss the wage and hour law (FLSA), the occupational safety and health act (OSHA), workmen's compensation, and unemployment insurance. What is the common theme of all of this legislation?

6. Why should children and teenagers be prohibited from working if they wish? Why should they be forced to go to school until a certain age if they do not wish to? Doesn't such action keep "undesirables" in school who are disruptive to learning?

7. What is "social security"? Why was such legislation passed?

8. What is the purpose and coverage of federal manpower training and development legislation and programs? How has this purpose and program coverage changed over time?

9. Why is employment discrimination based on non-job-related factors dysfunctional for a society?

10. Are affirmative action goals simply quotas? Why do you think that the affirmative action concept was adopted by the federal government?

11. Criticize the following quote:
    People just aren't equal. The federal bureaucrats can do all they want in passing and enforcing legislation to make people equal but it will all fail. Inequality will be always with us.

12. What are the coverages of the major labor-management laws in unionization and collective bargaining?

13. What is due process? What rights do employees have to due process? How can they enforce these rights? What obligations do employers have? What obligation does the federal government have?

14. Criticize the following quote made by a manager of a small manufacturing plant in Alabama:
    I'll be damned if I'll deal with those union agitators. They're communists and gangsters and their action is unAmerican. If I catch any of my employees involved in union activity, I'll fire them. If my workers don't like this philosophy, they can just quit and get a job elsewhere. If the government gets after me, I'll just move my plant or close down. I should have the right to deal with my employees as I see fit without any interference from an outside third party—be it a union or government.

ENDNOTES

1. Adolf A. Berle and Gardener C. Means, *The Modern Corporation and Private Property* (New York: Harcourt, Brace, and World, Inc. 1968), p. 294.
2. For a discussion of the historical events leading to this conclusion, see James W. Kuhn and Ivar Berg, *Values in a Business Society* (New York: Harcourt, Brace, and World, Inc. 1968), pp. 30-58.

3. Harvey H. Wellington, *Labor and the Legal Process* (New Haven, Conn.: Yale University Press 1968), p. 12.
4. For a particularly dramatic account of its effects see Rita James Simon, *We Saw the Thirties: Essays in Social and Political Movements of a Decade* (Urbana: University of Illinois Press).
5. Because of certain structural features and other characteristics of the labor force an employment rate much less than 4 percent is considered to be highly inflationary. See Lloyd Reynolds, *Labor Economics and Labor Relations* (Englewood Cliffs, N. J.: Prentice Hall 1974), pp. 127-138.
6. For example, it is estimated that in 1910 about 2,000,000 boys and girls between the ages of ten and fifteen were "gainfully occupied." See Ross M. Robertson, *History of the American Economy, 2nd ed.* (New York: Harcourt, Brace, and World 1964), p. 386.
7. Ibid., p. 387.
8. U.S. Department of Labor, *Handy Reference Guide to the Fair Labor Standards Act* (Washington, D.C.: U.S. Government Printing Office 1970).
9. U.S. Department of Labor, *A Guide to Child Labor Provisions of the Fair Labor Standards Act* (Washington, D.C.: U.S. Government Printing Office 1969), p. 5.
10. The definition of interstate commerce has broadened considerably over the years. People crossing state lines (motels), receipt of supplies from firms in other states, (even though the finished product is not shipped across state lines), and communicating across state lines can now classify a company as being engaged in interstate commerce.
11. For a more detailed discussion of these see Domenico Gagliardo, *American Social Insurance* (New York: Harper and Brothers 1949), pp. 368-374.
12. Ibid., p. 392.
13. John G. Turnbull, C. Arthur Williams, Jr., and Earl F. Cheit, *Economic and Social Security, 4th ed.* (New York: The Ronald Press Co. 1973), pp. 297-333.
14. For a more detailed discussion, see Ibid., pp. 205-243.
15. See Lloyd G. Reynolds, *Labor Economics and Labor Relations, 6th ed.* (Englewood Cliffs, N. J.: Prentice Hall 1974), pp. 51-64 and 153-157 for a discussion of some of these studies.
16. See William F. Glueck, *Personnel, A Diagnostic Approach* (Business Publications, Inc. 1974), pp. 189-192 and 537-565, for a more detailed discussion of affirmative action programs.
17. For a more detailed discussion of the law, see A. Howard Meyers and David P. Twomey, *Labor and Law and Legislation, 5th ed.* (Cincinnati: Southwestern Publishing Co. 1975).
18. In the *Enterprise Wheel and Car Corporation Case*, the U.S. Supreme Court ruled that the union or a company may not use the courts to set aside an arbitrator's decision. See Arthur P. Sloane and Fred Whitney, *Labor Relations, 2nd ed.* (Englewood Cliffs, N. J.: Prentice Hall 1972), pp. 222-223.
19. For an excellent discussion of this concept and its role in employee relations see James M. Black, *Positive Discipline* (New York: American Management Association 1970).
20. J. Fred Holly, "The Arbitration of Discharge Cases: A Case Study," in Jean T. McKelvey (ed.), *Critical Incidents in Labor Arbitration—Proceedings of the Tenth Annual Meeting, National Academy of Arbitrators* (Washington, D. C.: BNA, Inc. 1957), p. 16.
21. Edwin F. Beal, Edward D. Wikersham, and Philip Kienast, *The Practice of Collective Bargaining, 4th ed.* (Homewood, Ill.: Richard D. Irwin, Inc. 1972), p. 431.
22. For a further discussion of this concept and Commons' argument see William Gomberg, "Work Rules and Work Practices," *Proceedings, Industrial Relations Research Association,* Spring meeting, 1961.

ADDITIONAL READING

Aaron, Benjamin, Paul S. Meyer, John Crispo, Garth L. Mangum, and James L. Stern. *A Review of Industrial Relations Research* Vol. II. Madison, Wisc.: Industrial Relations Research Assoc., 1971.
Bakke, E. Wright, Clark Kerr, and Charles W. Anrod. *Unions, Management and the Public,* 3rd ed. New York: Harcourt, Brace and World, Inc., 1967.
Baratz, Morton S. *The American Business System In Transition.* New York: Thomas Y. Crowell Co., 1970.

Beal, Edwin F., Edward D. Wickersham and Philip Kienast. *The Practice of Collective Bargaining,* 4th ed. Homewood, Ill.: Richard D. Irwin, Inc., 1972.

Berg, Ivar. *The Business of America.* New York: Harcourt, Brace Jovanovich, Inc., 1968.

Chandler, Alfred D., Jr., Stuart Bruchey, and Louis Galambos, ed., *The Changing Economic Order.* New York: Harcourt, Brace, and World, Inc., 1968.

Cohen, Sanford. *Labor in the United States,* 4th ed. Columbus: Charles E. Merrill Publ. Co., 1975.

Davey, Harold W. *Contemporary Collective Bargaining.* 3rd. ed. Englewood Cliffs, N. J.: Prentice Hall, 1972.

Fishman, Betty G. and Leo Fishman. *Employment, Unemployment and Economic Growth.* New York: Thomas Y. Crowell Co., 1969.

Friedman, Milton. *Capitalism and Freedom.* Chicago: Univ. of Chicago Press, 1962.

Galbraith, John Kenneth. *Economics and the Public Purpose.* Boston: Houghton Mifflin Co., 1973.

Gallaway, Lowell, E. *Manpower Economics.* Homewood, Ill.: Richard D. Irwin, Inc. 1971

Ginsburg, Woodrow L., E. Robert Livernash, Herbert S. Parnes, and George Strauss. *A Review of Industrial Relations Research.* Vol. 1, Madison, Wisc.: Industrial Relations Research Assoc., 1970.

Hutchinson, Harry D. *Economics and Social Goals: An Introduction.* Chicago: Science Research Associates, Inc. 1973.

Leviton, Sar A., Garth L. Magnum, and Ray Marshall. *Human Resources and Labor Markets: Labor and Manpower in the American Economy.* New York: Harper and Row, 1972.

Magnum, Garth L. *The Emergence of Manpower Policy.* New York: Holt, Rinehart and Winston, Inc., 1969.

Miller, Glenn W. *Government Policy Toward Labor: An Introduction to Labor Law.* Columbus: Grid, Inc., 1975.

Mund, Vernon and Ronald Wolf. *Industrial Organization and Public Policy.* New York: Appleton-Century-Crofts, Inc. 1971.

Okun, Arthur M. *The Political Economy of Prosperity.* New York: W. W. Norton and Co., Inc. 1969.

Smead, Elmer E. *Government Promotion and Regulation of Business.* New York: Appleton Century Crofts, 1969.

Smelser, Neil J. *Theory of Collective Behavior.* New York: The Free Press, 1962.

Somers, Gerald G. (ed.). *The Next Twenty-Five Years of Industrial Relations.* Madison, Wisc.: Industrial Relations Research Assoc., 1973.

Torres, Juan de. *Government Services in Major Metropolitan Areas: Functions, Costs, Efficiency.* New York: The Conference Board, 1972.

U.S. Department of Commerce and U.S. Dept. of Labor. *The Social and Economic Status of Negroes in the U.S.,* 1974. (Washington, D.C.: U.S. Government Printing Office, 1974).

Weber, Arnold R., Frank H. Cassell, Woodrow L. Ginsburg, (eds.) *Public-Private Manpower Policies.* Madison, Wisc.: Industrial Relations Assoc. 1969.

MAXIMIZING HUMAN RESOURCE AND ORGANIZATIONAL EFFECTIVENESS

11

We have discussed some important issues in human resource management. Each of these issues is a critical area of concern for most organizations and needs constant, thorough managerial attention if human resource utilization is to be maximized. In this chapter we present a framework for effectively integrating human resources with organizations so that the performance of people, and therefore the performance and effectiveness of the organization, are maximized. We are concerned with the output and user boxes in our human resources model as shown in Figure 11-1.

The chapter is concerned with creating effective organizational structures and processes conducive to and stimulating for, human resource effectiveness. Within this environment or human resource climate, we will examine specific managerial attitudes, policies, and activities which will result in overall human resource achievement. Organizational structure, processes, policies, and human resource utilization are tied in with a contingency model of human resource management at the end of the chapter.

ORGANIZATIONAL EFFECTIVENESS

How do we judge if organizations are effective in society? How do we know when human resources are used effectively and efficiently? What criteria do we use? These are difficult questions. However, various criteria have been developed to measure efficiency and effectiveness.

EFFICIENCY AND EFFECTIVENESS

While some equate the concepts of efficiency and effectiveness, we make a distinction between the two. *Effectiveness* is concerned with whether a given goal or objective has been accomplished. It answers the questions: was the goal appropriate? and was the goal obtained? It is not concerned with the cost of goal achievement. *Efficiency* is concerned with the cost of obtaining a certain goal but not whether the goal is appropriate to begin with.

Suppose we have a goal of building an interstate highway through the

244

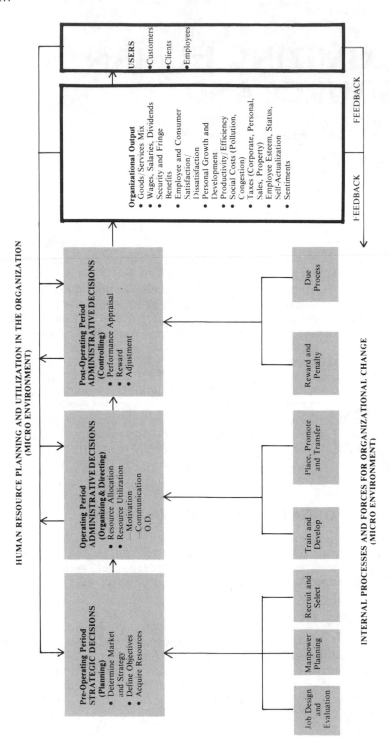

HUMAN RESOURCE PLANNING AND UTILIZATION IN THE ORGANIZATION
(MICRO ENVIRONMENT)

Pre-Operating Period STRATEGIC DECISIONS (Planning)
- Determine Market and Strategy
- Define Objectives
- Acquire Resources

Operating Period ADMINISTRATIVE DECISIONS (Organizing & Directing)
- Resource Allocation
- Resource Utilization
  — Motivation
  — Communication
- O.D.

Post-Operating Period ADMINISTRATIVE DECISIONS (Controlling)
- Performance Appraisal
- Reward
- Adjustment

Organizational Output
- Goods/Services Mix
- Wages, Salaries, Dividends
- Security and Fringe Benefits
- Employee and Consumer Satisfaction/Dissatisfaction
- Personal Growth and Development
- Productivity/Efficiency
- Social Costs (Pollution, Congestion)
- Taxes (Corporate, Personal, Sales, Property)
- Employee Esteem, Status, Self-Actualization
- Sentiments

USERS
- Customers
- Clients
- Employees

FEEDBACK

FEEDBACK

Job Design and Evaluation

Manpower Planning

Recruit and Select

Train and Develop

Place, Promote and Transfer

Reward and Penalty

Due Process

INTERNAL PROCESSES AND FORCES FOR ORGANIZATIONAL CHANGE
(MICRO ENVIRONMENT)

FIGURE 11:1 MAXIMIZING HUMAN RESOURCE AND ORGANIZATIONAL EFFECTIVENESS IN THE HUMAN RESOURCE SYSTEM

center of town within the next two years. If the highway is built within two years and meets all engineering and safety criteria, then we can say that we have been effective. We built the highway in the time forecasted. But if the highway costs twice as much to build than forecasted because we had to redo portions of the road, or because faulty material was used, or because the people we used were not well trained, were slow, and made many errors, then we certainly have not been very efficient. The highway was built, but at twice what it should have cost. We have been effective but inefficient.

Of course we may not even have been effective. Maybe instead of investing ten million dollars in a new interstate, we should have spent it on designing and putting into operation a mass transit system for the city. Maybe the goal was inappropriate to begin with. If this is the case, we have been neither effective nor efficient. This is the worst of both worlds.

The relationship between effectiveness and efficiency is shown graphically in Figure 11-2.

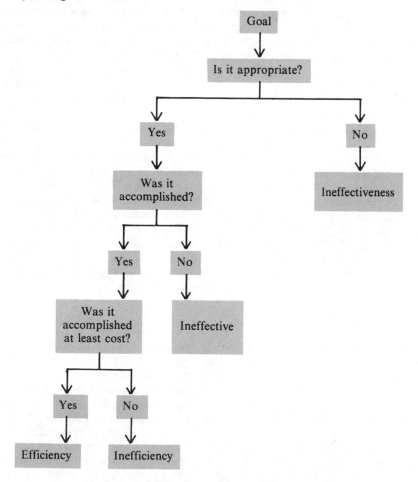

FIGURE 11-2   EFFECTIVENESS AND EFFICIENCY

CRITERIA AND PUBLICS

How do we know if appropriate goals have been set? How do we know if the cost is "least" cost? Criteria to determine the appropriateness of goals rest with the groups who are served by the organization. Chapters 1 and 2 looked at some groups in the macro, intermediate, and micro environments served by organizations. Each of these groups expects something from the organization. These expectations serve as the basis for goal determination.

The groups or publics which organizations serve can be broken down into two classes: those who are prime beneficiaries of the organization's actions and those who are not.[1] The key element in determining whether a group is a prime beneficiary or not is whether it benefits directly from the output of the organization. The prime beneficiary group for a business organization, for example, would be the owners who benefit from portions of the company's profits paid as dividends. For a service organization, such as a government welfare agency, it would be the clients served.

The prime beneficiary concept of an organization as developed by Blau and Scott can be expanded, however, beyond the identification of one major group for each type of organization. Using the micro, intermediate, macro approach developed in Chapter 2 and the task environment concept developed by Dill,[2] we can identify groups in the organization's micro and intermediate environments, which can be considered prime beneficiaries, and those in the macro environment, which are secondary beneficiaries.

Figure 11-3 depicts some of these groups and some of the particular goals each may expect from a business organization. We have not necessarily identified all of the specific groups in each environment, nor have we listed all the goals for each group identified. The intent of the figure is to indicate some of the major influences on organizational goal setting.

Notice that the prime beneficiaries who influence organizational goal setting exist both in the organization's micro and intermediate environment. Owners, employees, customers, distributors, suppliers, and government all have a major input into the setting of organizational goals. Even though government direct regulatory groups (such as the FCC, ICC, CAB, OSHA, EEOC, etc.) are not beneficiaries in the true sense of the word, the intent of their regulatory behavior is to provide a direct benefit for various groups in society.

Groups in the macro environment, even though not prime beneficiaries of a business organization, are affected in varying degrees by the organization's operations. The general public, federal, state, and local governments, competitors and public pressure groups all are affected in different degrees by the operation of a given business organization.

The concept of an organization's task environment also provides a way to determine groups which have a significant impact on the establishment of an organization's goals. The task environment consists of those components in an organizations' environment that are significant or potentially significant for goal setting and goal attainment. Dill identifies customers, suppliers, competitors, and regulatory groups as members of the task environment.[3] In our framework these groups exist in an organization's intermediate and macro environment. To these groups we would

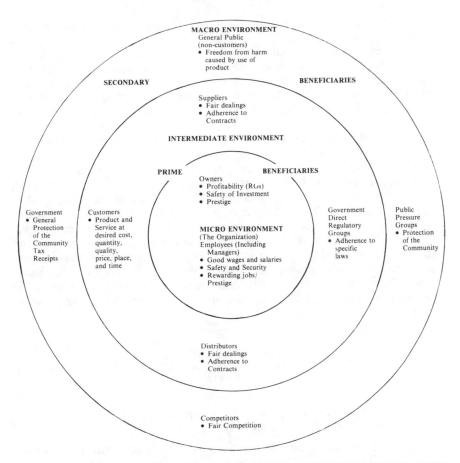

MACRO ENVIRONMENT
General Public
(non-customers)
• Freedom from harm
  caused by use of
  product

SECONDARY   **BENEFICIARIES**

Suppliers
• Fair dealings
• Adherence to
  Contracts

INTERMEDIATE ENVIRONMENT

PRIME   **BENEFICIARIES**
Owners
• Profitability (RUi)
• Safety of Investment
• Prestige

Government   Customers   Government   Public
• General   • Product and   Direct   Pressure
Protection   Service at   **MICRO ENVIRONMENT**   Regulatory   Groups
of the   desired cost,   (The Organization)   Groups   • Protection
Community   quantity,   Employees (Including   • Adherence to   of the
Tax   quality,   Managers)   specific   Community
Receipts   price, place,   • Good wages and salaries laws
                 and time   • Safety and Security
                                  • Rewarding jobs/
                                    Prestige

Distributors
• Fair dealings
• Adherence to
  Contracts

Competitors
• Fair Competition

FIGURE 11-3   SOME GOAL EXPECTATIONS OF PRIME BENEFICIARIES
AND SECONDARY BENEFICIARIES FOR A
BUSINESS ORGANIZATION

add members of the micro environment—owners and employees—as members of the task environment.

IMPACT OF GROUPS ON THE
GOAL SETTING PROCESS

The actual setting of goals for a given organization is done by the managers in that organization. Top management, aided by staff, has the major responsibility of overall goal setting. The top management goal setting process is influenced by the level of delegation in the organization, the permeability of an organization's boundaries, and the crystalization of expectations from prime beneficiary groups in the organization's task environment. To the extent that there exists extensive delegation of authority throughout the organization, permeable organization boundaries, and crystalized expectations from groups in the organization's task environment, this goal setting process of top management will be heavily influenced by significant others.

The pressures on goal setting and attainment from various groups are often conflicting. It is the responsibility of top management to balance these conflicting expectations in developing the final listing of overall goals to be achieved. This balancing act involves conflict and requires compromise. The final list of goals that results should reflect this compromise.

The sample objectives listed in Figure 11-4 reflect this compromise. These objectives were formulated by a division vice president of a large public telecommunications company in the southeastern United States. Notice that the first and fifth objectives relate to achieving a level of profitability specified in budget projections. This will assist in meeting the objective of profitability as desired by top management at the corporate headquarters and as desired by owners (stockholders) of the company. Objectives 2, 3, and 6 relate directly to improving telephone service to customers, thus meeting the expectations of this group. Objectives 4 and 6 relate to improved employee efficiency. Objectives 8 and 9 are designed to meet the expectations of two federal regulatory agencies. The last two objectives are concerned with meeting the expectations of the employees and the general public.

XYZ TELEPHONE COMPANY
SOUTHEASTERN DIVISION OBJECTIVES
FOR 1977

1. To meet operating budget projections through generation of revenues and control of expenses during 1977.

2. To maintain held orders for telephone installation at a reasonable level during 1977.

3. To reduce station installation intervals to a satisfactory level by December 31, 1977.

4. To reduce overtime to a satisfactory level by June 30, 1977.

5. To improve collection of accounts efficiency to a satisfactory level by June 30, 1977.

6. To reduce the trouble report rate on service to a satisfactory level by December 31, 1977.

7. To improve the quality of personnel performance throughout 1977.

8. To meet affirmative action plan objectives for 1977.

9. To meet OSHA and System safety objectives during 1977.

10. To improve employee—employer relations during 1977.

11. To improve company image in the community during 1977.

FIGURE 11-4   SAMPLE OBJECTIVES OF A MAJOR DIVISION OF A PUBLIC TELECOMMUNICATIONS COMPANY

Even though we can make this distinction among groups served by various objectives, it should be noted that all eleven of these objectives are closely related. In some cases they compliment each other. For example, by improving employee performance (objective 7), thereby contributing to reduced overtime (objective 4), the company will be better able to meet the budget and profitability objective (objective 1).

However, some objectives conflict with one another. Strict adherence to quotas regardless of qualifications on the affirmative action plan and to OSHA rules and regulations (objectives 8 and 9) is likely to result in difficulty in meeting the objectives of improved quality of personnel (objective 7) and reduced overtime (objective 4) and, thus, budget and profitability objective (objective 1).

The real meaning of these objectives lies in the way that they are implemented. The programs, policies, and procedures the organization develops to implement these objectives and the resources (people, money, materials) the organization commits to the achievement of each objective, determine the emphasis given the objective and the likelihood that the objective will be achieved.

GOAL SETTING, IMPLEMENTATION AND ACHIEVEMENT

We can summarize this process of goal setting, implementation, and achievement and relate it to a measure of organizational effectiveness as depicted in Figure 11-5. The expectations of prime beneficiary groups in the organization's task environment (customers, suppliers, distributors, owners, regulatory groups, employees) give rise to the establishment of organizational goals. These goals are made specific by operational and staff managers, throughout the organization. Programs or plans of action are developed that will lead to the achievement of these goals. Policies, procedures and rules are developed to carry out the programs. The performance of the organization is examined as it relates to the achievement of procedures, policies, programs and, ultimately, objectives. This, then, gives us a measure of organizational effectiveness and efficiency. If an organization reasonably meets the expectations of significant groups in its task environment, then it has been effective. If it meets these expectations with a minimum expenditure of resources, then it has been efficient.

ORGANIZATIONAL DESIGN AND EFFECTIVENESS

The preceding discussion focused on the development and accomplishment of organizational goals as criteria which are used to determine organizational effectiveness and efficiency. In this section we expand upon material developed in Chapter 7, Organization Development, to suggest ways of designing organizations to maximize effectiveness and efficiency. The focus here is on developing effective organizational structures which facilitate organizational goal achievement and, thus, organizational effectiveness and efficiency. The final section of the chapter examines effective ways to utilize human resource performance within

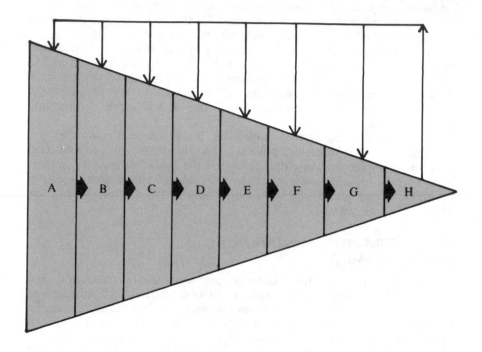

A. Expectations of Prime Beneficiary Groups in Organization's Task Environment
B. Overall Goals Established By Top Management with Input from Succeeding Levels of Management and Staff Groups
C. Specific Goals or Objectives Established By Remaining Levels of Management
D. Programs Designed to Implement Objectives
E. Policies Designed to Implement Programs
F. Procedures and Rules to Carry Out Policies
G. Organizational Performance
H. Organizational Effectiveness and Efficiency

FIGURE 11-5   GOAL SETTING, IMPLEMENTATION, PERFORMANCE AND EFFECTIVENESS

optimum organizational structures to maximize both the human resource performance and, thus, organizational effectiveness.

We can all think of organizations with competent people, noble goals, and sound policies that never seem to accomplish much. This condition usually occurs because of the way the organization is designed. Organizations should be structured or designed to facilitate goal accomplishment and to bring out the best in the people working in the organization. Often this doesn't occur. The structure of the organization actually *hinders* effective organizational performance rather than facilitates it.

Highly bureaucratized, large organizations often exemplify this condition. Originally, bureaucratic organizations connoted effectiveness and efficiency. Max Weber, who wrote extensively on the topic of bureaucracy, saw this concept as a way of improving organizational performance.[4] Chains of command, channels of communication, job descriptions, policies, procedures should be developed to make the organization function more smoothly and thus more effectively. Everyone should know what he is responsible for, to whom he is accountable, and how to handle given situations or problems encountered (procedures).

However, the concept of bureaucracy now has a negative connotation, at least among practicing managers. It connotes not efficiency but inefficiency; not effectiveness but ineffectiveness; not smooth operation, but lumbering, lurching operation.[5] Identifying an organization as bureaucratic today is an insult to the organization. Yet many organizations are, indeed, bureaucratic. This bureaucracy often can be traced to the way an organization is designed or structured.

CHARACTERISTICS OF BUREAUCRACY

While the literature varies as to the precise characteristics of bureaucratic organizations, we can list some commonly identified characteristics. This list reflects commonly held managerial perceptions of bureaucracies, not necessarily those developed by Weber.

1. Many levels of management between top management and operative workers
2. Highly formalized and inflexible rules and procedures
3. Highly formalized and inflexible policy
4. Inability to adequately and rapidly respond to external or internal change
5. Extreme specialization of jobs, particularly at lower levels in the organization
6. High levels of centralization of authority at the top of the organization.
7. Little concern for individual differences among employees or customers/clients of the organization
8. Poor communications, particularly from the bottom of the organization to the top
9. Extreme specialization and wide proliferation of staff positions
10. High emphasis on organizational loyalty, conformity and being a "team player"[6]

Organizations with these characteristics certainly don't foster effectiveness. These organizations are often large, heavily centralized behemoths that weigh heavily on the shoulders of its members with such oppressiveness that individual creativity and job flexibility are severely curtailed.

What can be done to reduce the tendency toward bureaucracy, especially in larger organizations? We pointed out some organizational development strategies and tactics in Chapter 7 that will help to reduce this bureaucracy and, thus, increase organizational effectiveness. These strategies include training and development programs for managers and other employees, changing organizational processes, and designing more effective organizational structures. We don't intend to rehash O.D. strategies previously discussed, but we will revisit the subject of organization design as it relates to effectiveness.

SITUATIONAL THEORIES OF ORGANIZATION DESIGN

There is no one best way for an organization to be designed or structured. The theories which recognize this and account for it in explaining organization design are the *situational theories of organization design.*[7] Situational theories rest heavily on the premise that the environment which an organization faces has a major bearing on the structure of that organization. Organizations which face unstable, highly differentiated environments tend to be structured differently from those which face fairly homogeneous, stable environments. Figure 11-6 depicts the range of organizational structures relating to a range of environments.

Environments which organizations face can be highly *differentiated* or relatively *homogeneous.* A highly differentiated environment is characterized by different classes of customers to be served each with significantly different needs, a diversified technology, perhaps multi-national operations, and having to deal with and meet the laws of various governments in carrying out organizational operations (U.S., foreign, state, city

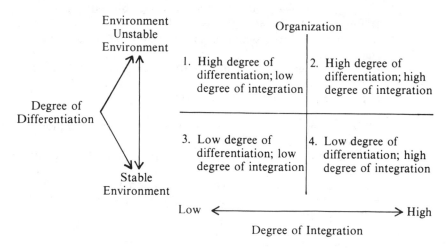

FIGURE 11-6 ENVIRONMENTAL STABILITY AND DIFFERENTIATION AND ORGANIZATION STRUCTURE

Source: D. Hellriegal and J. Slocum, *Management: A Contingency Approach* (Reading, Mass.: Addison-Wesley, 1974), p. 125.

and county). General Motors, through its worldwide operations, faces a highly differentiated environment. Apollo Plastics, which fabricates plastic products and employs about a hundred people located in Tallahassee, does not.

The environment might also be unstable or uncertain. If customer wants and desires, technology, and governmental requirements all change frequently, then the organization is in an unstable environment. This is particularly so if it is difficult to accurately predict the direction, intensity, and time of these environmental changes. A large state governmental agency, such as a department of vocational rehabilitation, faces an unstable environment. Expectations of the public and clients have changed greatly in the last five years. The "technology" of treating mentally and physically disabled persons has changed. Federal and state laws, in dealing with individuals who need rehabilitation, have also changed.

Organizations should structure themselves in response to the degree of differentiation and stability found in the environment. As seen in Figure 11-6, organizations that face a highly differentiated, unstable environment tend to be highly differentiated internally and have either low internal integration or high internal integration of functions. On the other hand, organizations which face a relatively homogeneous, stable environment tend to have low levels of internal differentiation and either high or low levels of internal integration.

Some examples may help in making this concept clearer. General Motors faces a highly differentiated complex environment and tends to have a high degree of internal differentiation and low integration. GM is decentralized along product lines and is better able to respond effectively to changes in its environment. Little integration is needed at the corporate level and most is achieved through the use of top management committees. Hughes Aircraft faces a highly differentiated, complex environment; but because of the nature of product lines, needs to be highly integrated at the top. Changes in contracts over time require changes in the number and types of managerial, professional, and technical people in the organization. To better bring about these changes as old contracts are completed and new ones are begun, high levels of internal integration are needed.

One type of integrative device used by aerospace firms and other companies facing a highly differentiated unstable environment is *matrix management* or *project management*. This concept is also known as product management, program management, task-force management, or system management. (Even though matrix management technically differs from these terms, we will treat the terms as representing the same concept.) Basically it rests on the attempt to integrate various functions required for a given product or project during its life-time. The characteristic of a given project usually requires that diverse organizational functions be brought to bear on the project for a given period of time. Project managers share authority with functional managers during the life of a given project.

Figure 11-7 depicts a project manager arrangement for a large aerospace company. Notice that the project managers report through a group vice president to the general manager of the corporation as does each of the functional managers. However, during the life of a given project,

254

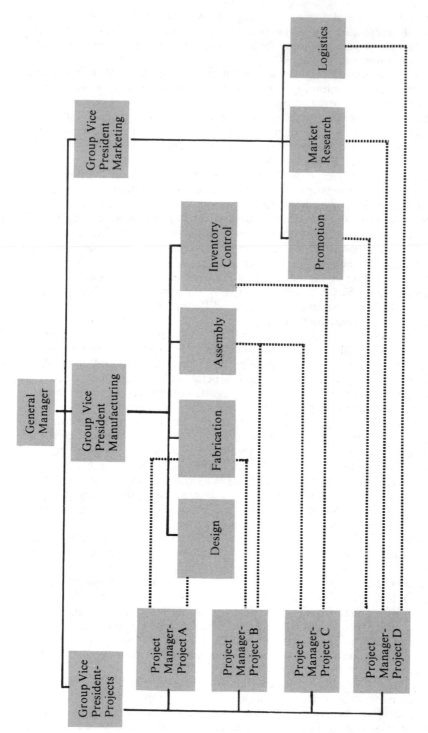

FIGURE 11-7 PROJECT OR MATRIX MANAGEMENT IN AN AERO-SPACE COMPANY

project managers have authority over individuals in functional areas as needed to complete various phases of the project.

Project management gives the organization flexibility in utilizing its resources to meet changing priorities and demands from the environment. However, it is not without its disadvantages. It usually requires frequent movement of people which breaks up friendship groups on the job, neighborhoods, and other established social ties. Individual managers may not be sure who is their immediate superior; thus, a violation of the unity of command principle occurs. Yet, there is much to recommend project management for organizations attempting to achieve integration in a highly differentiated, unstable environment.

The third case involves companies operating in a stable environment with low differentiation, which also have a need for low levels of internal integration. A glassware manufacturer would fit this model. Customer demand for glassware styles and amounts remains relatively stable. The manufacturing process has changed little over the last twenty years. Competitors tend to use the same process and machines in producing the glassware. There is little need for high internal integration since the environment and technology of the situation are so stable.

On the other hand, in the fourth case, a stable, low-level differentiated environment may give rise to organizations with a need for high internal integration. Franchised food operations tend to conform to this level. The industry is in a farily stable environment. Yet to maintain uniform quality and image of product/service offering, a great deal of standardized policies, procedures, and rules emanate from the home office on everything from display to store cleanliness, advertising, and personnel. All operations are standardized and apply throughout all stores.

These four models, then, suggest some design considerations that are appropriate for a given environment faced by an organization. Top management of an organization should attempt to ensure that the organization is designed to best meet the requirements dictated by a given environment. If this is done, chances are improved that the people who work in the organization will be more effective.

TALL VERSUS FLAT ORGANIZATIONS, DELEGATION AND LINE/STAFF

Another design consideration that has a significant impact on organizational and human resource effectiveness involves the degree to which organization structure facilitates delegation. *Delegation* refers to the passing down of decision making authority and accountability to lower levels in the organization, preferably to the point at which the actual task is to be carried out. The opposite of delegation is centralization. Centralized organizations require that all decisions, even minor ones, have to be made by top management.

Centralization can lead to many of the ills which characterize a bureaucracy, when this form of structure is used in an inappropriate environment. People throughout the organization lose their creativity, freedom, and individuality. They feel like robots, routinely following orders which emanate from on high. They're in mind-numbing, boring jobs which give them little opportunity to exercise any initiative. Delegating decision-making authority down through the organization will help in overcoming these ills. Job enrichment programs which are discussed in Chapter 4 essentially rest on the concept of delegation.

Organization structure can facilitate or hinder delegation. Flat organizations with wide spans of control and few managerial levels tend to facilitate high levels of delegation better than tall organizations with narrow spans of control, provided that adequate policy guidance and staff managers exist to facilitate the delegation process. In flat organizations each manager has from eight to fifteen people who report immediately to him. (See Figure 11-8.) There are also few managerial levels between operatives and top management. Since each manager has so many immediate subordinates to coordinate, he is more likely to delegate decision-making power to these subordinates so that they don't have to be constantly checking with him to get something accomplished.

If adequate policy has been developed by top management which set the parameters of decision boundaries, and if organizational goals have been clearly formulated and are understood by all managers, and if adequate staff exists to provide line managers with needed information and analysis, then flat organizations are very conducive to delegation. And organizations with high levels of delegation tend to maximize human resource effectiveness, provided the people are well trained and understand their jobs and provided that the environment encourages such differentiation through delegation.

MAPS, MBO, AND ORGANIZATION STRUCTURE

Recently, a method has been developed called MAPS (multivariate analysis, participation, and structure) which claims to effectively integrate goal setting behavior and organization structure so that an organic-adaptive organization is created.[8] An organic-adaptive organization is one that can respond effectively to environmental requirements and one that is so structured that it brings out the best in its employees. MAPS can be an effective tool to use in organizations that face a heterogeneous, unstable environment, especially if that organization needs to effectively integrate internal functions and operations (Block 2, Figure 11-6).

The MAPS method designs organizations around the tasks required to accomplish organizational objectives and groups people into subunit structures depending upon their preferences about tasks they wish to work on. More specifically, the MAPS procedure is:[9]

1. Members of the organization participate in defining the tasks needed to be carried out in order to accomplish organizational objectives.
2. The total set of tasks is separated into groups or clusters (using multivariate analysis, a statistical technique) so that interrelated tasks are placed together.
3. Members are placed into organizational units and subunits (using multivariate analysis) based upon their preferences about the task cluster assigned the subunit, so that members of each subunit can work well together.

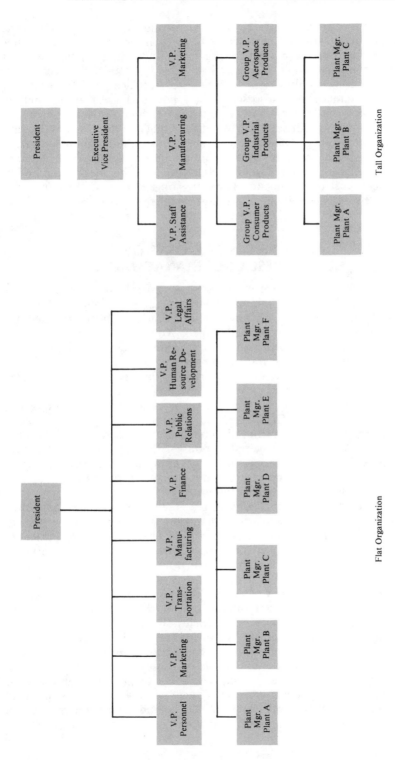

Tall Organization

Flat Organization

FIGURE 11-8 FLAT AND TALL ORGANIZATION STRUCTURE

The major advantage of the MAPS method is that it gives *explicit* consideration to tasks and member preferences in designing organizations to achieve objectives. Probably its greatest disadvantage is the need for organization restructuring as objectives, tasks, and member preferences change. The use of multivariate analysis as a statistical tool for grouping tasks and preferences may also scare away potential users of the method since they may not understand the statistical technique. However, it is a rational, reasonably efficient way to give explicit consideration to task accomplishment and human resource preferences in designing organizations. This will aid organizations in designing structures which enhance organizational and human resource effectiveness. The MAPS method is still in theoretical development. However, some testing of the concept is underway. Its actual usefullness, therefore, still remains to be determined.

CONTINGENCY MODEL OF HUMAN RESOURCE MANAGEMENT

So far in this chapter, we have discussed organizational goals, structure and design as they relate to organizational effectiveness. We have primarily been concerned with how organizations can facilitate effectiveness by the way in which they are designed. Now, we turn to what managers can do within this structure to maximize human resource performance of other managers and of operative employees.

In discussing organization design earlier in this chapter, we referenced the situational theories of organizational design. Actually, these theories are a larger part of a new management theory known as the *contingency theory of management.*[10] The contingency theory or approach to management rests on the concept that different environmental or situational factors require differing managerial responses. It recognizes that there are few principles or rules of management that apply in all cases. The appropriate management style and response depends upon the contingencies of the environment and particular situation.

The development of the contingency theory of management came about to explain the success of some managers who seemed to be managing improperly. Management textbooks would set forth a set of principles or rules to follow to be an effective manager. Yet, observation of real-world managers in organizations would turn up many examples of managers who violated the prescribed rules and yet were effective. Apparently these managers were effective because they were able to use a set of skills required by the particular situation in which they found themselves. They were able to adapt to the contingencies of the environment.

Management academicians began to realize that in the social sciences (of which management is a part), it has been difficult to develop laws and principles which are as valid and reliable as those developed in the physical sciences. We cannot predict with the same degree of accuracy what will happen if a new member is introduced into a group, as physical scientists can predict what will happen if a one-pound weight is dropped from a height of ten feet. Our problem in management has been the inability to:

1. Identify all significant variables which affect a given situation
2. Accurately measure the intensity of these variables
3. Determine which variables are independent, dependent, or covariant (cause and effect relationships)
4. Translate this information into suggested courses for managerial action

The contingency approach helps to overcome these limitations.

One of the earliest writers and researchers in this field is Fiedler who developed a contingency model of leadership effectiveness.[11] After several years of research, Fiedler was able to show that a manager's effectiveness as a leader is determined by the interaction of an employee's orientation with three variables:

1. The degree to which leader-member relations are good
2. The amount of structure of the task to be performed by the group
3. The position power which the leader has in the organization

If leader-member relations are good, there is strong position power for the leader, and the task is highly structured, then conditions are favorable for the leader and a task-oriented leader seems to be more effective in getting the job done. Similarly, a task-oriented leader seems to be more effective in very unfavorable conditions of low position power, low task structure, and poor leader-member relations. Thus, at the extremes of each variable, the task-oriented leader (one who is concerned primarily with task accomplishment) is more effective. However, in conditions of intermediate levels of leader-member conditions, medium task structure, and medium position power—conditions of intermediate favorableness to the leader—the employee-oriented or relationship-oriented leader (one who is concerned more with employee needs than the task) seems to be more effective.[12] Since most situations in most organizations are of the intermediate type, an employee orientation for leaders is often recommended.[13] Figure 11-9 summarizes these relationships.

Some examples may help to clarify this theory. Assume the leader of a military combat team has strong position power, a structured task, and good leader-member relations. Thus, the most appropriate leader would be a task-oriented rather than an employee-oriented leader. Assume the supervisor of a group of research chemists has weak position power, an unstructured task, and poor leader-member relations; hence, a task-oriented leader would be most effective.

However, assume an office supervisor of a secretarial pool has moderate position power, a semi-structured task, and moderately good leader-member relations; hence, an employee-oriented leader would probably be most effective. Finally, the head of a large state agency handling public welfare payments and services for a state probably has moderate position power (shares with the federal government and the legislature), a semi-structured task, and moderately good leader-member relations, and should, therefore, adopt an employee orientation.

Of course for each of these examples there are exceptions, and the theory may not hold. The key to the theory, though, is accurate assessment

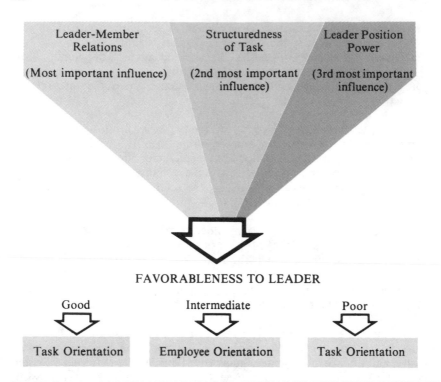

FIGURE 11-9   CONTINGENCY MODEL OF LEADERSHIP EFFECTIVENESS

of the state of leader-member relations, degree of structure of task, and leader position power. If such an assessment can be made, then the theory can be used to specify a more appropriate leadership style.

Although Fiedler's theory is promising and has yielded testable hypotheses, it is not without its weaknesses. For example, Shaw and Costanzo note:

> The major weakness of the theory is the definition of the favorability continuum. Although the experimental evidence generally supports the theory, there are wide differences between groups classified alike with regard to their favorability for the leader, suggesting that the three group-task dimensions are imperfectly measured or there are other variables which are relevant to the favorability continuum.
>
> [Furthermore] . . . situations in which the leader-member effective relations are extremely poor are probably very unfavorable to the leader even when the task is structured and his power position is strong. The description of the favorability continuum does not provide for this possibility.[14]

The real value of the contingency model of leadership lies not in its specific recommendation for a leadership style in every case. The recommendation may be wrong in some cases because of other variables that may impinge on a given situation that temporarily outweighs the three usually important variables identified. Rather, the value lies in the explicit recognition made by the theory of important situational factors that influence leadership style and orientation. This theory is the first to explicitly state that there is no one best style of leadership that always works, but there are some *suggested* styles that seem to work in a given set of circumstances. Additional research and practice with the theory is necessary before it can be further refined into a more prescriptive model of leader behavior.

USING THE CONTINGENCY THEORY

Even though additional refinement of this theory is necessary, we can expand upon it and make some preliminary suggestions for its use in maximizing human resource effectiveness in an organization. The first requirement of an effective leader is his perceptual ability. He has to be able to accurately perceive and make an assessment of a set of important variables. These variables which fall into six categories are listed below and are summarized in Figure 11-10.

1. The needs of the organization and its environment
2. The leader's needs, expertise, ability, and expectations
3. The needs, expertise, ability, and expectations of his immediate subordinates
4. The needs, expertise, ability, and expectations of his immediate superior
5. The needs, expertise, ability, and expectations of his peer managers
6. The demands of the task and the particular situation under which the task is to be performed

A given manager must accurately assess these variables and then adopt a leadership style that will maximize task accomplishment and employee satisfaction (his own, superior, subordinates, and peer managers).

The most important of these variables which must be examined in more detail are: (1) the task and situation, (2) the subordinates' abilities, expertise and expectations, (3) the leader's abilities, expertise and expectations. We will examine each of these three variables in more depth because of their critical nature in determining leadership effectiveness.

Task And Situation

A leader must must determine the complexity of the task to be performed, the amount of coordination required to complete the task, the time in which it is to be performed, the familiarity of himself and the group with the task, the complexity of the technology involved, the group for whom the task is to be performed, the quantity of the task to be performed, and the expected quality level of the task effort. All of these variables will influence the style of leadership he may adopt. For example; assume the task:

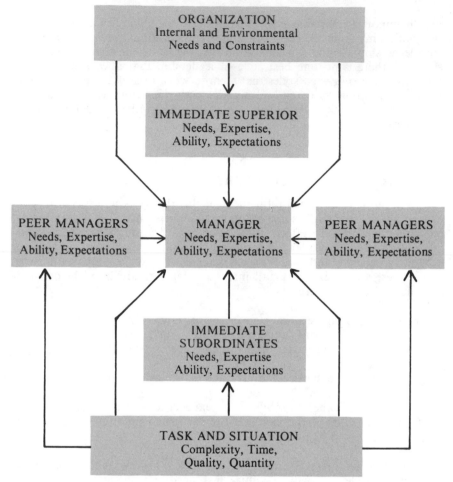

**FIGURE 11-10   THE IMPORTANT VARIABLES TO BE ASSESSED
BY A MANAGER**

1. Is complex.
2. Requires a high level of coordination.
3. Requires a high level of quality.
4. Is unfamiliar to the leader and the group.
5. Must be completed in a relatively short time period.
6. Employs a sophisticated technology.

In this case, a leadership style which emphasizes high initiating structure (role-behavior oriented toward goal attainment), creativity, flexibility, and a task orientation would be called for. A project manager on a new aerospace project, such as building the command module for the first Apollo moon landing, would fit this case.

On the other hand, an uncomplicated task, requiring little coordination, a routine technology, and a reasonable time in which to do it would suggest low initiating structure, an employee orientation, and a fairly routine approach. Supervision of a secretarial typing pool would fit this type of task.

Of course particular tasks may not fall neatly into one category or another, and most managers find themselves coordinating several tasks of varying types in varying stages of complexity. However, if a manager analyzes the tasks to be performed in an attempt to identify and determine which variables are more important, he will be in a better position to consider an appropriate leadership style.

Subordinates

A good manager thoroughly knows his subordinates and can accurately assess their strengths and weaknesses, abilities, interests, expertise, and expectations. Notice that the word *accurately* is important. Too often managers think they know their subordinates when they may have biased, incomplete information. They form prejudices and stereotypes on the basis of this biased information and proceed to manage on the basis of these prejudices. If managers have a good performance appraisal system with subordinates, a human resource information system with pertinent subordinate information, and open communication, they will be in a much better position to accurately assess these important characteristics of subordinates.

Let's look at a couple of examples as to how subordinate characteristics affect leadership style. Suppose the subordinates are highly educated, motivated, competent, have extensive knowledge of the task to be accomplished, and expect high output of themselves. A manager should then exercise a low initiating structure of supervision, employee orientation, and a flexible approach. Managing a group of Ph.D. research chemists would connote this style of leadership.

On the other hand, suppose the subordinates have low levels of education and motivation, questionable competency, and little knowledge of the task to be accomplished. Here a task-oriented, high initiating structure, fairly standardized style of supervision would be called for. Managing a group of new immigrants on a factory production line would call for this leadership style. (And in fact, this was the style of leadership predominant in the factories earlier this century.)

Managers must be careful that they don't permanently typecast their subordinates with a given set of characteristics. As these immigrants learned the language, the production process, and industrial work habits, their expertise, motivation and skills obviously changed. Even though a different leadership style was then called for, many managers continued leading on the basis of the characteristics previously shown by the group.

The Leader

A leader has to know himself. He has to know his strengths and weaknesses, motivation, interests, abilities, expertise, and competency. Suppose in a given situation a leader has little knowledge of the task to be done, little interest in the task, no previous experience with it, a low educational level, and generally low levels of motivation in accomplishing the task. This leader must rely on the expertise, interests, and motivation of others (perhaps a staff assistant, or informal group leader) in getting the job done. A low initiating structure, employee-oriented, fairly routine leadership style would seem most appropriate. The installation of a computer-based billing system in the billing and collection unit of a retail operation would exemplify this case. Chances are that the existing manager of that unit would have little expertise and interest in computer technology.

On the other hand, if the manager has extensive knowledge of the task, high interest and motivation, and much past experience, he is likely to supervise closely and be task-oriented. He may or may not be flexible, depending upon his ability to perceive requirements of the task which are different from those in the past. A former all-American basketball player who is now a coach would fit this model. So might a successful salesman promoted to a sales manager's job or an outstanding professor of management promoted to a dean's position.

Summary

We can summarize the specific variables for each of these characteristics—leader, subordinates, and task—and indicate which leadership style is most effective for maximizing task accomplishment and employee satisfaction. Such a summary is presented in Figure 11-11. Note that each variable exists on a continuum and that it is seldom that a manager finds himself at either end of the extreme. Also note that a manager usually finds himself toward one end of the extreme on some variables and toward the other end on other variables. There are very few "pure" cases. However, a manager must accurately assess the direction of each variable and determine their importance in a given situation. This is where managerial judgment is crucial. There can be no "cookbook" approach to management which specifies the correct ingredients appropriate in each and every case.

Finally, this summary in Figure 11-11 is strictly hypothetical. Although building upon some research done by Fiedler and others, the relationships shown in the figure between certain key variables and leadership style have not been substantiated by research. However, perhaps this series of hypothetical relationships will encourage further research which examines some previously unexamined variables.[15]

LARGE ORGANIZATIONS AND HUMAN RESOURCE EFFECTIVENESS: CAN THE MARRIAGE LAST?

Today's organizations are becoming increasingly larger than those of the past. This is happening for several reasons. The primary reason, however, is the economies of scale that accrue to a large organization. Size allows specialization, the purchase of large productive machinery (e.g., computers), wider markets, higher salaries to attract topnotch managers— all of which contribute to greater efficiency and effectiveness. Of course there are other reasons why organizations grow: to be more competitive in the market place (market power); to reduce market risk through product diversification; to provide greater prestige and social power for its top managers; and to compete more effectively for funds in stock, bond, and lending markets. However, the primary reason is overall economic efficiency. But is the efficiency through size at the expense of member satisfaction?

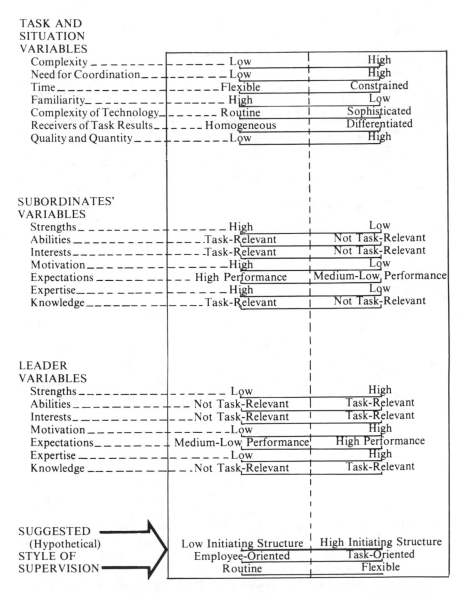

TASK AND SITUATION VARIABLES

Complexity	Low	High
Need for Coordination	Low	High
Time	Flexible	Constrained
Familiarity	High	Low
Complexity of Technology	Routine	Sophisticated
Receivers of Task Results	Homogeneous	Differentiated
Quality and Quantity	Low	High

SUBORDINATES' VARIABLES

Strengths	High	Low
Abilities	Task-Relevant	Not Task-Relevant
Interests	Task-Relevant	Not Task-Relevant
Motivation	High	Low
Expectations	High Performance	Medium-Low Performance
Expertise	High	Low
Knowledge	Task-Relevant	Not Task-Relevant

LEADER VARIABLES

Strengths	Low	High
Abilities	Not Task-Relevant	Task-Relevant
Interests	Not Task-Relevant	Task-Relevant
Motivation	Low	High
Expectations	Medium-Low Performance	High Performance
Expertise	Low	High
Knowledge	Not Task-Relevant	Task-Relevant

SUGGESTED (Hypothetical) STYLE OF SUPERVISION

Low Initiating Structure	High Initiating Structure
Employee-Oriented	Task-Oriented
Routine	Flexible

FIGURE 11-11 IMPORTANT VARIABLES TO ASSESS IN DETERMING LEADERSHIP STYLE

Throughout this book we have tried to show that organizations should not only be economically efficient and effective; but that in the long run, they should satisfy employee and customer-client expectations. Neither productivity at the expense of human satisfaction nor human satisfaction at the expense of productivity is a desirable long-term goal. Organizations of the future are more likely to achieve this dual goal if they adopt the suggestions we have made in this chapter and in other portions of this book.

To meet these challenges, organizations will need to do at least the following:[16]

1. Be less fixed and rigid and more flexible and change-oriented.
2. Be more participative-democratic and less authoritarian at all levels
3. Invest more in human resource development of employees at all levels to achieve competency.
4. Adopt a situational approach to design and managerial style.
5. Develop, implement and measure clearly defined goals and objectives.
6. Frequently evaluate the expectations of prime and secondary beneficiary groups to determine how well they are being met.

In short, the large organization needs to become more *humanistic* in its quest for economic efficiency and member satisfaction. We hope some of the suggestions made in this book will help.

CASE 1
LITTLE CHILDREN

Ernie: I'll tell you what our problem is around here. Everyone is too tradition bound. No one wants to try anything new. We're practicing the traditional style of management, and it's inappropriate today with the type of employees we have. These employees are more educated, want meaningful jobs and careers, and want challenge and the opportunity to participate. What do we give them? We treat them like little children.

Bert: Come on now, Ernie. You know our workforce. Most are not that educated. They don't like to work, and therefore a manager has got to keep on their back if any work is to be done. Let's face it, there are very few employees who want creative, responsible jobs. They should be treated like children. The traditional approach is the only one that will work. The human resources approach might work in some advanced company like IBM or AT&T but they will never work in our organization.

Ernie: They act like children because we treat them like children. It's a self-fulfilling prophecy. As long as the vicious circle continues we'll never see any improvement in work output.

Questions

1. What are the real issues Ernie and Bert are discussing?

2. Explain the self-fulfilling prophecy that might be operating here. How could it be broken?

3. How does a person tell when to use a particular management style? Can a style be switched "off and on" like a light switch?

4. What would you say next if you were Ernie?

CASE 2
DONALDSON CONSTRUCTION COMPANY

The Donaldson Construction Company is a family owned venture started by Ray Donaldson and two of his three sons. The third son, Tom, chose to enlist in the armed forces rather than join the family business right after school. The business held its own for twenty years, specializing in all forms of construction. After Tom retired in 1968, he, too, joined the company. He had a natural ability at all phases of the work and excelled at job estimation, architectural drawings, and salesmanship. In five years, he was carrying the majority of the work load. The two brothers decided to move into other jobs and sold their interests in the business to Tom. Tom then set about initiating new branches of the business, of which his father did not approve. The transition period proved to be tight financially, and Ray felt Tom would run the company into bankruptcy with his new notions of specializing in pole barns, pre-fab garages, and home remodeling. He wanted no part of financial failure, so he sold his part of the business to Tom and asked to stay on in an hourly wage position.

Ed Garvey, a good finish carpenter, bought into the business shortly after Ray sold out. Ray did not like the idea of an outsider in the company and voiced his objections to anyone who would listen. Despite all his forecasts of doom, the company began to really grow and achieve good profits. It was agreed that Tom would sell, estimate, and lay out jobs, while Ed would run the four crews with Tom dividing the job of supervision when time permitted. Ed soon found that he had little influence over the men. Since it was important that Ed get to all four jobs each day, the members of the crews had to listen to Ed's or Tom's instructions and obey them to the letter. It always seemed that one crew would fail to do what they were instructed to do. At first Ed thought the workers were incompetent, but after observing the men he felt they were all good workers. Ed decided to rotate the membership of the crews periodically. As time passed, Ed noticed that the membership of the group that failed to meet their objectives always had one thing in common, Ray Littleton. Ed hesitated to mention this to Tom and decided to try to overlook the situation.

The next week Ed left specific orders with Ray's crew to raise a barn off its foundation. Tom told Ed, who was inexperienced in this form of construction, to place two jacks every twenty feet to support the weight of the structure safely. Ed told the crew what he and Tom wanted done and left the job for a remodeling job on the other side of the county. When Tom stopped by the job later that afternoon, the north side of the barn had slipped off its jacks, and the men were desperately trying to shore up the corners to keep it from falling. This attempt was to no avail and the barn fell and was partially demolished. Tom, who was furious, asked why the jacks had not been set as he instructed. Ray spoke up and said that he had set the jacks exactly as Ed had told him too, one every twenty feet.

At this time Ed returned to the job looking for Tom. Tom insisted on knowing why Ed had changed his recommendations for the barn. Ed denied having done so and began arguing with Ray about his sloppy work and changing of orders given to him by his superiors. Ray then informed Ed that neither he nor Tom knew what they were talking about, and if it were not for him (Ray) the company would not be here today. Ed turned to Tom and said something had to be done with "that senile old man." Tom stood helplessly between the two men not knowing what to do as the entire work crew stood and watched.

Questions

1. What are the factors that should be examined in this case to determine the appropriate leadership style?

2. What role does Ray play in this case in determining a leadership style?

3. Are the men who do the work "incompetent?" What evidence do you have?

4. What issues besides leadership style does this case raise?

5. If you were Tom, what would you do now?

CASE 3
THE SENATOR AND THE SECRETARY

Lew: Your problem, Mr. Secretary, is that you never know when your agency has done a good job. You have so many layers of management, such a large budget and so many employees you can't keep track of what's going on.

Joe: Senator, sir, we are making an effort to do better. We have installed a management by objectives system, a management information system and a Planning Program Budgeting System. Hopefully all of these systems will help us to better determine how we're doing.

Lew: Well, sir, you know that no government agency has that one hard measure of performance that business has, and that's profit. All of these systems may not do a damn bit of good. Your organization is too big, too fat, and too lazy, and I don't think all these fancy systems you installed will improve that. You've got to cut, streamline, and reduce the bureaucracy. There's no question in my mind that your people are not as effective as they could be. The bureaucracy stiffles them. Where are your leaders? All you have are a bunch of paper pushers and rule followers.

Joe: Senator, you are not being fair. We have some very capable leaders in our agency. We have attempted to streamline and cut the red tape, but it's difficult to do overnight. As far as efficiency, our program planning budgeting system will allow us to determine how much it's costing us to reach our program objectives. We'll never have the flexibility of a business, though, because the congress is constantly changing the law we have to follow. That's why we have so many people who "go by the book." The book keeps changing so we have got to constantly keep our nose in it. This is not a condition that inspires great leadership.

Questions

1. Do the senator's comments apply to most government agencies?

2. Is profit a good measure of effectiveness and performance for a business? Why or why not?

3. How should a governmental agency ultimately measure its effectiveness?

4. In your opinion do managers in government agencies tend to exercise different leadership styles compared to managers in private industry?

5. Examine the secretary's rebuttal to the Senator. Are his arguments sound?

STUDY AND DISCUSSION QUESTIONS

1. Define the following terms: effectiveness, efficiency, prime beneficiaries, and task environment.

2. What is the relationship among these terms: the expectations of prime beneficiary groups, goal setting, program determination, policy making, procedure implementation, and organizational performance.

3. What is bureaucracy? What are its advantages and disadvantages?

4. How does an organization's environment affect the organization's design and structure?

5. What is matrix or project management? Under what conditions is it an appropriate organization design? What are its limitations?

6. What is MAPS? How is it related to MBO and to organization design?

7. What is the contingency model of human resource management? How does it relate to the contingency model of leadership?

8. What are the key issues to consider between a leader and each of the following: subordinates, superiors, task to be done, and peer managers. How should these be analyzed in specifying an appropriate leadership style?

9. What do we mean when we say organizations of the future must be more "humanistic"?. Is the current trend in that direction? Should organizations really try to satisfy their employees?

10. Criticize the following statement:
    All of this stuff on leadership is for the birds. A guy is either a leader or he isn't. Some people will never be leaders no matter how much training they are given. A good leader gets people to follow him anywhere. He doesn't need to consider the environment, task, etc. he just knows and people follow him because they respect him. He knows how to get people to toe the line.

11. What do you see as the major challenges for a human resource manager in the future? Are all managers human resource managers?

12. How can managerial effectiveness be determined?

ENDNOTES

1. Peter M. Blau and W. Richard Scott, *Formal Organizations* (San Francisco: Chandler Publishing Co. 1962), pp. 40-58.
2. William R. Dill, "Environment as an Influence on Managerial Autonomy," *Administrative Science Quarterly,* Vol. 2, No. 4 (March 1958), pp. 409-443.
3. Ibid., pp. 409-443.
4. Max Weber, *The Theory of Social and Economic Organizations,* trans. by A. Henderson and T. Parsons (New York: The Free Press 1947).
5. See Keith Davis, *Human Behavior at Work, 4th ed.* (New York: McGraw-Hill 1972), pp. 202-203.
6. See William F. Whyte, *Organizational Man.*
7. Ideas for portions of this are from D. Hellriegal and J. Slocum, "Organizational Design: A Contingency Approach," *Business Horizons,* Vol. 16 (1973) pp. 59-69, and D. Hellriegal and J. Slocum, *Management: A Contingency Approach* (Reading, Mass.: Addison-Wesley 1974), pp. 122-137.
8. Ralph H. Kilman, "An Organic-Adaptive Organization: The MAPS Method," *Personnel* (May-June 1974), pp. 35-47.
9. Ibid., p. 37.
10. See Henry L. Tosi and W. Clay Hammer, *Organizational Behavior and Management: A Contingency Approach* (Chicago: St. Clair Press 1974), and Hellriegal and Slocum, *Management: A Contingency Approach,* op. cit.
11. Fred E. Fiedler, *A Theory of Leadership Effectiveness* (New York: McGraw-Hill 1967).
12. Fred E. Fiedler, "Style or Circumstance: The Leadership Enigma," *Psychology Today* (March 1969), p. 41.
13. Davis, op. cit., p. 116.
14. Marion E. Shaw and Philip R. Costanzo, *Theories of Social Psychology* (New York: McGraw-Hill Book Co. 1970), p. 320.
15. For an excellent discussion of most of these variables from a more rigorous point of view and with some well presented hypotheses for research, see Steven Kerr, et al., "Toward a Contingency Theory of Leadership Based on the Consideration and Initiating Structure Literature," *Organizational Behavior and Human Performance* (August 1974), pp. 62-82.
16. Ideas for some of this are from Harold J. Leavitt, William R. Dill and Henry R. Eyring, *The Organizational World* (New York: Harcourt Brace Jovanovich, Inc. 1973), pp. 316-330.

ADDITIONAL READING

Bryant, Clifton D., ed. *The Social Dimensions of Work.* Englewood Cliffs, N. J.: Prentice Hall, 1972

Burack, Elmer. *Organizational Analysis: Theory and Applications.* Hinsdale, Ill.: The Dryden Press, 1975

Cummings, L. L. and Donald P. Schwab. *Performance in Organizations: Determinants and Appraisal.* Glenview, Ill., Scott Foresman and Co., 1973

Fiedler, Fred E. and Martin M. Chemers. *Leadership and Effective Management.* Glenview, Ill.: Scott, Foresman and Co., 1974

Hall, Richard H. *Organizations: Structure and Process.* Englewood Cliffs, N. J. Prentice Hall, Inc., 1972

Hostiuck, K. Tim. *Contemporary Organizations.* Morristown, N. J.: General Learning Press, 1974

Lorsch, Jay W. and Paul R. Lawrence. *Managing Group and Intergroup Relations.* Homewood, Ill.: Irwin-Dorsey, 1972

Mott, Paul E. *The Characteristics of Effective Organizations.* New York: Harper and Row, publishers, 1972

Rice, George H., Jr. and Dean W. Bichoprick. *Conceptual Models of Organization.* New York: Appleton Century Crofts, 1971

Sedwick, Robert C. *Interaction: Interpersonal Relationships in Organizations.* Englewood Cliffs, N. J.: Prentice Hall, 1974

Swinth, Robert. *Organizational Systems for Management: Designing, Planning, and Implementation.* Columbus: Grid, Inc., 1974

Thompson, James D. *Organizations in Action.* New York: McGraw-Hill Book Co., 1967

NAME INDEX

SUBJECT INDEX